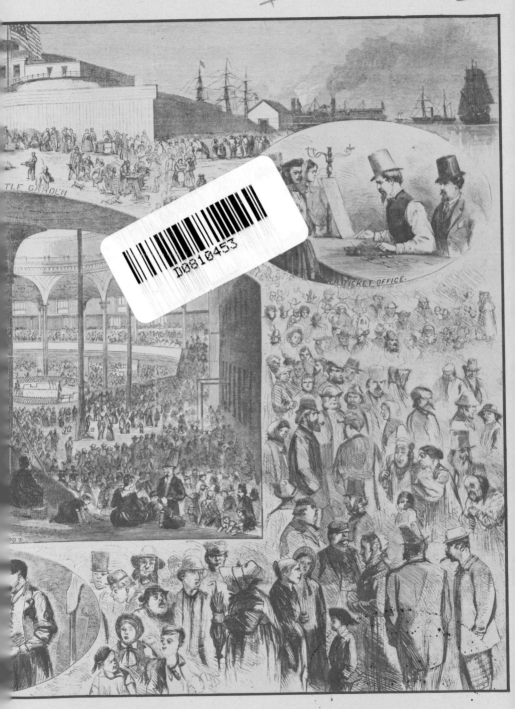

TLE GARDEN

R.R. TICKET OFFICE.

THE GLITTER &
THE GOLD

THE GLITTER &
THE GOLD

THE DIAL PRESS · NEW YORK · 1971

*A spirited account of the Metropolitan Museum of
Art's first Director, the audacious and high-handed*
LUIGI PALMA DI CESNOLA

by
Elizabeth McFadden

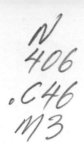

Library of Congress Catalog Card Number: 78–131178

Printed in the United States of America
Book design by Thomas Clemens
First Printing 1971

For
Gene and Conchita Collins
Patrick
Eugenia
John
Andrew
Maria
Amanda
Kieran

Appreciation

In a book of this type, which depends for much of its worth on historical facts, the assistance of those who have the records is essential, and this I have had in full measure. Particularly valuable was the cache of Cesnola material at Dartmouth College, two cartons of personal letters to Hiram Hitchcock, Cesnola's close friend. Hitchcock, who intended to write a biography of the director, had saved not only the letters but also a store of other matter that traced Cesnola's life. It is a pity that he died before Cesnola and was thus unable to carry out his project. For more than half a century, Dartmouth saved the material, and Professor Emeritus John B. Stearns had the writer notified of it when her author's query appeared in *The New York Times*. With the generous consent of Mrs. J. Bradley Cook of Sharon, Connecticut, Cesnola's granddaughter, and the great help of Kenneth C. Cramer, Dartmouth archivist, and Jan Ouellette, his assistant, this material became the backbone of the biography. Newspaper reporters of the Victorian era fleshed it out with their long and graphic reports.

Much of the background on New York and the Civil War came from the New York Public Library and the New-York Historical

Society. At the library, Walter Zervas provided space for typing. Frank Bradley and Lillian Zwyns of the local history room and Leon Weidman of the American history room gave continual vital aid. John Hawkes and others at the central desk suggested productive sources, and Joseph Mask saw to it that the books were delivered. Marion Wiethorn made a complicated picture collection meaningful.

The Historical Society provided an eminently comfortable, pleasant and effective working place and special thanks go to Nancy Hale, Joseph Schwarz and Wilson Duprey for their very real help.

The Metropolitan Museum of Art, through its director, Thomas P.F. Hoving and its vice-director for administration, Joseph V. Noble, opened its archives after a slight nudge, and John Buchanan, archivist, and Patricia Finley supplied letters and documents the museum has preserved from the Cesnola era. Elizabeth R. Usher, museum librarian, provided a typing alcove and Patrick Coman sent down some marvelously useful old scrapbooks.

It was Dr. Dietrich von Bothmer, curator of Greek and Roman Art, who gave an introduction to the head of the Leningrad State Museum, Dr. B. B. Piotrovsky. My warm thanks go to him for his assigning me a capable translator, Dr. Sophia Boriskovskaya, through whom I was able to get copies of letters between the museum and the Russian Imperial Court regarding the purchase of the first Cesnola Collection.

In Italy, where Cesnola was born, Dott. Carlo Bona took me to the Cesnola stronghold and to the Cesnola home and introduced me to an archivist, Celeste Ferdinando Scavini, who had amassed a trove of Cesnola data. Romolo Lanna USIS officer at the American Consulate in Turin put me in touch with Dott. Mario Trinchera who, with Dott. Narcisse Nada pinned down Cesnola's Army record in Italy, a task that only their professional skill could accomplish.

In Washington, I had the help of Elmer O. Parker of the Old Military Records Division, National Archives, George Metcalf of the Smithsonian Institution, Roy P. Basler, chief, manuscript division, the Library of Congress, and Dr. William N. Franklin, director, Historical Office, the State Department. Ensign Clinton Garber, USN, checked out some vital information at the British Museum.

Finally, my thanks go to my friends who listened, encouraged and did odd and needed chores. My special thanks go to Charles Cummings for his general advice in the field of biography and to J. Stewart Johnson for the clarity of his ideas on the demands of history.

E. McF.

One

In the rich land below the jagged mountains of northern Italy, the cobblestoned hamlet of Cesnola, fragrant with honeysuckle and roses, is set in the side of a hill. From it mounts a moss-bound path to a ruined castle, a gorge on one side and stuccoed brick houses on the other. Curved, ascending lines of grape arbors outline the hillside. A farm, still used, stands below the peak on which a castle reaches upward like an ivy-shrouded spire.

The stronghold itself is in two sections: one a single-story building with two ancient oak doors, the other two small rooms with a lofty watchtower, open to the sky on a prominence several thousand feet above the valley, an eagle's nest of defense against intruders. It was the feud of the house of Palma in Piedmont, and its name, in the person of a Civil War colonel, consul to Cyprus, archaeologist and the first director of the Metropolitan Museum of Art, was to flash briefly across the Victorian sky with dazzling brilliance.

Rivarolo Canavese where Emmanuele Pietro Paolo Maria Luigi Palma di Cesnola was born June 28, 1832, is south of Cesnola, gentler country in the heart of Piedmont.[1] The countryside is one of contrasts, of solitary awesome peaks and of towns set out in square,

Roman style with low classical stone buildings, elegant and austere.

The boy's parents were strangely matched: the father, Luigi Maurizio, though the descendant of a noble medieval family, was poor, a revolutionary who worked actively for the unification of the Italian states and their freedom from Austrian and French rulers; the mother was the Countess Eugenia Ricca di Castelvecchio, wealthy, a lifelong conservative, daughter of Count Giuseppe Ricca, for many years the vice-regent of Sardinia for the House of Savoy.[2] When Luigi was born, his mother was twenty-four years old and his father was fifty.[3]

Luigi's mother ran a comfortable home. She was a cultivated woman, complacent, fond of embroidery, who wrote to her friends in French and whose priest kept Mass waiting until she arrived.[4] As her children were born, she sent them to a wet nurse in the country until each was weaned at two years of age.[5] Though they were often separated and the marriage was not a happy one, the couple had four sons; Luigi was second. While their father moved in the revolutionary backwaters of the Piedmont capitol, Turin, the boys lived with their mother in Rivarolo.

The official family biography, published in 1905, comes directly to the point:

"The marriage of the Count-Captain Maurizio, the Napoleonic veteran become a liberal and a Carbonero, with a woman of noble family, could not, in all realism, have been a happy union." They were not in discord; they were simply not together.[6]

Despite their father's absence, it was chiefly of his family, a long line of cavaliers stretching back to 1262, that the boys heard tales.

The first Palma recorded was a Spaniard, Giacomo of Borgos who went to Italy early in the thirteenth century as a "captain of fortune." His son, Pietro, lived in cold quarters in the narrow un- paved streets near the fort in Salassa (Ivrea), the center of the unend- ing feral struggle between the counts of Savoy and the marquises of Monferrato. So tormented with discord was their territory that Dante wrote that the constant ruptures between the two great families "made Canavese cry." Ivrea stood at the entrance to the Aosta Valley which led to the two major passes—the two St. Bernards—over the Alps. Above it only a few miles was the towering stronghold of Cesnola, in the territory of the Savoys whose lands straddled the great mountains. This family had known for generations and at first hand that political power followed control of the great highroads of conquest and trade. They led bands of warriors—Palmas among them—to keep West Lombardy, as Piedmont was then known, within their sphere. A second lesson was nearer home: advancement or decline came with the favor of the powerful. The sharp contrast between the fortunes of Count Giuseppe Ricca and the boys' rootless father Maurizio made that clear.

Best of all, they heard of the dim origin of their name. Somewhere in the clouded past, whether in the steep-cliffed valleys of the Alps or on the sun-dried flats of the Near East on crusade, the Palmas earned the coat of arms that the family uses to this day. There is no account preserved of the exploits that won it for them. The palm may symbolize either straight victory, or the place where the device was gained. The eagle to one side represents aggressive valor, the lion, the nobility of the sword. Below the palm, set on a green field, is the telling motto: *Oppressa Resurgit*—"Oppressed, he rises again."[7]

Whatever forgotten disaster the ancient family had survived, the motto signified in the mind of little Luigi glories of the past, fed by a date here, an anecdote there, a sword of conquest cherished, a badge of honor that recalled a lost and heroic cause.

The slow centuries flashed with occasional renown. The first mention of the family, by Bertolino, the Count of Valperga, is of Giacomo's son, Pietro, formally invested in 1262 with partial jurisdiction over the huge walled and turreted castle at Rivarossa.[8] One of Pietro's three sons, Ottavio, was a commander of cavalry, the very role his nephew would fill fifteen generations later—in 1862-64—in the southland of a continent not yet discovered.

Through the Renaissance, the Palmas, as many others, were submerged among the nameless minor nobles who fought and lived and watched the great fêtes that gave respite from battle. As they learned of their ancestors, the growing Palmas found a third practical lesson. Not only was advancement for those who grasped it or who had strong protectors who rewarded their services. It came also through "good" marriages.

The Palmas had always followed the Savoys, and that family,

finally the rulers of Italy, had added to their lands and standing by both marriage and conquest. The interaction of the two had been enough to tide them over heirless dukes, conspiracies, invasions and wars. By the eighteenth century, the House of Savoy had not only survived but was flourishing. Through them, the Palmas flourished also. Emmanuele Palma, the first Count of Cesnola, received his title from Vittorio Amedeo III in 1789, just a few years before such honors were abolished forever.

The Duke of Savoy was to lose his duchy to France but not before he had given the Palmas their reward for many generations of fidelity. With the title went the feud of Cesnola. The crumbling, medieval stronghold, one of many in the great valley where the mountains turned from north to east, was to pass to Emmanuele's sons, to men, ironically, who strove not to protect the state of things as they were but who wanted, even at crucial cost to themselves, to bring to Italy the modern notion of liberty. One of these was Luigi's father, Maurizio.

It was over the passes, down the valley and past Cesnola that Napoleon moved, and on the same route, following the French Revolution, came the forces that ignited Italians with a passion for unification. Past the ancient stones of the stronghold had flowed uncounted centuries of history. To this day the mere shell on its towering peak makes a powerful impression. Years later, in describing a hill on which Luigi said he found a fabulous treasure of gold, silver and alabaster—the controversial "Treasure of Curium"—he gave to that gentle eminence on the southern coast of Cyprus the physical characteristics of this steep peak, the eagle's nest of Cesnola.[9]

Perhaps throughout his youth the fabled peak brought dreams that salved reality. It seems likely. When his father made an appearance in the narrow treeless side street where the family home had stood for centuries, Maurizio left on his sons an impression that would reverberate down the generations.

Mrs. Violet Baker Cook of Sharon, Connecticut, Luigi's granddaughter, recalls her mother standing over the dinner table, spitting out admonitions in traditional imitation of the Napoleonic cavalier: "You eat that! Every bit of it! Every single bit of it! You be glad you have it! Coming back from Moscow, *we* would have been glad to have it. But we didn't. What we had was *rats*. Now, eat!"

The boys ate. But Luigi hated his father for it and felt relieved when Maurizio returned to Turin, leaving the Rivarolo household under the mother's quiet control. The boy studied at home under tutors, learning French and English as did most of his young friends.

He awaited his father's return with fearful apprehension. It seemed to him that of all four sons, he was unfairly singled out for punishment.[10] In the first few hours at Rivarolo his father usually parceled out punishment for things the boys had done during his absence. He used a cane or horse's crop. On one occasion the father, sixty-one then and in the last year of his life, stood across the room from Luigi, a tight grasp on the cane.

"Come here, sir!" he commanded. The boy stared at the tall figure, at the cane, at the anger, at the wide stance.

He paused a moment. Then, bending his head like a charging bull, he ran full tilt between the old cavalier's legs and turned him over, sprawling on the floor. Luigi was eleven years old. His youth was over.[11] When, later that year, Maurizio was killed trying to stop some runaway horses, Luigi was "glad of it."[12] After his revolt, the family sent Luigi away to school. He was exiled to Ivrea, with its huge, four-towered, medieval fortress-castle, and put under the control of the Jesuits, favorites of the House of Savoy. His father intended him for the priesthood. It also seems likely that another compelling reason Luigi was sent to the Jesuits, who were, after all, reactionary and opposed to Maurizio's libertarian views, was that they were, first and last, disciplinarians. He endured it for a time, one of many shrill boys looked after by men who must have seemed a whole phalanx of black-clad—and hated—fathers. He knew immediately that he was on his own.

The resentment, the "unquiet spirit" his granddaughter speaks of, shaped his anger into a tool of constant conflict with these superiors. He did not become a disciplined obedient boy. He was a young man in revolt. He was expelled.

His next school, this time a military one, gave Luigi an advantage among the youths trading stories in the quadrangle: he had a hero in his family, a real, live, practically consecrated hero, his uncle the Count Alerino, one of the revered "martyrs of 1821."

Luigi and all his companions knew the story, how Count Alerino had led Carboneri in revolt, been exiled, hung in effigy and gone to a pleasant exile in Greece.

The hero's younger brother, Maurizio, emaciated veteran of the Moscow march, galled with anger, adored the radical Alerino and followed him with the spirit of an old man caught up in a glorious, barely possible, gambit of youth. For his part in the 1821 revolt, Maurizio was sentenced to several years in exile. Eventually, he was pardoned and allowed to return to Rivarolo, but the rents from Rivarosso and the other properties were confiscated.

In Luigi's generation, the cause of unity and liberty seemed to be in the hands of the beloved "Pio Nono," Pope Pius IX, who had seemed at first to respond to the throng's longing for a leader of the liberal cause. That cause was now flaming up and down the land. Thousands rushed into arms, youths running off to war in a common, ecstatic rush of patriotic feeling.

The Pope, the King, Carlo Alberto, an ascetic of medieval intensity, the exiled leaders like Mazzini and the young leonine Garibaldi, writers, musicians, artists, all roused the titled and the humble to the Cause that would inevitably bring them freedom from foreign control.

Luigi Palma, moved by the general rush of patriotism, left school on September 9, 1847 to join the Fourth Infantry Regiment as a volunteer. He was then fifteen years old.[13]

Officially, in the Sardinian Army of the Savoys, Palma was one of thousands under Carlo Alberto who, like a ruler of the Middle Ages, followed the Pope's lead. He granted freedom of the press and police reforms. Although his attachment to Austria remained deep, that autumn for the first time he challenged Austria, his wife's homeland, over import taxes. But the King was still favoring Austria in other ways. When the people of Turin broke into Rossini's "Hymn for Piux IX," Carlo Alberto had the police scatter the crowd.

Pressure from the patriots—the rising Cavour chief among them—brought a new constitution in early 1848, a two-house legislature and a civil guard. Reform was in the air that year, shaking ancient standards on the capitols of Europe. In Italy, Milan was the first city to break into open revolt. During its "Glorious Five Days" in March

1848, Milanese insurrectionists took over the Lombard city from the Austrians. The eighty-one-year-old field marshal of Austria, jovial, wily, the "Papa Radetsky" of his devoted troops, was forced to withdraw.

Spurred by Cavour, Carlo Alberto pursued the Austrian army. Though he was torn between the new libertarians and his royal family ties, the king took his army and his recruits—Luigi for the first time in military comradeship—eastward to Lombardy.

Luigi Palma became an under-corporal on April 21, 1848. A few weeks later, May 6, he was a corporal.[14] He and his comrades rode in support of the strongest revolt in Italy against the established order, Milan's break with Austria.

But, once aid from Austria reached Radetsky, the Savoyards were no match for the plump marshal who had beaten Napoleon himself at Leipzig. The Piedmontese army behaved gallantly but sued for an armistice in the summer. By August 7, Carlo Alberto and his forces were back in Piedmont; there they stayed, while the troops underwent training. In the following spring the king decided on a desperate, last attack.

Radetsky's troops were confident. Their bands blared. The men tucked green sprigs, a sign of victory, in their cockaded hats, as they moved west into Piedmont.

It was a poignantly brief six-day campaign. The Piedmontese fought the Austrians with a fire that showed their Savoy captains a new day had come. On the first day of the engagement between the two forces—March 17, 1849—Luigi Palma was promoted from corporal to under-lieutenant for gallantry on the field. He received the silver medal of bravery on the spot, a sixteen-year-old hero, brimming with pride, alive with the roar and the fanfare and the rousing clatter of the fight.[15]

On the field of Novaro, where the expanded Austrian forces attacked, Carlo Alberto outdid himself. He was continuously in the roughest part of the battle, almost, it seemed, as though he was hoping to die. But he did not die. He and his forces were thoroughly routed. Carlo Alberto abdicated. His son, Vittorio Emmanuele, then twenty-eight years old, outgoing, impulsive, short, with wide mustaches sweeping to his chin, succeeded to the throne. The old king fled to Portugal, where he went into complete seclusion. In four months he was dead.

The new king moved the broken army back to Turin from where the new lieutenant often made the easy ride home to Rivarolo. His brothers, Alerino, then eighteen years old, Flamino and Alessandro, listened to the cavalier's tales of campaign life.

When, after summer in camp, the corps was reduced, Under-Lieutenant Palma and a few others were sent to the Royal Military Academy at Cherasco[16] to become fully trained Savoyard cavaliers, defenders of the fortunes of the family their ancestors had served and from whom Luigi's grandfather still held high position.

It looked as though Luigi's future would be secure. He had proved himself in his first, rasping brush with battle. Family connections with the House of Savoy strengthened his position, and he was rising in the army of a practical, provincial monarch who one day would become the first king of modern Italy. When he emerged in 1851, at nineteen, from the leading military academy in Italy, he was a cavalier of the most powerful house in the peninsula.

Italy, during this period, steamed with activity. The Pope had been forced to leave Rome in the fall of 1848, seeking refuge in Naples, and the papal city had been ruled by a triumvirate, one of whom, Mazzini, proved a capable and compassionate leader. Rome's assembly announced its government in February 1849, as a "pure democracy," and in taking the "glorious name of the Roman Republic" guaranteed that the Pope would have a papal state of his own.

Garibaldi, the "forest oak," stirred patriots to join him in exile when Rome was retaken by French and Austrian troops. Exhorting a throng in St. Peter's Square in July 1849, he cried:

"Soldiers! You who have shared with me the labor and the dangers of fighting for our fatherland, you who have won a rich share of glory and honor, all you can expect if you now come with me into exile is heat and thirst by day, cold and hunger by night. No other wages await you save hard work and danger. You will live in the open, without rest, without food, and there will be long night watches, forced marches, and fighting at every step."

Garibaldi knew whereof he spoke. Securing the unity of Italy, by

1852 filled with a disillusioned set of partisans, was to be an affair of operatic proportions with heroes' deaths—Garibaldi's included—in every act. Patriots were bickering. Combat had uncovered sharp differences between regions that were the heirs of old, rival city-states, between monarchists and republicans, between Catholics and anti-clerics. The Pope returned to Rome, a bitter man, ever after hostile to liberalism. It required the influence and power of the Bourbons of France and the Austrians to maintain his temporal power.

In the north, Austria regained its old position as overlord, and Italy was again subject to foreigners. But the hostility of the people, often resulting in terrorist acts, made the country unsafe for the Austrian soldiers. Of all the Austrians, only old "Papa Radetsky," friendly and lively, could ride in an open coach through a Lombard town.

For the young Cavalier Palma, now twenty and equipped for the life of a Savoyard officer, it was a period of full-blown pleasure. He was treated in Rivarolo like a young lord, anything he did admired and recounted with approving laughter. He had all the means to indulge himself and the looks—the sturdy body with the finely mod-eled nose and ears and the wide brow of his forebears—to attract young women. And since his father was dead and his uncle in Greece, he was on his own, as, indeed, he had been for many years.

In the spring of 1852, Palma was recalled to his old regiment, the Ninth Infantry. Ten months later—March 27, 1855—a minister's dis-patch, presumably representing special treatment, transferred him to the Sixth Regiment. And a year and a half later, in September 1854, it was by "royal discretion" itself that he put on the richly ornate uniform of the aide-de-camp to the Lord Major General, the brigade commandant who handled ministerial arrangements.[17]

Epauletted, mounted on a fine horse, Palma clattered over cob-blestones beside the Lord Major General's coach as it sped to the embassies. Under arched gateways topped with wrought-iron fes-toons of whimsical design, the dark gilt-trimmed coach carrying the general, slowed, then finally came to a halt. It would stand, horses of the outriders snorting beside it, in front of a palazzo of the famed Piedmontese baroque. The door would open to a world where the

valor, good connections, and means of the powerful were the common currency.

In September 1854, Palma was named lieutenant, also by "royal
discretion," of the House of Savoy and was soon appointed secretary
to the commanding officer, a general in the personnel division.

Little more than a month after his promotion, in one calamitous
episode—whose particulars remain a mystery—Palma's burgeoning
career collapsed. By "royal permission" on October 17, 1854, Lieutenant Palma was allowed to "graciously accept voluntary dismissal."[18] He was to admit later that in a "moment of madness" he
had thrown his position, his future, away.

The only reason given in the files of the State Archives in Turin
is that he failed to pay a usurious loan. But his mother's family was
wealthy, and he always had plenty of funds for normal expenses. Why
would he have to get a special loan at the astronomic rates then
demanded?

He never gambled. He never drank much, liking a glass of wine
with his meals but no more. Once only, and then years later in a letter
to his future wife, Palma merely hinted at the cause—a love affair—
that caused his downfall.

The day of his "voluntary dismissal" coincided with the first
British attack on Sevastopol in the Crimean War. And the cavalier,
presumably on the strength of family ties in London, was able to
secure a commission in the Anglo-Turkish Army which was serving
in the eastern Mediterranean.

There also, as in Piedmont, he was aide-de-camp to a general, on
this occasion, General Ansaldi, a Sardinian serving in the English
forces, [19] who, though young, was surrounded by a grand staff.

At the end of July of the following year, 1855, Vittorio Emmanuele wanted to join France, Britain and Turkey against Russia,
hoping to lead his army in battle and rid himself of the increasingly
powerful Cavour. The Prime Minister, however, countered by getting the Piedmont parliament to enlist its army in the Crimean War
on its own. Palma sought readmission to his old forces, but he was
refused.

He remained with the British, then, as Ansaldi's aide, until the
general, with no fewer than eighteen other generals, fell in the Sep-

tember 8, 1855 assault on Sevastopol. Moving from Balaklava to Constantinople, Palma remained in the Middle East, becoming acquainted with the customs and nature of the Turkish population.

Just when Luigi left for New York is uncertain. To most of the world, to his friends and acquaintances, to the men who questioned him for encyclopedias when he had become an important figure as the director of New York's Metropolitan Museum of Art, he would say that he came to the United States in 1860. But there is strong evidence, as will be shown, that 1858 is the more likely date.

In all probability he did not return to Rivarolo after the Crimean campaign. Later he wrote to his dear friend, Hiram Hitchcock, that "the others could stay at home and live off Mother's fortune," but he had decided to make his own.[20]

Two

The change was abrupt and bruising. From the Alps of his beloved homeland where thick-walled, solitary fortresses housed the descendants of the great feudal sires, to the pulsating city of Manhattan was a distance that could not be measured in mere miles. It was an entirely new world, and its newness was raw.

The Irish potato famine in the 1840s and the continental wars of 1848–49 had brought a flood of Irish and German immigration to the United States. So many of these hapless people had been fleeced by runners for boarding houses and sellers of bogus railroad tickets that the State of New York had finally set up an "Emigrant Office" at Castle Garden in New York's Battery Park for the "landing of strange populations." In the hall where Jennie Lind made her American debut in 1850, state agents sold transportation tickets and gave advice on lodgings. By 1892, when Ellis Island became a federal center for the handling of immigrants, more than three million Europeans had passed through the old Fort Clinton's sturdy interior.

Louis Palma stepped ashore at Castle Garden, letters of introduction in his pocket, flute under one arm, and not very much money.[1] He was in that curious, metropolitan situation of sharing an experience with a crowd of people and, at the same time, being very much alone.

Palma knew English and now pronounced his first name in the British manner, Lewis. However, he spelled it *Louis*. This change symbolized his exile from his past, from his life as an Italian cavalry officer to that of an émigré, twenty-six years old, alone, passing under sail into the far-off foreign port of New York.

Frigates moved like solemn, silk-clothed prelates in the procession of ships on the wide rivers which emptied into the New York port. Others, their sails furled to their masts, nuzzled bowsprits over clamorous downtown streets. Smaller vessels brought produce through the Sound to the noisy bickering market, and almost a score of ferries provided the only link between the island of Manhattan and the neighboring towns of Brooklyn, Williamsburg and Jersey City.

Palma's first two years in New York were spent in poverty and solitude. They formed such a painful memory that in later years he spoke of them only to his closest friend, Hiram Hitchcock, and then only in general terms.

He lived, his granddaughter tells us, in a succession of cheap boarding houses. The New York *Herald* on the first of that year 1858 ran an ad offering room and board at 340 Seventh Avenue, between Thirty-first and Thirty-second Streets, "for respectable men" for $2.50 a week. At 121 Bleecker Street, at Broadway, was "A delightful suit [*sic*] of rooms, handsomely furnished on first floor with chandeliers, etc; also a parlor and bedroom on second floor; a few pleasant rooms for gentlemen with fire, large and small; gas, baths, etc. Dinner at 6 o'clock. References required." Higher up the scale was a "Pleasant second story front room" at 3 Fifth Avenue, "suitable for two gentlemen at $4 each per week, gas and fuel included. References exchanged."

He first sought work as a translator, then, when that failed, he wrote music, and tried to sell his scores in an unreceptive market.[2]

The trouble was not simply that his talents and training were not fitted for the volatile city. Business, generally, was at a standstill. The collapse of the stock market in August 1857 had been a full disaster.

Palma unknowingly chose one of the least promising years in a decade to come to America.

"Business is dismally stagnant. There is little sign of its revival," George Templeton Strong, lawyer, and patron of the arts wrote on March 27, 1858, referring to the Panic of 1857. To replace their "wonted excitement in Wall Street," the astute diarist observed, people were building up a major "Revival of Religion," seeking a substitute there "in the sensations of the prayer meeting."[3]

All through the spring of 1858, the Great Religious Revival drew thousands to mass meetings, to prayer sessions at the noon hour, to long sermons in the evenings. All sects felt the surge of feeling. The Roman Catholics were inclined to credit William Aspinwall's importation of Murillo's "Madonna," whose authenticity was questionable, with having brought about the stir. The graceful figure, her foot on a crescent moon, roused strong religious feelings. Others pointed out that about two hundred Protestant ministers, chiefly Presbyterians, had met in Pittsburgh sometime after the crash and had actually planned to set the revival in motion.

It was plainly a time for relief of sorrowing spirits. New York was two worlds: the world of the rich—those who lived "uptown" around and above Washington Square, their carriages waiting for them outside brownstone homes filled with comforts; and the world of the poor—the young women who answered ads for "A SMART TIDY GIRL TO DO GENERAL housework, planning, cooking, washing and ironing; is kind to children,"[4] or the men who were sought to manufacture steel springs for ladies' skirts.

William B. Astor was building a château on Fifth Avenue at 33rd Street, and the city's 1,250 patrolmen were making eight hundred dollars a year. The wealthy went to Saratoga for the summer or traveled abroad. Their manner of life, bolstered with plenty of immigrant-servants, grew more self-indulgent, more elaborate, as it was pampered by the flourishing trade, with imported food, wine and clothing.

There was no real union between the two groups, no common set of ideals and aims for New York's 700,000 people. Professional politicians ran the city government, often to their own corrupt advantage, and few of the old and cultivated families took any real role or notice.

People were generally on their own, each building up his own, frequently vast, fortune, or scratching out a mean marginal life. Men sought to move from one group to the other in a pervasive war of wits, as capitalist-adventurers pulled fortune and power from a close-fisted fate.

And yet, in a way that seemed almost supranatural, New York City was coming into its own. In April 1858, a plan called "Greensward" won a $2,000 first prize for Frederick Law Olmstead and Calvert Vaux. Their design for a central park was America's first attempt to offer its people a public and unspoiled area for pleasure within the confines of a metropolis. Nelson's *Guide to New York*, a popular directory for strangers, had called the city "inferior to many of the great cities in Europe in regard to free, open spaces." New York was feeling its first impulses of competition with the old, revered world.

It was a strange year, one of towering hopes and ultimate dismay, exemplified in Palma's own experience in coming to a new, raucous, expanding land, finding no workable way of life and existing in desperate, evermore disheartening poverty. He could not, like others around him, help to find promise—and final failure—in the two major events of 1858, the successful laying of the Atlantic cable and the destruction of the Crystal Palace.

The cable, an insulated, rubber-wrapped tube of wires, was being spread out on the ocean floor by two ships, one from America, one from England. The practical dream of Peter Cooper, whom Strong called "the millionaire glue boiler,"[5] and Cyrus W. Field, a retired businessman, the project had faltered the previous year when the thick metal tube holding the wires broke on three separate occasions. There was doubt the government would continue its support. But the word on New Year's Day, as society made its calls, was that Secretary of the Navy Toucey had written Cooper and Field of the New York, Newfoundland & London Telegraph Co. that President Buchanan was reauthorizing the use of a steam frigate to tackle the job anew that coming summer.

At last, the New York *Herald* reported, "The cable is laid. To God be all the glory." People went wild with joy. Bells pealed. Cannon boomed. Fireworks sprayed the night sky with fountains of light.

"All Yankeedom," the *Herald* said on August 9, "was rolled up in the British and American flags and nearly ready for a straight jacket."

Victoria sent a message to Buchanan. From New Orleans to Portland, demonstrations celebrated the success of the endeavor. In his diary, Strong looked ahead to see the world one hundred years later, "a strange place in 1958, most unlike what it is now. The diverse races of men certainly seem tending toward developing into a living, organic unit with railroads and steam packets for a circulating system, telegraph wires for nerves and the London *Times* and the New York *Herald* for a brain."[6]

Others were opportunistic. Atlantic Cable Bouquet cologne went on the market in September, advertised as "distilled from ocean spray and fragrant flowers especially for the national ovation held in New York September 1."

On that day the choir and organ of Trinity Church sang a *Te Deum*. Mayor D.F. Tiemann presented Cyrus Field with a gold box in an elaborate ceremony at the Crystal Palace. Colored lanterns by the thousands hung in trees up Broadway for a parade whose heroes were the sailors from the cable-laying frigate, the *Niagara*. City Hall, center of the "noblest fete ever witnessed in New York," was lit by so many fireworks and illuminations that its roof caught fire and its windows cracked.

Even as the litter of the celebration was being cleared away, the insulation in the cable began to fail. By October, the telegraph lines were silent. They were not to be in general working order again until 1866. But America had other things ahead.

By October, also, the spectacular Crystal Palace had crashed to the ground. The huge structure stood in Reservoir Square behind the Croton Distributing Reservoir at Fifth Avenue between 41st and 42nd Streets. It was a copy of London's Crystal Palace in Hyde Park, a sensation in 1851 when it was the scene of England's Great Exhibition, and it marked anew America's consciousness of old world feats.

In the showplace, workmen put together 1250 tons of steel and 9000 panes of glass in a building whose ground plan was in the shape of a Greek cross. It was the scene of huge concerts, fairs, and balls. Visitors circled the premises on three steam calliopes, gaped at jewelry from Tiffany's and showed an interest, however perfunctory, in surveying machinery.

Then, in early October, fire destroyed the landmark in twenty minutes. Flames rushed along its pitch-pine floors. Heat exploded gas pipes. The 100-foot dome plunged to the ground in a tidal wave of shattering glass. The building that *The Stranger's Guide* called "the biggest thing in town" was a heap of rubbish.

To Palma, it was symbolic. Unemployed and probably hungry, he was in desperate straits. In these early Manhattan days, the cavalier from Piedmont finally lost heart. Oppressed, he could not rise. He had no stomach for the problems that faced him and, ultimately, in some dank moment of despair, took a dose of laudanum in a suicide attempt.[7]

On many street corners, pharmacy shops offered nostrums: "One for a man, two for a horse." Laudanum, or tincture of opium, readily available, was highly popular and touted regularly in newspaper advertisements. Drug manufacturers were not required to list the exact amount of the opiate's strength in the various batches of its solution in alcohol. It was plainly dangerous and, being relatively quick and painless, was a favorite of suicides.

Known as the "sleep of death," laudanum's effect, in overdose, depresses the central nervous system to unconsciousness. With the vital functions slowed almost to a halt, the patient becomes cold, his pulse barely palpable, and his skin livid with the engorgement of blood that the heart is unable to pump through the system.

Some were saved from death by doctors and relatives who walked them through the initial period of deep drowsiness; in some cases, flagellation kept the would-be suicide alive; in others, a new system of artificial respiration came to the rescue.

The *Chicago Medical Journal* of 1860 reported one case of an attempted suicide, a nineteen-year-old man who had taken one ounce of laudanum at 11:30 A.M. The doctor arrived at noon and "got him taken up immediately and persuaded him to have his stomach pumped." By 1 P.M., however, the victim was cold, livid and comatose. The physician began respiration, keeping it up all afternoon "without any apparent amendment" until 6 P.M. when the patient suddenly "threw up his arms and raised up in bed, and, of course, recovered."

If Palma had a physician who spent five hours resuscitating him, if he didn't take enough laudanum, or if he was stronger than he thought, we do not know. We know only that he recovered, that he put 1858—and 1859, for that matter—out of his mind and confided only to the impressive, kindly and, perhaps, fatherly William H. Seward, Secretary of State when Palma was a consul, that he had, indeed, even been in America in those two, tremulous years before the Civil War.[8]

Totally untrained to be anything but a cavalry officer, Palma had to find a way to rebuild his life. Music hadn't worked. Translations were too few to tide him over even the low rent charged in boarding houses. He finally decided to use his knowledge of languages, the fruit of long, easy-paced hours in Rivarolo Canavese, in another way —teaching Italian and French.

Most of his pupils were women. "It is well understood that a woman shouldn't work," wrote the Brussels physician, Dr. N. Reiss, in a book on his trip to New York in 1850. "She should keep herself occupied only with adoring her husband and making him happy."[9]

The doctor observed a curious corollary to this custom, common before the typewriter was manufactured in the 1870s: women managed to get mighty interested in things outside the home. They also began to do things in such "natural" fields as education and the arts, but in no time at all were working not only to get Sunday schools opened but to have the slaves emancipated. The outspoken American woman was a wonder to the European man.

Tammany Hall gave young girls, immigrants or daughters of immigrants, a chance to meet young men at dances without chaperones "and without fear of the least wrong." The girls, the doctor observed, were set on marriage, and the Tammany dance was a "favorite husband-seeking place. If she didn't make out there or on Sunday excursions to Harlem or Hoboken, or, if rich, winter trips to Washington, she usually went into missionary work and could very well wind up in China, with a missionary husband. They leave for the Far East after the nuptial ceremony."[10]

Palma, then, met his share of housewives with time on their hands and girls with wedding rings in mind. But it was not until the following spring—after April 1860—that he met the outspoken and forthright American woman who would become the Countess, or Madame, Cesnola.

Far away in the Lombardy town of Magenta, the allied French and Piedmontese under Napoleon III defeated the Austrians. An aroused world gloried in the victory. In New York an opera benefit raised $3000 at the Academy of Music for the wives and children of the "heroic soldiers who are fighting so gallantly and gloriously for the independence of a great people on the plains of Lombardy."[11] Palma would have been among them had he been in Italy. He would have been revenged on the defeat of Novaro, as part of the forces that gave the Hapsburg army, no longer led by "Papa Radetsky," one of its most telling defeats. In July the two emperors, Napoleon III and Francis Joseph, signed the Peace of Villafranca making Italy a confederacy.

But Palma was in Manhattan watching the rise of a remarkable new hotel at Madison Square, and becoming a close friend of one of its proprietors, Hiram Hitchcock. A tall New Englander with sympathetic—and ailing—grey-blue eyes, a goateed beard and full mustache, Hitchcock became Palma's confidant and warm supporter.

The two had much in common. Each had been born in the same year and each came from an old family. Hitchcock, born in Claremont, New Hampshire, was descended from Matthias who came from London to Boston in 1635.[12] And each had started out in life in a profession he prized and had been forced to abandon. For Hitchcock it had been teaching, but failing eyesight put an end to that career. Moreover, each had just about the same amount of formal schooling.

In 1852, Hitchcock had gone south for the winter and took a job in the office of the St. Charles Hotel in New Orleans. There he discovered French cooking. At a resort hotel, the Nahant House near Boston, in a setting of well-regulated services, he introduced Southern and French cooking to New Englanders, and the establishment had been so successful that he had been invited to run New York's Fifth Avenue Hotel. He had achieved, by his native Yankee orderliness and his driving ambition, a reputation as one of the leading hotel men in the East.

The Fifth Avenue Hotel was a marvel of its day: six stories of white marble in neoclassic style with a "perpendicular railway intersecting each floor." This was the world's first passenger elevator, only one of the new, technical inventions that, with time-tested amenities, made this hotel, at the northwest corner of Twenty-third Street, the leading one in America for decades. The showplace, which some thought too far uptown, had accommodations for one thousand. There were one hundred luxury suites each with a parlor, bedroom, a dressing room and bath.

The public rooms, carpeted with oriental rugs, decorated in classical orders, served by a carefully trained army of waiters, captains, porters and bellhops, were soon to welcome the privileged of the world, from Edward, Prince of Wales, a jolly youth of nineteen, who broke up a ceremonious day by playing leapfrog with companions in a corridor, to Presidents of the United States.

From the day it opened in 1859, the Fifth Avenue Hotel was a center for the social, financial, and political worlds of New York. Here was held the dinner at which it was decided to nominate General Grant for the Presidency. Here the Amen Corner bar drew the shapers of the changing times. A stock ticker tape stood in a plush, first-floor reading room which was so busy with action that it became a regular, spontaneous stock exchange on its own. The management put up a sign: "Gentlemen are requested not to buy or sell stocks or gold in these rooms." But the gentlemen did, nevertheless. Even in the post-panic market, the buzz of business crackled around the new traders, the men who dealt, unlike the well-bred and well-read brokers before 1857, not in thousands but in millions, who broke most of the old rules and opened a completely new and ruthless era in American finance.

The classic dining salon had long tables that could accommodate twenty to thirty people. Elaborately served, the meals heartened couples whose carriages carpeted with Alaskan fur robes waited outside. After dinner the ladies retired to the finely furnished drawing room on the second floor to amuse themselves with games while the men, below, grasped the main chance.

Some of this feeling for the expedient, profitable course—and the devil take the niceties—took hold of both Palma and Hitchcock.

The New Englander was later to lose a good deal of money as head of the Nicaragua canal project. The atmosphere around the Fifth Avenue Hotel would make it possible for both, as it had for the men in from unpaved Kansas City, to grab at luck and make it hand over a fortune.

It was a way of life that was the absolute antithesis of the one Palma himself lived at the time. It would not be for many years that he would be able to utilize some of its obvious lessons. Now, pulling himself laboriously upward from the depth of his suicide attempt, he sought only to keep as steady a keel as he could in this swirling sea of change. He did his teaching and rested in his rented room. Life remained uneventful and somewhat monotonous.

Sometime after April 1860, a new pupil, Mary Jennings Reid, presented herself for French lessons. She was plump, earnest and observant. Her father, Samuel Chester Reid, a hero-privateer of the War of 1812, had died recently and, with a good inheritance, she had gone to keep house for her brother Will, a rising newspaper editor.

Her reaction to her teacher was simple and her course direct. She liked him, and she asked him home for tea. This was a substantial affair even in a single woman's household, and the young woman— she was thirty, two years older than Louis—provided an ample plateful of small sandwiches.

Though he had not confided in her, her guest ate those sandwiches with such open relish that she knew he was going through a hard time. And, from the sight of him sitting on a hard, though upholstered chair, eating those tiny sandwiches, Mary Jennings Reid felt she had a chance to marry the cavalier.

She too came from an old family, one of soldiers and sailors, captains and commodores, who had fought in King Charles' navy in England, at Bunker Hill, at Trenton, and, most memorably, at Fayal in the Azores. There her father had held off a British fleet long enough to spare Louisiana from being invaded by the English. Later, in 1818, harbor master in New York and father of ten children, he had suggested that the stripes in the American flag be kept constant and that stars be added for new states. Congress adopted the format in 1859, making Reid the designer of the present American flag. Socially, the family, though not exceptionally wealthy, moved among the conservative, prerevolutionary English settlers.

When he walked into Mary's home for tea, then, the cavalier from Rivarolo Canavese went into a room where military men were esteemed. He found there a pretty woman who could readily appreciate what he had to tell about action in Piedmont and the Crimea.

They saw each other frequently. Seated in the parlor heated by a coal fire, their talk often turned to war. Everywhere, just then, there was talk of secession. At one time, Horace Greeley of the New York *Tribune* suggested that the Southern states be allowed to secede. Later he recanted. Lincoln, cadaverous, deeply eloquent, came to Cooper Union on the East Side appealing for understanding but taking the clear position that slavery should not be extended to newly opened territories. In May 1860, at their convention in Chicago, the Republicans rejected the former New York governor, William H. Seward, as their candidate because he had been for too long an ardent opponent of slavery. Instead, they chose Lincoln who, later that fall, won the Presidency without carrying a single border or slave state. As the new year opened, eleven Southern states seceded from the Union. The outgoing President, Buchanan, felt powerless to prevent secession by federal force.

Lincoln left Springfield with a task before him "greater than that which rested upon Washington," and moved slowly to the capitol. His first inauguration was on March 4, 1861.

About a month later, April 1, 1861, Palma was visiting at Fort Washington in the capitol. He had seen Mary the previous Saturday, and she had taken the lead and brought up the subject of love. The gist of her talk was that she didn't think he knew what it was.

In a room crowded with more than fifty people, the cavalier sat down and in his small, Spencerian script drew for her a frank and detailed picture of his emotional past and its probable future. He wrote:

My dear Miss Mary
Please be kind enough to interpret this note of mine as you can, for I have neither a Dictionary to select my words & phrases nor

if I had it I would have time to do it; still I beg you to be quite
sure that in this note I do not intend to say anything desagreable
to you and if so it shall be unintentionally indeed.
Last Saturday *at last* you have taken up again a discours which
I was from a long time waiting for. You plainly told me that I do
not know what is *love* & you are quite at a loss to guess what
name must be applied to the feelings I have for you. Well then.
Will you have patiens enough to read all over this note and I shall
endeavour to find its name, not for me because I have it already
from my childhood but for you only. I won't give you any definition of the word—Love—because it has so many meanings as
there are human beings on the Earth able to feel it. I shall only
try to draw a faithful picture of what I really feel for you & you
afterwards will apply one yourself.
Suppose a man comparatively young that from the age of 14 had
been petted by a society of friends and relatives in middle of
which he grew up quite master of his own will and not
thoroughly deprived of that taste for the refinement of human
nature; suppose him with a virgin & warm heart in a land which
love has been created expressly for its inhabitants; what could
have been his life? Very *fast* I think you will say, and so too I
believe. A man in such a position must have felt love in several
different gradations; at 14 the love *angellike*, all illusions &
dreams; at 20 the love of passions with means to satisfy it on the
largest scale; at 25 he began to find his heart tired if I can
properly use the word, of the first as well as of the second;
therefore he was already able by experience to give full appreciation to both; what the result? a third kind of love, the
positive life—Now take this man that the Providence made him
born in a privileged class. In which all his nonsenses were considered as proof of *wit* and admired by a second class as a superior
young man (although he had good sense enough to know of what
he was worthy) give him a strong character & a great inclination
to independence; give him a good enviable social position which
in a moment of madness he throw away & take him away from
his country and put him in another hemisphere as an outcast
obliged to degradate himself in earning his daily bread, do you
believe that he will be able still to love as at 14 or at 20? No
certainly not. He may have for the woman which he considers
superior of the others, the *greatest affection*, he can give his life

up for her sake, he can devote himself all his life in rendering
happy the woman he selects, he will be at last the most faithful
& kind husband, but he shall never be a lover like when fourteen
or twenty years old. Now you believe that such a kind of man will
never be a good husband, but you are in error he shall be ten
years afterwards what he was the day of the wedlock be sure of
it, and his wife is happy as a being maybe in this valey of tears
—While a marriage begun with love & passion shall in a short
time be followed by indifference & afterwards by hate & sometimes divorce. I am a man like the above sketch and unable to
feel anything stronger for all my life than a true affection durable
till life will last, and if I cannot find a superior woman who is able
to understand me, I will die bachelor. I can enur it. I have so
many things to say in corroboration of what I said before that I
would have more room here to explain myself better but this is
at present impossible; moreover to day this private office of Mr.
Bennett is crowded by guests I think we are more than 50. Mrs.
B. gave a great dinner to the Bride of Commodore Levy. I don't
recollect the name. Mrs. Livingston, Tailor & Rosevelt are
amongst the guests. Believe me ever
Your most affectionate
Luigi P. di Cesnola[13]

Although Mary's family and friends opposed her marrying the
impoverished Italian, the two were wed on June 11, 1861. The Rev.
Henry E. Montgomery, the bride's rector, performed the Episcopal
ceremony at the Church of the Incarnation. In the minister's certifi-
cation, the two are called "Luigi Palma and Mary Isabel Reid."[14]

The cavalier, however, put a classified notice in the paper under
MARRIED: "On Tuesday, 11th inst. in the city of New York, by the
Rev. Henry E. Montgomery, the Cavaliere LUIGE PALMA DI CES-
NOLA of Piedmont, second son of the late Count Maurice Victor
Palma di Cesnola, to MARY ISABEL, daughter of the late Capt. Samuel
C. Reid."[15]

Three

From Fort Sumter, lying on a small island near the harbor entrance, Charleston, not ten feet above sea level, seemed a mirage. Its live oaks, its lindens, the spires of its many churches, its old, comfortable homes, all looked as though they were rising from the sea. There was something unreal—and unthreatening—about the sight.

But to Major Robert Anderson, a Southerner who commanded federal forces in Charleston, danger was real. When South Carolina seceded in late December 1860, he cautiously moved his garrison from Fort Moultrie, nearer the shore to Fort Sumter.

By spring of 1861, his supplies were low. Salt pork came to the breakfast table. The drink with it was water. He called for provisions.

And in Washington, Seward, the powerful Secretary of State, and the new, and some thought, diffident President, struggled over different ways of meeting the rebellion.

Seward proposed a series of foreign wars against Spain and France to provide a unifying force within the nation.

On a more practical level, he wanted Lincoln to abandon Sumter and instead, reinforce Gulf ports. And he pointed out in a memorandum to the President April 1, "Either the President must do it [the foreign war] himself, and be all the while active in it, or Devolve it on some member of his cabinet." [Seward was leaping to stage center.] The President replied the same day and set the Secretary straight. He repeated the phrase: "devolve it on some member of his cabinet," then wrote: "I remark that if this must be done, I must do it." He was never to be troubled by Seward's ambitions again and was free to run his own administration.[1] Deciding against sending arms to the Carolina fort, one of only four that remained in Federal hands, Lincoln notified South Carolina on April 6 that he was sending a peaceful expedition there to deliver supplies.

But the state's leaders drew back in disbelief and alarm. They were not going to be caught by any guile. They would avoid federal occupation, the taking of their low-lying, vulnerable city by Union forces coming under whatever name of need. On April 11, South Carolina demanded that Major Anderson surrender the fort on the spot and received in return his offer to surrender once his supplies gave out. This, he reminded the Confederates, was just a matter of days. Fully aware that provisions were on the way, the leaders of South Carolina refused the offer.

At 4:27 A.M. on April 12, as the first graying of the sky exposed the fort and its two towers, the first shot was fired into Sumter from the Stevens battery. With it, the Civil War began.

Some twenty-six hours later, at daybreak on April 13, fire ignited the officers' quarters, and soon that entire section of the fort was in flames. By noon the flagstaff was hit, and the standard fell.

Robert Anderson, Major, First Artillery, commanding Fort Sumter, "marched out of the fort Sunday afternoon, the 14th instant, with colors flying and drums beating, bringing away company and private property, and saluting my flag with 50 guns."

The war was on. Lincoln declaring an insurrection existed, called for 75,000 troops and sanguinely set enlistments at three months.

Massachusetts, the first to respond, sent her Sixth Massachusetts Regiment heading for Washington on April 16. As they passed through New York, the marching men seemed a "triumphal parade," applauded, garlanded and cheered.

In Baltimore, the story was different. There, as the new soldiers marched through the streets, a mob of Southern sympathizers attacked them in fury, pounding them with paving stones and taunting them with a Confederate flag.

With growing seriousness New York said good-bye to its favorite, the Seventh Regiment, which traveled from Philadelphia to Baltimore by water. Maryland officials, as a bar to further riots, had burned the bridges on the direct roads between the cities.

In an account of the passage in the New-York *Times*, Fitz-James O'Brien gave a bright picture of the trip aboard the steamer *Boston*. These were the sons of the elite of New York, and says O'Brien, "I never saw a more good-humored set of men in my life. Fellows who would at Delmonico's have sent back a *turban de volaille aux truffes* because the truffles were tough, here cheerfully took their places in file between decks, tin plates and tin cups in hand, in order to get an insufficient piece of beef and a vision of coffee. But it was all merrily done ... I say to those people in New York who have sneered at the Seventh Regiment as being dandies, and guilty of the unpardonable crimes of cleanliness and kid gloves, that they would cease to scoff and remain to bless, had they beheld the square, honest, genial way, in which these military Brummels roughed it ..."[2]

By this time, Cesnola had what he practically considered a regiment of his own.

He and Mary had married in the first flush of the war excitement, in June 1861, just after Sumter, when the cheerful troops were marching South with bands blaring. The war had finally come and put an end to countless questions of policy and direction and presidential powers and the legal rights of the states leaving the Union. The issue was joined, and, as in every war from the beginning of time, the man who was going off to the front wanted profoundly to leave behind him a wife at home.

In discussing the future, Mary suggested to her husband that he take into account his background. "Louis," her granddaughter quotes her as saying, "you seem to know more about cavalry than about anything else, really. You ought to go into teaching officers because we need them desperately."[3] Louis put an advertisement in the paper under the name of Palma, offering to train men for one hundred dollars each. Mary was most practical. "Payable in advance," she suggested. The count-cavalier thought that was "dreadful."

"But I know my countrymen," Mary said. "They'll think more of you if you get them to pay in advance. Anyway, we can use it."

As a result, he had $1000 in pocket after the first advertisement.[4] His wife had a clear notion of what to do with the money as, indeed, she had of many matters. The couple moved to the Maison d'Or, an establishment of stature on Union Square. It served superb French food, and it gave Palma contacts through whom he could meet men and organize a troop—by training recruits in cavalry and infantry warfare and the logistics of supplies.

The couple soon was poor. Evidently they were spending every cent that came in, as is shown by the story of Mary's embarrassment when, making a formal call, a pawn ticket fell out of her pouch bag as she was leaving her card.[5]

But they were very definitely making progress in the world. The cavalry school was flourishing. The war and those who knew about warfare were being taken more and more soberly. Cesnola, it became clear, could realistically expect substantial rank in service.

The national turmoil opened up a great many roads to fortune, and Wall Street was crowded with financial buccaneers eager to join in corners, wash sales, pools and raids. Men could pay others to serve for them, and to many of the speculators and the serious students of the flourishing commerce, the war years were important only as their events affected prices.

"There was as little look of public distress as of popular excitement," wrote Edward Dicey, an English journalist, of New York in 1862. "The port and quays were crowded with shipping. . . . Splendidly-equipped sable-covered sleighs were to be seen at ever turn." Ladies wore imported finery. "New stores and streets were still building."[6]

The initial enthusiasm for the war was over. A few recruiting offices tempted young men with offers of a hundred dollars' bounty, but few military bands played; when regiments went through town on their way South, "only a few idlers were gathered to see them pass." In fact, the show-time of the war had passed away.[7]

In Washington, things were different.

Dicey saw Lincoln with three others, all of whom knew the President well. Dicey looked at the President closely:

"He works hard, and does little; and unites a painful sense of responsibility to a still more painful sense, perhaps, that his work is too hard for him to grapple with. . . . If you take the stock English caricature of the typical Yankee, you have the likeness of the President."[8] Wendell Phillips, the Boston patrician and orator, had recently described Lincoln as a "first-rate second-rate man," and Dicey thought this cutting witticism one that would stick to its victim forever.

It wasn't, in fact, until the last year of the war, when Lincoln's resolve had become unmistakable, when his face had become as ravaged as an old rabbi's painted by the aging Rembrandt, that people took him for the savior of the Union.

Washington in 1862 was much more touched by war than Manhattan. For lack of funds, which had been diverted for the war effort, building on the Capitol had utterly stopped. Dicey saw "blocks of unhewn marble on every side, scattered over the pleasant grounds. . . ." And its "immense iron dome [like St. Peter's in Rome], rising grandly over that hilly campagna country, is still a bare framework of beams and girders surmounted by a crane."[9]

It was in Willard's Hotel that Dicey, who had been a correspondent in the Italian revolution felt he was in a warfront capital. It reminded him of the Hotel Victoria in Naples in the days of Garibaldi. The hotel had "the same collection of all sorts of men from every country, the same Babel of languages, the same fusion of all ranks and classes, the same ceaseless conversation about the war . . . the same series of baseless contradictory rumors and the same feverish restlessness and excitement."[10] He saw many Italians there. Cesnola was to know it well.

In February 1862, Cesnola volunteered for the Eleventh New York Cavalry Regiment, known as "Scott's 900."[11]

Its colonel, James Barrett Swain, a full-bearded man of forty-one, was a journalist who had a way with words and a flair for people, among them, Abraham Lincoln.

He had a roving life with more than its share of ups and downs, going from one newspaper to another until the New-York *Times* sent him to Washington. There, before the days of the wire services, he introduced the correspondent system of added coverage. He also met Lincoln. And he helped the President, probably aiding him with his many speeches.

When Lincoln took office in 1861, he appointed Swain a first lieutenant and in that October authorized him to raise a regiment of cavalry for federal service. The one-time editor and reporter set up recruiting booths in downtown Manhattan and got together several hundred future cavalrymen, bakers, boatmen, farmers, clerks and students. The group of about four hundred spent the winter in Staten Island where regimental headquarters were set up in a balconied, two-story building close to the water at Quarantine Landing.

It was there that G.A. Nicholetts, a New Yorker who enlisted as a sergeant-major and became captain of "D" Company, met Cesnola. In the history of the regiment Nicholetts describes his interview with Colonel Swain. During his conference, Nicholetts wrote, he noticed an officer smoking a cigar on the balcony outside.

When his enlistment was decided, the officer came into the room. "I recognized at once that he was a trained regular officer," Nicholetts wrote. "This was the Chevalier Louis Palma di Cesnola, a Sardinian officer who had served in the Crimean War and also in the War of Italian Independence; as I had the honor of serving in the Crimea, the lieutenant-colonel spoke very kindly to me and said he thought I had made the right move in enlisting in the ranks and he had no doubt that I would receive an early promotion."[12]

It was some months later, in April 1862, that Cesnola went recruiting to the home of Henry Murray Calvert whose mother and father wanted to be sure their son was joining a "crack cavalry regiment." Henry later described Cesnola, then almost thirty years old, as "about 27," well-knit, "his face full of intelligence and sprightliness," and his Italian accent giving his speech a foreign fillip. Happily at his best back in military service, the lieutenant colonel was simply "magnetic."[13]

During the long dinner, Cesnola talked about his beloved Italy, and it was only after the dessert that he came to the business of the evening and asked Henry and his friend George Pearson, also a possible recruit, the key questions.

"Do you look on the war as a frolic, something for you to laugh

and joke about," he asked, "or do you consider that the country is engaged in a conflict from which she may emerge as a degraded third-rate power?"[14]

The family group took that question into the drawing room where Cesnola called for an atlas and showed that the United States was in "terrible danger of being broken up." His finger traced the Confederacy's Atlantic seacoast, which gave her half the seaboard. Her control of the Mississippi represented, in large measure, control of the inner continent. As things stood then she had absolute dominion over the Gulf of Mexico. Should the South keep the Confederacy and the Mississippi the United States of America could very well be limited to the northeast quadrant of the land.[15]

The strapping, impetuous cavalier said he was a scientific soldier who had studied the war from its outbreak, "as a spectator watches a game of chess." The youths and their parents were soon won over to the idea of the young men following such an officer South.

Once that was settled, Cesnola's laugh rang out, and he sang Italian operatic airs as the Calvert daughter, Edythe, accompanied him on the piano. His rendition of "Tempest of the Heart" impressed his audience most.[16]

The evening closed on a realistic note; Cesnola would like, of course, to be able to tell them that the war would be finished by Christmas but he was forced to admit, "That would be miraculous and hardly likely." General George B. McClellan's campaign against the Confederate capital of Richmond, which made Northerners hope for a quick victory, was failing in the face of the general's timidity. Cesnola's bleak forecast was the professional—and accurate—one.

Several days later, the Calverts, the elder Pearsons and the two young men gave Cesnola a lavish lunch at the fashionable Astor House, and the table conversation again turned to Italy. With the coffee came the direct question: "And now, will you enroll?" They would. Cesnola rose and left the dining room. He returned with a recruiting officer who swore the young men in on the spot, privates in Scott's 900 Volunteer Cavalry.

Cesnola, "a born soldier" in the eyes of the admiring young men, gave them some of his enthusiasm for the coming fight. He drilled them incessantly. Although they had no horses as yet, he hardened

them by taking groups for long walks over the hills of Staten Island. "I can vouch for it," Calvert wrote later, "that on such occasions, he was the pivot of attention."[17]

How well this was taken by Colonel Swain is an open question. The commanding officer was then struggling to keep his unit of nine hundred in the federal service by blocking its transfer to state control as he had been ordered. He simply ignored the new orders, preferring his direct link with the White House. It was two years before he finally recognized the authority of the State of New York to control the regiment.

By May 1862, the Eleventh New York Cavalry moved to Washington, bypassing Baltimore on water and encamping on Meridian Hill at the end of Seventh Street. From there they had a distant view of the unfinished Capitol, and their presence in the vortex of martial activity filled them with fervor. Their horses arrived, matched animals of single color for the various companies. The regimental band rode its black mares around the parade ground. Sometimes at night they could hear firing outside the city.

But as the days passed, more and more routine work, guard duty and the like, became the regiment's lot. One group, A Company, provided a guard for the President; but in general, the assignments were custodial and dull. They were not at all to Cesnola's liking. They had none of the panache of actual battlefield conflict. And he was second in command when, plainly, he felt much the superior of the journalist-colonel. On June 20, 1862 after only four months of service, Cesnola resigned. The recruits Calvert and Pearson wanted to leave with him but were not allowed to.

The regiment, however, had not heard the last of the cavalier. Less than three weeks after his departure from the regiment, on July 8, 1862, Cesnola was hustled off to Old Capitol Prison. His arrest was an emotionally charged episode in which his temperament as well as his accent must have flourished. On his commitment record, his name is given as "de Arnola, Lewis Palma de Cesnold, de Cesmoli" and several other Yankee versions of Piedmontese.[18] The charges were interfering with his old regiment in a way "calculated to produce a mutiny."

Contemptuous of Colonel Swain, a man he considered a rank

amateur in the cavalry saddle, as, indeed, he was, Cesnola had apparently encouraged men of the Eleventh to formally petition the army and the State of New York that they be mustered out of the regiment. That could very well have been a move by which Cesnola, also free, could muster them into service anew and get his most earnest wish, his own full command.

Now, in an anonymous letter, advocates of Cesnola in the Eleventh protested his arrest to the War Department praising him as "both *Soldier* and *Gentleman.*" Swain, in their view, was "an old robber who without military talent or skill has assumed the title and position of Col. to make money."[19] He had withheld their pay for months, the men charged.

Jailed, Cesnola did not mope away his week in prison.

He wrote immediately to the commander of the Union forces, General George B. McClellan himself, and his message was not only that of one professional soldier to another but of a cultivated North Italian to a man of the world. Graduated second in his class at West Point, McClellan while traveling abroad to study European armies and especially the Crimean War had learned the principal European languages and acquired an appreciation for continental men and affairs. Like Cesnola, he was a diligent student of military tactics, an observer of other leaders' strategy. Some considered McClellan the thoughtful practitioner of "masterly inactivity," as the New York *Herald* put it, but he was the head of federal forces. To him, Cesnola wrote: "Colonel J. B. Swain is as ignorant as a new recruit."[20]

In handwriting that was noticeably larger than that he normally used, the angry cavalier said the head of the Washington services, General James S. Wadsworth, had simply ignored his complaints about Swain. That officer, he told McClellan, had "robbed the U. S. government and no justice was done against him."[21]

In his counterattack, Cesnola wrote flatly, "I am American citizen." This, of course, was simply not so. He undoubtedly felt that he would make more headway with his complaint if he could show he was not only fighting for the country but had given up his own nationality for it.

As for his own future, Cesnola told McClellan with no undue modesty that he wanted either to be "chief of staff or colonel of a cavalry regiment.²² He wanted it perfectly clear that he would turn down an offer of another post as lieutenant colonel. In that rank, he told McClellan, he could not "display my knowledge as an officer."²³

The man knew his own mind. He wanted to serve either under McClellan, a not injudicious desire under the circumstances, or under Major General Franz Sigel, graduate of the German Military Academy, and, like Cesnola, veteran of the European revolutionary fighting in 1847. General Sigel had rallied the German community to the Union side, his men fighting under the slogan, "I fights mit Sigel." Cesnola told McClellan that General Sigel knew him and would like him on his staff. His appeal successful, Cesnola was released from Old Capitol Prision about a week after entering it.

Southerners, rich and poor alike, were practically born on horses, and when war erupted, riders and horses went together. Finely attuned, moving in their home country, the Southern cavalry swooped over the rich hillsides and wide meadows, splashed through streams and runs and rivers and, under the leadership of flamboyant men like General James Ewell Brown ("Jeb") Stuart, struck the Northerners piercing, deadly blows.

"Jeb" Stuart, a West Point graduate, had come to Virginia with a Kansas frontier regiment. To the public, he had a flamboyant, idiosyncratic style. His wide-brimmed hat was plumed with a black ostrich feather. In the field he might wear a warm, loud plaid shirt, buttoned in brass. Riding into a city, however, he dressed in a gold-braided jacket, a golden sash at his waist, his famous cinnamon beard, fine buff gauntlets to his elbows, tall cavalry boots and the spurs of gold given him by the ladies of Baltimore.

In the North, the reputation of its own cavalry was a far different matter. The cities teemed with horses, but they were doing plodding work, drawing carts, omnibuses, and coaches. Equestrianism for the masses was, in effect, a lost art. Only those with the wealth to support a stable could feel as much at home on a horse as on foot as the Southerners did. Since it was not the wealthy, but the bakers, school teachers, clerks, and students who flocked to join the cavalry, the men had to learn first to ride, then to work together with their horses as a fighting unit and, finally, to swing a sabre from the saddle. It took time.

For many it was, at first, just too much. Edward P. Tobie of the cavalry of the Army of the Potomac, in which Cesnola would now serve, wrote of the compounded trouble that came when green men mounted green horses. The horses reared, kicked, snorted. The men paled. Many pulled back from the advancing line to avoid the rearing horses that excited their own.

Tobie told of Rhode Island's Governor Israel Washburne Jr. reviewing a fresh troop of sailor-cavalrymen led by a sea captain colonel. "Come on there, Joe! What in hell are you falling astern for?"[24] That was in April 1862, a time when Cesnola, for a lack of any horses at all, was marching his men up and down the hills of Staten Island.

While Cesnola was supervising men on guard duty in Washington, Tobie's mounted sailors were doing what they felt was degrading duty in Virginia. They were working to the rear of the infantry, patroling to prevent the soldiers from wandering off. Between riflemen and cavalry there grew a fierce antipathy, the hatred of a group of exposed and embattled men, crouching behind low stone walls, who were at the mercy of the Confederate cavalry. At this time the union mounted troops were, in effect, military police. As they passed, the infantrymen would shout: "Who ever saw a dead cavalryman?"[25] It was a common taunt, so common that it reached general headquarters.

Through the summer and fall of 1862, as the infantry and artillery dominated the fields at the second Bull Run, Antietam and Fredericksburg, the unproductive Union cavalryman in Virginia "grew more and more disgusted and was inclined to be ashamed."

Though gaining in experience, a cavalryman still knew from time to time, more rarely now than before, the sinking feeling of the sailor on horseback, out of his element. The use to which commanders put him contributed to his unease. Cavalry battles in the Civil War were rare. The action—and the glory—went to the infantry and the gunners.

Now a new general, the West Pointer Ambrose Everett Burnside, an artilleryman, gave the cavalry its supreme opportunity. He created the unified cavalry corps of the Army of the Potomac, a famed, spirited unit pulled together from the disorganized, disparate bits and pieces of cavalry attached to the infantry throughout the East.

Organized into brigades and divisions, it was put under the command of General George Stoneman, another West Pointer and a dragoon, who led mounted infantrymen to the battlefield where they dismounted to fight. Both Burnside and Stoneman, experienced in Mexican and Indian fighting, had other ideas. They wanted a mounted force capable of matching "Jeb" Stuart's. It was a tall order.

Throughout the winter of 1862, the new corps drilled and trained, getting used to working as members of a single force. As a unit, they looked promising, and Burnside's successor, General "Fighting Joe" Hooker, was said to have rubbed his hands together in joy at the prospect, more certain now, of a dead cavalryman.

In October, at the request of Governor Edwin D. Morgan of New York, "Louis Palma de Cesnola" was mustered into service as Colonel of the Fourth Regiment of New York State's Voluntary Cavalry.[26]

He had his command.

In taking it, he succeeded Colonel Christian F. Dickel, organizer of the troop known as "Dickel's Mounted Rifles." Cesnola brought a party into service with him and then set up two recruiting offices, one at 62 White Street at his own expense, the other at 27 Broadway which the state paid for. He discouraged bounty jumpers by developing strong regimental pride.

By the end of November 1862 Cesnola led his men to Virginia where he was in command of four cavalry regiments: Connecticut's First, his own New York's Fourth, and the Ninth, and Ohio's Sixth. At home in Hooker's newly organized cavalry, he was glad to be in the thick of things.

Skirmishing in the rich Virginia farmland between Washington and Richmond brought Cesnola and his troops face to face with glum prisoners, hardship in getting forage and the exhilarating first clashes with the enemy. With the veteran Brigadier General Julius Stahel, trained in Kossuth's army of 1848, Cesnola and his men took Berryville, across the Shenandoah in northern Virginia, streaming into a line of defending rebels in a rush of surprise. "I did not give them an opportunity to see the difference in numbers but charged them," he wrote later. "They broke and ran in receiving our sabres."[27]

By the end of November, Cesnola, soon to receive command of Pennsylvania's Seventeenth Cavalry, had orders to "hold your command in readiness to march at a moment's notice."[28] The high command was obviously relying more and more on the Savoyard.

The new year began with Lincoln announcing the Emancipation Proclamation. To the President, it seemed that the battle of Antietam, where the Northern forces hurt the South just a bit more than the Southern hurt the North, justified his taking such a step. Even though it lacked immediate great importance—the Proclamation abolished slavery only in the South where its provisions could not be enforced—yet it altered the basis of the war from the challenge of secession to the moral issue of slavery. This shift and a need for the North's wheat had much to do with diverting England's original sympathies from the South and lessening the risk of her intervening in the war.

On the home front, prices, production and profits spired over pre-war levels and huge supplies of manpower—800,000 souls—came from the old world to take the places of the men who were at war. Then, as McClellan's expected dash for Richmond failed and the fighting settled down to a long struggle, people began to hoard. Later they profiteered. Cornelius Vanderbilt leased his fleet of ships to the Federal government and began acquiring rails.

The men on the fields of Virginia had no such chances. Instead, they had what Cesnola prized, an important part in the flowing, strident action of the Army of the Potomac. In early 1863, his command was a vital part of the strategic force with which General Hooker probed Confederate lines, pulling its cavalry offside and getting useful information on rebel troops. His men were becoming hardened, experienced scouts and campers.

Young Second Lieutenant Jack Townsend Ketcham, a Quaker farmer from Long Island who commanded the Fourth's Company "M," wrote to his mother that "Virginia mud is like grafting wax." At camp near Falmouth in a "beautiful piece of wood," the mud was "even with the top of our boots when you step on it; six mules have to look sharp to get along with a light load, and on each side of the road the soil is as nice and dry as the 'long pond' woods in summer.

... I can hardly realize yet that I'm with the Grand Army."[29]

The men and their colonel were doing more than enjoying the Virginia countryside. Soon Cesnola sent a report back to his command of an engagement on January 26, 1863 at Grove Church, Virginia. "We have men killed and wounded," he reported. "Because of the want of forage, I am compelled to send out quite a force each day."[30]

The report of the dead cavalrymen went straight up the line, through General Sigel of the Eleventh Corps and Major General Daniel Butterfield, chief of staff, to "Fighting Joe" Hooker, commander of the Army of the Potomac.[31] The bite of the old question, who ever saw a dead cavalryman, began to fade.

Cesnola's brigade collided again and again with the Confederates, suffering wounds and death from firearms and sabres. It was becoming intimate with the terrible, swift sword, and respectful of the enemy. The wealthy sportsman and planter, General Wade Hampton, one of "Jeb" Stuart's lieutenants, moved his troops, one thousand men in infantry and cavalry with two huge guns, before Cesnola's forces. It was a sight to rile the temper of the Piedmont cavalier.

The day Cesnola's forward patrol watched the well-provisioned Hampton, two of his horses died of exhaustion. He minced no words with General Stahel: "My horses were tired out for want of several days' forage."[32]

Though his enfeebled forces were attacked almost daily, Cesnola was, in fact, at the peak of his rise in the cavalry. He was in the front lines commanding a cavalry brigade of five regiments—the First Maryland, the Fourth and Ninth New York, the Sixth Ohio and the Seventeenth Pennsylvania—close to five thousand men. His situation was such that he would warn his division commander, Brigadier General Carl Schurz, to hold his troops in "readiness in case of an emergency."[33]

It was at this juncture that, for Cesnola, the greatest engagement, though not a battle, became his own.

On January 31, 1863 the judge advocate general sent a report to Secretary of War Edwin M. Stanton:

The shameless plunder of the public property which is known to prevail in the service can be suppressed only by the most prompt and summary punishment of the offenders. A receiver or a dealer in public property, marked as his own as such, which has been stolen or fraudently disposed of should be as unhesitatingly expelled the service as if he were the primary offender. The present is a flagrant case & it is recommended that Col. Cesnola be dismissed.[34]

The charge was a simple one. In early January the provost marshal's office reported to the Assistant Secretary of War, P.N. Watson, that an officer had found at the Adams Express Co. in Washington, a box Cesnola had addressed to his wife at 37 West 30th Street in New York. It held not only some of the colonel's clothing but six new Remington Cavalry pistols and their holsters "belonging to the government."[35]

From "Headquarters Fourth New York Cavalry commanded by Colonel L.P. Di Cesnola," the cavalryman shot back a quick answer to his accuser, Col. L.P. Baker of the provost marshal service. He had sent the firearms north, he asserted, for use by guards to check desertions at his induction camp at Quarantine Landing on Staten Island. New York State had failed to supply the needed pistols and "exorbitant bounties" were stimulating desertions. Only by the strictest discipline had the camp produced three much-needed new companies for his regiment.

Cesnola failed to explain why he had not forwarded the pistols directly to the camp. Surely the commanding officer of a brigade was not obliged to wrap up his own packages. His only reference to the mailing address was that Major August Pruyn, given an order for the pistols by Cesnola, was to pick them up at the Cesnola home.

From his letter to Colonel Baker it was apparent that Cesnola felt that the backing of influential friends—he mentioned Generals Sigel and Stahel, Senator Ira Harris of New York, the railroad magnate Erastus Corning and ex-Governor Morgan of New York—would extricate him from the net of circumstance. In a final and naive reference, he enclosed a newspaper article "in which my name is mentioned favorably as a corroboration to my words."[36]

Such an easy way out was not to be his. The secretary of war, a

lawyer who had been attorney general in Buchanan's cabinet, took
the adjutant general's advice. In the name of the President of the
United States, Cesnola was dishonorably dismissed from service on
February 2, 1863.[37]

He went straight to Willard's Hotel in Washington, close to his
powerful friends, and poured out his anger.

To Assistant Secretary of War Watson he wrote:

I feel so keenly the wrong that has been done to me, so barbarian like
and without reason, that I beg you with all my heart to see that this
protest is handed to the Secretary of War immediately.

I have no friends. [What happened to the public figures and the
generals?] I am a foreigner, and I am an innocent man you have
shown me kind interest when I had trouble with Col. Swain. I hope
you will assist me once more in getting what I am entitled to.

The newspapers since I am in the field had made my reputation
as a soldier one of the highest. . . . [Again, he gives publicity prominence.] General Sigel gave me the command of a Brigade of cavalry
& calls me an excellent cavalry officer. I have captured rebel prisoners, arms & horses more than any other Colonels have done yet and
when my dismissal came I was in the very advance skirmishing with
the enemy at the Rappahannoc since a month while the Army of the
Potomac was complaining of the mud & bad weather. If officers who
are fighting for their country have to be treated in such a way the war
will never end.

He enclosed some "extracts from the papers to show how Col. Cesnola has always done his duty."[38]

By middle February, Cesnola had letters of recommendation
from the two foreign generals, Stahel and Sigel. Both attested to his
good name and wanted to see him restored to duty in the field. But
no redress came from the War Department.

Now, for the first time, Cesnola quit relying on friends and publicity to save himself and attended to the legal aspects of the case. He
had already convinced Colonel Baker that the pistols belonged not
to the federal government but to New York State. Baker, in fact, had
sent the package and the pistols on to Manhattan, presumably to
Madame Cesnola. How could the colonel, then, be dismissed for
appropriating property of the federal government when the items

involved were actually state property? Cesnola now went after Stanton in earnest. He had been "unjustly condemned to a moral death," he wrote the secretary of war. He had in his possession a receipt he had signed for the pistols to the New York State Arsenal. He was still responsible to the arsenal for them.

His wrath at the War Department overflowed. "Without a hearing, without a reason, I have been a week ago publicly disgraced by your order," he told Stanton. I have remonstrated through the proper channel, soldierlike, in hope that you would immediately restore my honor which neither you nor the President of the U.S. nor God have a right to deprive me of unjustly. . . . I bore the stigma of thief upon my brow patiently to give time to repair a gross mistake. . . ."[39]

He then solemnly protested his dismissal without full prior investigation and the protection of civil and military laws. His fine military reputation, "second to none," had been "in a moment blasted by some gross error and I have apparently to sue and beg for that justice which the Secretary of War should be the first gladly to extend." He signed himself "late Colonel 4th N.Y. Cavalry, Commanding Cavalry Brigade."[40]

To Assistant Secretary of War Watson he sent an affidavit from his recruiting officer, Major August Pruyn, attesting he had requested the pistols in December. However, no copy of the December letter accompanied the affidavit. The major swore also that the colonel had sent him an order by which he could get the pistols from the Cesnola home. But, again, no copy of the order was produced. Watson sent the affidavit on to the judge advocate's office. And Cesnola, waiting, fumed.

Writing to Stanton from Willard's Hotel on February 25, he referred to himself in the third person and neglected both opening and closing salutations:

Col. di Cesnola, 4th N.Y. Cavy. is since three weeks suffering from the effect of a gross mistake; his name heretofore one of the purest in the U.S. Army is disgraced, his family in desolation, his reputation soiled and yet no redress is coming to him.

Col. Cesnola therefore most respectfully request [sic] you to see that full justice be done at once to him and his good name be returned.[41]

He sat in bewildered silence and disgust for two more weeks. Finally, on March 3, 1863, by General Order #50, Cesnola's dismissal was revoked and he was "reinstated in his command, provided the vacancy has not been filled, he having shown that the property was not stolen, and that in irregularly and improperly forwarding it to an officer of his regiment no wrong was intended."[42]

He went back as colonel of the Fourth New York Cavalry but not as commanding officer of the brigade. He was to yearn and struggle from then on for a restoration of the full brigade to his authority.

Restored to but a part of his former command with no apology, Cesnola was unhappy. He was so distressed that he was thinking of going off to become a farmer "and live an independent life."

He had had his full of inspectors and adjutants general and he told his patron, the Albany railroad chief, Erastus Corning, who had once recommended him for command of a New York regiment, that he would now like a new state appointment. He wanted no part of continued federal service. "With what aching heart I return to my regiment few persons can appreciate it," he told Corning. "I tried ever to my utmost in well deserving from my adoptive country and the rewards I received from the Administration I may say were nothing but kicks. . . . It is impossible for me to continue in the service as tho I have been restored. I have not received from the Administration that full justice I was entitled and Leery Stanton says 'it is all he can do.' " He had returned to the Fourth "with a broken heart" to stay only a few weeks. It was only a lack of money that forced him to go back at all. He had spent the little money his wife had to recruit troops, he told Corning, and he had to now find a suitable job to enable him to leave the regiment without becoming "a beggar out of service."

If it was true, as he had heard, that New York was about to set up a military training camp, he would seek a post there, as he was just as capable as "any of the West Point Professors" at instructing trainees.[43]

But these hopes and his daydreams of farming never materialized and he entered a dark period, fixed in his reduced place in General Hooker's Army of the Potomac as commander of the Fourth New York Regiment.

Other regiments were led by cavalrymen of lesser rank. Many and many a brigade, which Cesnola had headed before he sent the pistols off to Mary, was commanded by a brigadier general, and the longing for the rank which he had held in fact if not in title mulled like soured wine in the bitterness that filled Cesnola after the pistol episode.

He was plainly disheartened and disgruntled. "Here things go badly," he wrote Hitchcock in May, "everybody commands but nobody wants to obey. I have as yet all those men I recruited in New York 9 months ago all dismounted and I do not see any steps taken to mount them." Of the 737 men in the Fourth New York at the time, 461 had no horses. "This & thousand other wrong things dishearten me that I shall not be able to stand great deal longer this life of humiliation, never revenged, and injustice."[44]

He felt he was being passed over in promotions. "I am the senior Colonel in Averill's Division," he wrote his friend, "and since he left, other Colonels [Americans] were put in command when the law & any Regulations give me as by seniority of rank the command of it. Oh my heart is everyday more sore! Nobody was more enthusiastic in fighting than I was. They succeeded now to make me cold like a stone."[45]

In spite of the aggravations, it was good to be again in the field, to jump on a horse even if it was not the very best of mounts, and to see to it that his men got horses.

Up north in New York, however, matters other than the war diverted the public. Excitement over the wedding of the midgets "General" Tom Thumb and Lavinia Warren still bloomed like an exotic, miniature rose. Some had their doubts as to "whether the whole affair would not turn out a sham—an advertising hoax on a large scale, designed and executed by the smartest tactician on this side of the Atlantic."[46] But "the great Barnum himself, who looked excruciatingly happy," led the doll-size man and his tiny bride into the reception at the Metropolitan Hotel after their wedding.

In the windy, wide, rolling country of Virginia and in its steep mountain passes, the life was one of fighting off hunger, of struggling daily for enough forage for the horses, of a hardening that, though

barely perceptible from day to day, was culminating in a power that
would soon make itself felt.

The cavalry was now under Stoneman, who was proving to be
a daring, almost rash, man. He headed a corps of three cavalry divisions, some 11,500 men, on forward outpost duty in northern Virginia. Raiders who jabbed at the enemy, his patrols were the eyes of
the army. While Cesnola was away in Washington, they had stood up
to the Confederate cavalry under Stuart himself. Rhode Island troopers and the Fourth New York had straddled a road at Hartwood,
ignored the curdling rebel yell and pushed back the renowned horsemen of "Jeb" Stuart who had encircled McClellan's army.

The cavalry men were elated and ready for more. On the afternoon of March 15, General William W. Averell, thirty-one years old,
head of the Cavalry Corps' Second Division, reviewed his now-
mounted troops, "a beautiful sight." Then brigade officers, Cesnola
among them once again, went to Averell's headquarters. Their instructions: to be prepared for the start of a raid at 8 A.M. the next day.
They were to carry three days' rations and one day's forage.

They were on their way to the battle of Kelly's Ford, a clash in
an open field, the first time in America a sizeable cavalry force fought
sabre-to-sabre. It proved an indecisive contest between two groups,
"yelling like demons," then charging with drawn sabres and meeting
like counter-whirlwinds.

"The two forces came together at full speed—horse to horse—
man to man—sabre to sabre. What a fight! The conflict was short,
determined, deadly. The enemy—the famed Stuart and his boasted
Virginia Cavalry—was broken, rolled back, utterly repulsed, with
very severe loss."[47]

The Union cavalry exulted. Historians do not see the encounter
as a Union victory. But the men did.

"Near sunset the enemy retired; the day had been too much for
their cavalry," the troop's chaplain, Frederic Denison wrote. The
Union troops moved quietly back across the river, proud that they
had weathered charges by General Fitzhugh, "Fitz" Lee, nephew of
the Confederate commander, the young "laughing cavalier," a fierce
fighter and a major general before he was twenty-eight years old.
Stuart himself had galloped against them.

The colonel then commanding the brigade, Colonel A.N. Duffié, told his men the fight would become famous not so much for the numbers in it, "but as a demonstration, beyond a doubt, that in an open fight the Rebel cavalry cannot stand Yankee sabres."[48]

By April, the spring sun warmed the rich Virginia soil, and great plans stirred the commanders. "Fighting Joe" Hooker prepared to surprise the enemy by curving around through Kelly's Ford and outflanking Lee and the strong force he had posted in defense of Richmond.

Hooker sent General Stoneman and his cavalry to rip the Southern rail and telegraph lines and hit at Richmond. It was the first such organized expedition into enemy country, a bruising, fearsome raid that ravaged the land and exhausted the men. Bad weather led to several false starts before the cavalry swung around to the rear of Lee's army, tore up his communications with Richmond and laid to waste and useless desolation railroad lines, canals, grain warehouses and Confederate government property. One small band of raiders penetrated the outer line of Richmond's defenses. The sabre-swinging men "carried consternation everywhere."[49] With the others on Stoneman's raid, Cesnola and his men of the Fourth wreaked havoc in a concentrated preview of Sherman's march in Georgia. They slashed ahead for four days and three nights, managed one night's good sleep, then returned in four more sleepless days and nights. The very physical aspects of the raid won respect.

While the raiders streaked through Virginia behind him, Robert E. Lee unconventionally cut his force in two and, in what is called his masterpiece battle, the Chancellorsville campaign, threw one at Hooker and the other at General John Sedgwich who was making a flanking attack on Rebel forces. Hooker's Army of the Potomac suffered more than twice Lee's losses.

The Southern leader had begun moving to the west. Hooker then ordered General Alfred Pleasanton, new head of the cavalry, to find out by reconnaissance what Lee was up to. Federal troopers found Stuart holding a shield of land along the Rappahannock. Surprising the Southerners, they attacked before dawn on June 9, rousing them from sleep. But the Confederates reorganized, and the two forces of regimental troopers, Cesnola's Fourth New York among them, met on a wide plain at Brandy Station. It was the largest cavalry engagement of the Civil War.

Lieutenant Tobie wrote,

The whole plain was one vast field of intense, earnest action. It was a scene to be witnessed but once in a life-time, and one worth all the risks of battle to witness. But we could not stop to enjoy this grand, moving panorama of war. On we went, amid a perfect tangle of sights and sounds, filled with such rare, whole-souled excitement as seldom falls to the lot of man to experience, and thoughts of danger were for the time farthest from our minds. Even the horses seemed to enter into the spirit of the occasion and to strain every nerve to do their full duty in the day's strange deeds, obeying the least motion of rein or spur with unusual promptness, as if feeling the superiority of their riders in this terrible commotion.[50]

Finally, horse and man were one. The battle *made* the federal cavalry in the opinion of the Civil War historian H.B. McClellan. Until then admittedly inferior to the Southern troopers, the cavalry won at Brandy Station that confidence in itself and its commanders that fitted it to fight so ably on the battlefields of June, July, and October.

After the engagement, the federal cavalry could report that Lee was headed not only west but north. He might, indeed, be heading for Pennsylvania.

A week later, the cavalry corps of both armies, each keeping close watch on the movements of the other's forces, met head-on farther north at Aldie, Virginia.

In their route north, the Confederates had come to the steep and sheltering hills of the Catoctin Mountains. Against them, squads of sharpshooters crouched behind low stone fences, taking pot shots at roving Rebel cavalry. The rivalry between the federal cavalry and the infantry still flared in the fire of guerrilla warfare and the hard-riding Cesnola, bent on moving his own men and unsolicitous of the infantry, angered an infantry general. His sword was taken from him. He was put under arrest.

At this point, on June 17, 1863, in the hill country of western Virginia, at Aldie, some forty miles from Washington, as they were pushing north, the Fourth New York Cavalry, under General Judson Kilpatrick, came face-to-face with Stuart's cavalry.

This was to be one of the most savagely fought engagements on Lee's historic route from Chancellorsville to Gettysburg two weeks later.

Kilpatrick ordered a charge. Bound by his previous arrest, Cesnola was forced to stay behind. His men thundered forward, yelling and sweeping the clean air with their sabres. Cesnola could hear the metallic clash of sword-to-sword combat, the shrieking Rebel yells, the thud of horses falling.

Then his men, driven off in desperate fighting, limped back. They called to him to go with them. Without a moment's hesitation, he did. Jumping to his mount, he galloped around the routed Fourth, his accent heavier than usual in the thick emotion of the moment. The men rallied, and Cesnola led them on toward Stuart's cavalry. He went without his sabre, a brash, desperate gesture, and the Fourth, with the daring Italian at their apex, rode like a living spear into the side of the Confederate troops.

When the skirmish was over, the Fourth returned to their main forces, and Brigadier General L.G. Estes, astounded at Cesnola's act, reported to Kilpatrick that the cavalryman, unarmed, had just returned from a charge against the enemy. Kilpatrick told Estes to get Pleasanton to relieve Cesnola from arrest so he could take proper command of his regiment.

Estes rode off and procured the colonel's reinstatement. Then, rushing up to Cesnola who sat mounted among his men, General Estes handed him his own sword.[51] The Fourth then charged again. But when the regiment returned for the third time to their headquarters, their colonel was not with them.

Cesnola lay under his dead horse, a sabre cut three inches long in the crown of his head, a large cut in the palm of his right hand and a gunshot wound in the upper part of his left arm.

After nightfall, when the Confederates returned to the field to retrieve their wounded and dead, Cesnola was captured.[52] He was sent with others to a prison center in Winchester, Virginia, and there he found a friendly fellow-prisoner, Captain Thomas Morley of the Twelfth Pennsylvania Cavalry. Morley saw Cesnola was helpless. The colonel was lying on the ground, "unable to do anything for himself."[53] Cesnola asked for water. Morley gave it to him, and, seeing the "dirty bloody rags" with which his wounds were bound, heated some over a little fire and bathed Cesnola's head. Then he cut off the hair around the wound and pulled the wound together, fixing it in place with sticking plaster.

Cesnola, his uniform streaked with mud, leaned back in sheer fatigue. Although a transfer of prisoners was about to take place, he wanted to stay where he was. It was Morley who impressed on him the need to go with the rest. The main Rebel prisoner center in the area was at Stanton, some miles away, and Morley knew that Cesnola could never walk there.

Cesnola managed to hire a horse and wearily mounted again, going South to prison.

Four

Imprisonment struck Cesnola as a personal insult, the more so since, had he won his way with Corning, he would have been training troops in New York. Ordered to remove his grimy boots for inspection when he arrived at Libby Prison in Richmond, he told the Confederate sergeant making the demand that he "always had a servant to perform that service."[1] He glared at the reluctant sergeant and would not budge from his refusal.

The sergeant's avarice won out over his pride since he had recovered much Northern money in the lining and soles of Union officer's boots. He removed Cesnola's and became furious.

"He was angry because he could not find any greenbacks on my person," Cesnola told the United States Sanitary Commission that investigated prison conditions in early 1865. "He asked me what I had done with my money, and if I had any watch." Cesnola told him a "chivalric Southerner" had stolen his watch and money on his captive ride to Richmond. The sergeant flared and took from him "every little trinket" he had, his meerschaum pipe and matches, his penknife, a bunch of small keys, even his eyeglasses.

"I therefore entered the gates of a Confederate prison stripped

of everything except my spurs, which being screwed into the boots
could not be removed."[2]

Most of the prisoners who hiked into the old, brick tobacco
warehouse on the canal beside the James River suffered the same
treatment. The wounded Cesnola found himself without a blanket
and for some five months had not even a piece of paper on which to
write a letter. Though his wounds troubled him constantly, he
avoided the prison hospital, having heard that patients, especially
foreigners, received poor treatment there. Instead, he relied on the
care given to him by Captain Morley. To it, Cesnola later credited his
life.

The Pennsylvanian, who slept next to Cesnola for nine of the
latter's ten months in prison, tried to help the disabled man.[3] The
New Yorker, afflicted with rheumatism and asthma as well as the
battlefield wounds, was relatively helpless and lay in his uniform on
the bare floor. The glass having been knocked out of the window near
him, he suffered bitterly from the cold when winter came.

In the prison, one of the most notorious in the Confederacy and
second only to Andersonville in its harshness, some twelve hundred
United States officers lived in six bare rooms.

Each man had a scant ten-feet-by-two in which to exist within
the miserable gloom, with meager rations and foul, verminous conditions. The men named the rooms after their lost leaders, and Cesnola
was one of many in the room of "Kilpatrick's Raiders."

The scene from their windows over the James, however, was one
of an urban center softened by the varied, gentle landscape of Virginia. One prisoner of war described the view:

Immediately below is the canal; beyond it flows the river with a
rapid, murmuring current, reflecting here and there the purple flush
of the morning clouds; there is a cluster of tall factories on the opposite bank; beyond these is the village of Manchester on one side and
on the other are broad fields, and the rolling hills which fringe a
distant curve of the river.[4]

He saw a "lovely little island" upstream and, in the distance, "a full
mile off," the foul Belle Isle Prison where enlisted men died from
starvation and cold.

Shooting at prisoners who even approached the windows at Libby Prison was a sportive pastime of their bored jailers. Terrified, the Northerners learned to stay far within the low-ceilinged rooms. As many as fourteen shots snorted toward the windows in a single day, and the sequel, seen from a cautious distance, was that of the "sergeant of the guard ... bringing out a dead or wounded soldier."[5] When a lieutenant was shot in a small enclosure where there was no window, the commander of the prison snapped, "The boys are in want of practice."

The diet, as Cesnola first entered the prison, was relatively good. So was the morale. Most of the prisoners were newly captured and their spirits buoyed by chaplain L.N. Beaudry of the Fifth New York Cavalry. A full-bearded, husky cavalryman of consistent, modestly cheerful outlook, Beaudry was taken at Gettysburg and forced by "Jeb" Stuart himself to say "I surrender."[6] Beaudry, imprisoned in July, set to work at once to hearten the prisoners. He led some to the roof where in the cool of the evening they spent some time away from the stench of the rooms below.

Dick Turner, the "hard keeper" of Libby discovered the men taking this respite and put an end to it.

One aspect of prison life remained constant. A wild insect population flourished on and around the prisoners and gave rise to the daily activity of "skirmishing" during which they took off their wretched pieces of clothing one at a time and picked them.

To take their minds off this, Beaudry established the "Libby Lyce-I-see-'Em."

Essentially a debating society, the Lyceum enabled the men to sound off on their ideas on such subjects as whether "the Fear of Punishment has a greater influence upon mankind than the Hope of Reward." They set up classes, then, on a variety of subjects: arithmetic, algebra, philosophy, history, theology, medicine, and a wide span of languages, Greek and Latin, German, Italian, Spanish and French. Beaudry, a native Frenchman, had one hundred in his French class. The most popular study was phonography. Colonel Cesnola taught cavalry tactics to a number of prisoner-pupils.

On most evenings the men gathered to sing English, French, German, Irish, and Italian songs, attracting a huge audience of prisoners within Libby and guards and Richmonders without. When the crowd outside was large enough, the pent-up men belted out the popular, "Down with the traitors! Up with the Stars!" Libby was fast becoming known as the "Prison Palace of the Confederacy," more for its inmates' spirits than its prison fare.

The main work of the Lyceum was its "publication," *The Libby Chronicle*, written chiefly by the chaplain who used it as a pulpit, a confessional, and a reminder of civilian joys. Once a week the reading of *The Chronicle* would be announced throughout the building and the prisoners would rush to listen to its contents. The men formed a circle on the floor and Beaudry, standing in the center, would read the various articles aloud. Such "publication" proved safe.

At one session a paper described the celebration of July 4, 1863, at Libby, about a fortnight after Cesnola's arrival. Orators were legion; all they needed was a Union flag. Some captured flags hung upside down in the prison's central offices. But the danger in recapturing them was too great. Perhaps one could be bought in Richmond; almost anything could be, in fact, with Yankee dollars.

But the men finally decided to make their own. Though they had no red cloth, they managed to fashion a flag from a white shirt and blue pants. The men were kept from one room the morning of the Fourth as a few saw to it that the flag was hung high from a beam. The place selected was under the peaked roof, the highest place within the prison. Then the men were called to enter.

"Men wept and laughed and stamped and clapped and shouted," *The Chronicle* reported. "These old walls trembled, and for a while, like those of ancient Jericho, seemed ready to fall."[7]

Dick Turner, the keeper, rushed into the hall demanding that the blue-striped banner be taken down at once. The men's silent refusal stared him down. He finally put his orderly to the task, and Beaudry recorded the moment:

At last the arrant Rebel held in his sacrilegious hands the sacred emblem of a great nation's pride. . . . But he could not wrench from the hearts of these undaunted men what to them was a priceless boon, love to God and Country. Tell me now if these prisoners have not in them the stuff of which heroes are made?[8]

Rivarolo Canavese, in the heart of the Piedmont, is a town set out in square, Roman style with low, elegant and austere buildings.

The Cesnola coat-of-arms.

OPPRESSA RESURGIT

From the hamlet of Cesnola mounts a moss-bound path to a ruined castle, the feud of the house of Palma. (From C. F. Scavini, Torri e Castelli Canavesani, Torino, 1964.)

Opposite Page: City Hall Park in 1858 was a lush little oasis with a superb fountain. (Lithograph and drawing by Bachmann. Courtesy, The New-York Historical Society, New York City.)

Opposite Page: New York's suburbs in 1858 were rural; its harbor filled with ships. ("Bay of New York from Hudson City, 1858" by William R. Miller. Courtesy, The New-York Historical Society, New York City.)

Right: Mary Reid Cesnola. (Courtesy, Mrs. Violet Baker Cook.)

Below: Hiram Hitchock of the Fifth Avenue Hotel, Cesnola's "dear old friend." (Courtesy, The Metropolitan Museum of Art.)

Diners at The Fifth Avenue Hotel sat twenty or thirty at a table. (From Harper's Weekly, Oct. 1, 1859. Courtesy, Dartmouth College.)

After dinner, the ladies withdrew and men traded stocks. (From Harper's Weekly, Oct. 1, 1859. Courtesy, Dartmouth College.)

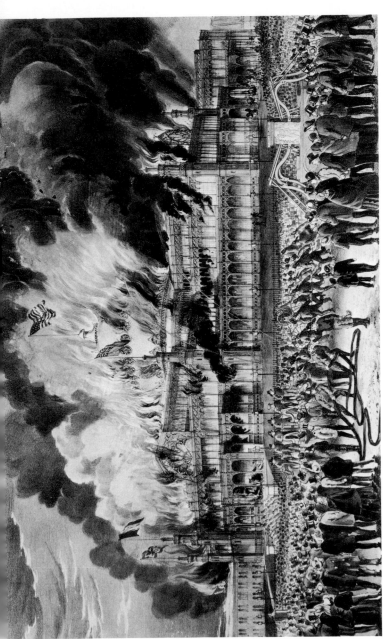

In early October 1858, New York's Crystal Palace was destroyed by fire in twenty minutes. (Currier & Ives lithograph. Courtesy, The New-York Historical Society, New York City.)

Above: War brought tents and uniforms to New York City. Soldiers drilled in the camp on the Battery. (From Frank Leslie's Illustrated Newspaper, July 11, 1863. Courtesy, Dartmouth College.)

Below: Stoneman's Raid, during which Rebel warehouses were burned. (From Frank Leslie's Illustrated Newspaper, May 30, 1863. Courtesy, The New-York Historical Society, New York City.)

Above: Stoneman's Raid. Canal locks exploded in blasts of Federal dynamite. (From Frank Leslie's Illustrated News-paper, May 30, 1863. Courtesy, The New-York Historical Society, New York City.)

Below: Stoneman's Raid. Troopers streak through Virginia behind Lee's lines. (From Frank Leslie's Illustrated Newspaper, May 30, 1863. Courtesy, The New-York Historical Society, New York City.)

Above: At Aldie, Virginia, General Estes restores confiscated sword to Cesnola. (From: James Moore, M.D., Kilpatrick & Our Cavalry *[New York, 1865]. Courtesy, The New-York Historical Society, New York City.) Below: On June 17, 1863, Cesnola fell wounded and was captured at Aldie, Virginia. (From* Frank Leslie's Illustrated Newspaper, *July 11, 1863. Courtesy, Dartmouth College.)*

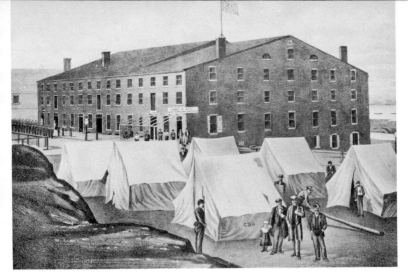

Above: Prison for Cesnola and hundreds of other Federal captives was the old brick tobacco warehouse of Libby & Son in Richmond. (Bella C. Landauer Collection. Courtesy, The New-York Historical Society, New York City.) Below: In Libby Prison, one of the South's most notorious, some 1200 Union officers lived in six bare rooms. (From: Harper's Weekly, October 17, 1863. Courtesy, The New-York Historical Society, New York City.)

Left: The journalist-cavalryman James Barrett Swain, colonel of Cesnola's first regiment, irked the Savoyard and forced him to retire. (From Thomas W. Smith, Story of a Cavalry Regiment [New York, 1897]. Courtesy, The New-York Historical Society, New York City.)

Opposite: In the spring of 1864 everyone with any wit or talent joined in working for the Metropolitan Fair. (From Harper's Weekly, April 16, 1864. Courtesy, The New-York Historical Society, New York City.)

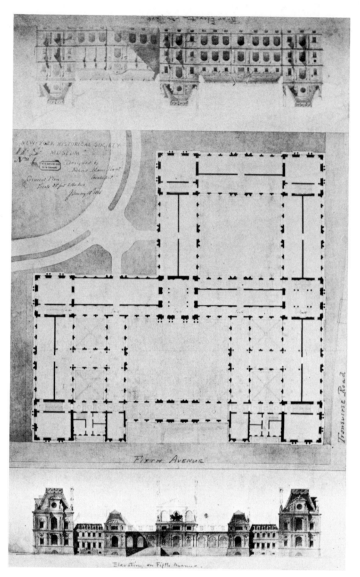

Richard Morris Hunt drew Louvre-like plans in 1866 for The New-York Historical Society's museum in the park. The proposed site was exactly where The Metropolitan Museum of Art now stands. (The New-York Historical Society elevation and plan, January 15, 1866. Courtesy, The New-York Historical Society, New York City.)

Captain Beaudry, plainly, was too great a morale builder. On October 7, 1863, the chaplain, his feet in boots made of a torn blanket, his body in clothes that were thin with wear and eaten by vermin, a jaunty gray slouch "Stonewall hat" on his thick hair, was released to Northern forces of the steamer *New York*, a truce ship resting at City Point on the James River. He wept at the sight of the Union flag. With his departure, a nugget of life's spirit left Libby.

Each man looked out for himself. Differences in rank all but disappeared as each officer struggled for his own best place within the strictures of the overcrowded, foul-smelling, planked-floor prison.

Cesnola remained in what he later called "this deplorable condition, without a book to read or a sheet of paper to write, for over five months, nursing my grief during the whole day, using my boots for a pillow during the night, and sleeping on the bare and often damp plank floor, with neither blanket nor overcoat, nor any other covering. Dogs had certainly better sleeping accommodations in their kennels than I had there." His only consolation was that other officers shared the "wretched conditions."[9] It was not until October 1863 that Cesnola received blankets.

All the prisoners were under orders to scrub the floor, the tables and the sinks, and it usually happened that it was just when the officers were performing these demeaning tasks that Southern ladies somehow appeared at the windows.

They did not see Cesnola on his knees. "I must confess," he told the Commission later, "such service was revolting to me, and I always found some good-hearted fellow prisoner who, for sake of exercise, would perform it in my stead."[10] Clearly, the colonel could cajole as well as lead men.

In the fall of the year, the quality and amount of the ration fell to the point when the corn bread served was so hard it was called "iron clad, solid shot, railroad iron." Meat came in servings of a few ounces, only four or five times a month. Soup, passed around in the dark of night, turned out, by day, to be filled with maggots rather than rice.

In November 1863, Major Turner called Cesnola to the commandant's office to tell him he would replace General Dow, a friend and fellow-prisoner, as commissary of distribution. Dow had offended the military governor of Richmond, Confederate General J.H. Winder, and the prison officials were told to get another officer to handle distribution of goods received from the North. Cesnola was given the job of supervising delivery of boxes to Belle Isle Prison where Yankee enlisted men were kept. With the order went instructions not to talk to any of the men there. The colonel chose two assistants, Lieutenant Colonel Joseph F. Boyd and his friend, Lieutenant Colonel Alexander von Schrader, who had been inspector general of the Fourteenth Army Corps.

As Cesnola and his aides prepared to take the boxes to Belle Isle, Dick Turner told Cesnola that he, Cesnola, would be personally responsible for paying the transportation costs. Boyd, who had had some money taken from him by the Confederates on entering the prison, offered to allot that to the purpose. The next day, November 12, that solution was accepted. To all three, the project promised relief from the tedium of prison.

Accompanied by two guards they went to Belle Isle at 10 A.M. each day and returned about 4 P.M.

They found 6434 Union prisoners in dire straits at the camp. Dorothea L. Dix, the impassioned reformer later found that Belle Isle prisoners suffered more from hunger than from rapid marches, exposure to bad weather or lack of clothing. The enlisted men there told her that one hundred men received but "one iron-bound bucket filled with packed meat" a day, twenty-five pounds in all.

As winter deepened, the bucket of meat appeared only twice a week, and the usual daily ration consisted of roughly baked corn meal. Many died of simple starvation. They found that the hospital offered "a little boiled rice, to which was sometimes added a very small quantity of brown sugar or molasses." About twenty-five died daily, their graves stretched out along the island's shore.

Cesnola found the officer in charge, Lieutenant Bossieux, "gentlemanly, humane and generous-hearted." The French-descended Richmonder "cheerfully afforded me every facility in his power,"[11] Cesnola remembered later, and the project of distributing the clothes, food and blankets sent by the United States Sanitary Commission and by the United State Government itself, got under way in earnest.

Soon Cesnola felt too much time was lost commuting from Richmond to Belle Isle and sought permission to sleep at Belle Isle, "in order to be at work early in the morning in distributing, as the cold weather is terribly felt by our poor men." General Winder's reaction was a sharp, "*No, certainly not.*"

The incident demonstrated Cesnola's compassion, that of the professional soldier, for the suffering of the men. He wrote later, describing the period:

We would have very willingly distributed day and night in order to shelter with good warm clothes the thousands of half naked bodies, shivering from head to foot from cold and hunger.

I am a soldier by profession since my boyhood. I have been in several wars in Europe; I am familiar with death and have seen it in all its different aspects, but my heart has never been moved as it was by the condition of these men at Belle Isle. Their frozen feet wrapped in a piece of blanket or an old flannel shirt, in place of the boots which were taken away from them by their captors, those long, pale, hungry faces, with hair and beard uncut for months; a kind of perpetual motion given to their bodies by the millions of vermin that devoured their very flesh; their emaciated forms, telling at first sight how many long and weary, weary months they had been there fighting against death in the form of scurvy, low fevers, diarrhoea, congestion of the lungs, etc; their feeble voices saying, "Oh, Colonel, do give us something to eat, for God's sake," etc.[12]

Desperate, the men at Belle Isle ate rats and dogs. One unwary Rebel officer took his pet dog into the camp. "He did not miss it until he was coming out; but, alas! it was too late, and by that time he could only see one man gnawing with voracity his dog's last bone!" The next day, the Richmond *Enquirer* wrote of the incident under the headline, "Dogs eat dogs." Its editor made the point that Yankee prisoners at Belle Isle, though given plentiful diets, "preferred to eat dogs."

Many of the men—some seven hundred of them—suffered from a lack of tents, and, weakened by starvation, died of the cold. Cesnola sought to have the heavy wooden boxes sent from the north used as flooring in some tents and as construction material for shacks.

Some of the boxes, arriving too late, became coffins.

The reckless despair that grasped the prisoners made them prey to the suggestion by the Rebels that four hundred of them exchange their miserable state for parole. Better food was promised them if they would make shoes for the Confederate army. Southern officials promised to give more a similar chance.

Cesnola's reaction was characteristic. And it was dangerous. He had been ordered specifically not to speak to the men. But it made no difference. He took the matter in hand immediately.

"I decided at once to do what I considered the duty of a U. S. officer and interfere in this matter," he said. He sent for the squad leaders. Inform your men, he told them, "that by going to work for the Rebels, they are breaking their oath towards the U. S. government and are helping instead of fighting the enemy of their country." What they were doing would bring them certain court martial as soon as they reached Union lines, Cesnola informed them through the leaders. "I consider it my duty to inform them of it."[13]

The message got through.

When the Rebels tried to get a second group of shoemakers, they found that not a single, starving Union soldier would accept the offer.

The reason—Cesnola's warning—proved easy to discover. And the Southerners wanted no part of this firebrand professional.

About the same time, they had a second display of the Italian colonel's volatile nature.

With other officers, Cesnola was ordered to leave the "Kilpatrick Raiders" room, one day somewhat earlier than usual so the place could be scrubbed by Negroes. His messmate and friend, Lieutenant Morley, had left a piece of ham on a shelf, and Cesnola called him back, telling him to put it out of reach. He told Morley he was "as much afraid of Negro thieves as of white ones."

The Negroes did not react overtly but, to Cesnola's amazement, the white overseer who, unknown to the colonel stood behind him as he made the remark, took the slur personally.

The Southerner pulled Cesnola around by his shoulder, blurting: "God damn you, do you mean that I am a thief?"

"If a hot iron had touched my skin," Cesnola said, "it would not have maddened me more that his insolent touch did." He turned fully to the Rebel, "and in a second I had him by the throat with both my hands, down he went on the floor, and I struck him many times as hard as I could on his face, until my rage was satisfied."[14]

Cesnola was summoned to Major Turner's office. By his grave and courageous disobedience in warning the desperate enlisted men at Belle Isle not to make shoes for the Rebels and by his rash reaction to the overseer's touch, he had forfeited any chance of ever leaving Libby again before his release. Such daily relief was canceled. Once again, his imprisonment became total and would remain so until he was exchanged. Intractable, increasingly glum as the slow weeks crept on, Cesnola was considered "obnoxious" by the man whose good opinion of him was most consequential at the time. That was the Confederate prisoner-exchange commissioner, Colonel Robert Ould. The Southerner told the colonel plainly that he didn't want to send him North at all. So, while others who had been there a shorter time made the trip to City Point, Cesnola remained.

As was usual when he was disheartened, he became sick and thus could take no part in the escape of one hundred twenty-nine captives. They had dug a tunnel which led from the cellar under the cobbled street to a storage building near a gate, and the irony of the adventure was that if, indeed, any guards had seen them moving out in the night they would have thought them Southerners taking some of the provisions stored there.

Mary wrote to Hitchcock, saying she had gotten letters from her husband that made her very gloomy. Louis told her that younger officers with less prison seniority than he were being daily liberated. He did not seem to have received her letter asking whether an offer to exchange him for a Colonel Lucius Davis of the Tenth Virginia Cavalry was still open. In fact, she wrote Hitchcock, her husband did not seem even to remember that his own regiment—his cherished New York Fourth Cavalry—had petitioned for his release in a special appeal.

The fact of my husband's health & spirits giving way renders me extremely anxious on his account & I therefore beg of you to ask what influence you have to secure his speedy release.

If the government would only give me the power to negotiate the exchange, I am sure I could at once effect it. Why will they not?[15]

It was a not unusual complaint. From January on, packages of food from the north were not delivered although they were tantalizingly within the prisoners' sight. Diarrhea and pneumonia enfeebled the men. Starving, they suffered from delusions. One felt a burning sensation within him. "I grew so foolish in my mind," he said later, "that I used to blame myself for not eating more at home."

The inhuman conditions at Libby Prison were to take a turn for the worse. Kilpatrick and his cavalry worked out an impetuous plan for the rescue of prisoners in Richmond, officers and men alike, and the assassination of Jefferson Davis himself. His chief lieutenant, Colonel Ulric Dahlgren, moved an advance party toward the Southern capital, pulled up tracks of the Virginia Central Railroad, rested briefly and, at midnight March 1, 1864, saddled his men up again to hit at Richmond itself.

But his guide led the troop into Rebel pickets. Dahlgren strung him up on a tree, then sought out and found the right place to ford the river. He was moving ahead against only slight resistence when the Southerners, alerted by fast outpost riders, brought up their artillery under the command of Robert E. Lee's son, Custis. The Union cavalry could now stand up to the Confederate cavalry, but it could not challenge artillery. Dahlgren withdrew, beset by the doggedly determined Southern horsemen. He was killed in ambush.

As a result, at Libby, the Confederates placed two hundred pounds of gunpowder in the cellar, and Major Turner told the captives, "I would have blown you all to Hades before I would have suffered you to be released." Hundreds of prisoners were removed daily, not to the north, but to the dreadful Andersonville Prison farther south.

Cesnola's wife and Hitchcock pleaded his cause with Brigadier General Judson E. Mulford, United States Agent for Exchange. Luckily, Mulford "chanced to discover in a detachment of Rebel prisoners" on board the exchange ship "a personal friend of Jeff Davis in the person of Col. Jack Brown of Ga." Mulford paroled him as a "special equivalent for Col. Cesnola." If the transfer were not reciprocal, Mulford stipulated, then "Col. Brown was to return and report himself a prisoner of War within 20 days."

The maneuver brought many objections, official and otherwise, but on March 21, 1864, Cesnola was released at City Point. He reached Camp Parole, Maryland, four days later and was again a free man.

Five

After the slow journey home, Cesnola took his first-born child, Eugenia Gabriella, named for his mother, in his arms, her long, soft, white dress and petticoats spilling over his rough uniform. He settled into the flat Mary had taken at 236 West 22nd Street,¹ rested, and began planning for the future. Still smarting from the disapproval of his wife's relatives and friends, he had no intention of becoming friendly with them. At the same time, he encouraged his wife to see them and was glad that they eased her loneliness.²

The couple planned to live as economically as possible so that when the war was finally over he could take her to Italy "in that manner that is becoming to the wife I have chosen in this country."

There was not the slightest doubt in Cesnola's mind where the good society existed. "The society you have to visit in Italy is not a compound of rags dealers or ex-shopkeepers made rich by swindling and so forth as in this country. The society you have to enter there is pure from filth and belonging to the caste to which you are a member now yourself." He explained to her that she would have to "keep up that show and appearance which the poorest nobleman in Italy does."³

Once again Cesnola lived in one world, that of decorous poverty, while he moved freely, with the entree his friendship with Hitchcock allowed him, in another, the assured world of New York society. George Templeton Strong had members of both worlds working with him on the Metropolitan Fair that spring of 1864. Everyone with wit or talent or energy joined in working to raise money through the Fair for the U. S. Sanitation Commission. Strong, treasurer of the Commission, called on the leaders of society to help the commission fulfill its aim of taking nursing and health services to the Union forces in the South. The public in New York rushed to help in the work involved in setting up booths in the commission's 14th Street Fair. The artist, Albert Bierstadt, designed a wigwam in which musicians performed everything from Beethoven to Indian war dances. "Dick Hunt has put all his taste and all his indomitable energy," Strong wrote, "into decorating the Union Square building in his best Beaux Arts style."[4]

Life in Manhattan was in vast contrast to that in Virginia. On the battlefield, men were scrubby, unkempt and raw. In New York the waistcoats of businessmen out for the evening sparkled with diamond buttons. More money was spent in New York each night on pleasure and entertainment than in Paris. Gold flowed into the metropolis from the mines of California.

As easy money raised prices, thus making life in the slums more unbearable, tensions tightened between the rich and the poor. Officers of a Russian fleet anchored in the North River gave $4760 to buy fuel for the needy. But William B. Astor raised his rents thirty percent.

It was clear to Cesnola that living in New York required money, enough money to do more than just keep up the tasteful appearance required in the Piedmont. Family background—when it was noble and European—was important here, it was true, but the Colonel's experience in Manhattan made it obvious that money, and plenty of it, was the key to a civilized life in post-war Manhattan.

Cesnola hardly had time to get to recognize the new men who had gained authority in Wall Street and in commerce before he was back in military service. He carried with him glimpses of Cornelius Vanderbilt, now in his seventies, commonly called the "Commodore," though the only rank he held was that due to a fortune won by his own wits; of J. Pierpont Morgan, the financier, who had become a partner in a new investment company; of the affable society architect, Richard Morris Hunt.

By the end of May, Cesnola was again in Virginia, moodily in charge of 6000 dismounted cavalrymen and 3000 Rebel prisoners in a camp at Belle Plain. His own Fourth New York Cavalry, afoot like all the rest, had welcomed him back, the first time they had seen him since Aldie, "as they would their own father."[5]

Cesnola, with the pistol episode followed so quickly by prison, with his hopes of combat command not realized, was suspicious. "They" took his men's horses, he felt, in order to put a colonel junior to him in command of the brigade. But as soon as he could get free from some of his responsibilities, he told Hitchcock, "we shall see." He was still bucking for brigade command and the rank of Brigadier General.

The first step toward that rank was obviously to get horses for his men and, he exulted to Hitchcock, "luck or Providence sent me here in the right time." Major General Albert T. A. Torbert of the infantry had appointed a quartermaster to receive horses "and mount other favorite regiments."[6]

The Major General didn't know Cesnola.

As the Commissary officer, Cesnola ordered Torbert's quartermaster to report to him for orders, "and in *24 hours* I had my dear old Regiment completely mounted & equipped, and I did not allow one single horse to be given to any other Regiment until I had the 4th N.Y. Cav. completely mounted. So now my regiment is *allright* again. I will see what man will have the *hardihood* of dismounting again my Regt."[7] The course he took hardly endeared him to General Torbert.

Even though Cesnola failed to reach the rank of Brigadier General, he was back in the war in earnest. General Grant, deep in the Wilderness Campaign, hit Lee with a frontal attack, then released his grip and, in a perilous move against the unpredictable Lee, arced around to his rear. It could have been the maneuver that ended the war, but Grant's front-line commanders failed to act aggressively enough. Though Sheridan and his troopers, Cesnola and his Fourth New York with them, raided behind Lee constantly, they failed to cut the Southerners' supply lines by breaking the Virginia Central Railroad.

By June 24, in a cramped, small hand, Cesnola was writing Hitchcock that he and his reduced regiment of 321 had not taken off their shirts or boots for thirteen days. In addition, he was in trouble again. Although his regiment had been fighting at the "very front" in a battle with Wade Hampton's cavalry at Trevilan Station, he was accused of firing into General Gregg's forces. They weren't anywhere near him, he insisted, being "a thousand yards in my *rear.*"

"But I made a big row at Genl. Sherridan's [*sic*] HeadQrs and *there* they found out that it was *not* the 4th N.Y. Cav. who had fired into other regiments."[8]

Next his troops, who suffered 51 casualties in two hours' fighting were accused of falling back without orders. Cesnola went to General Sheridan's headquarters again and "told him clearly that the scandalous slandering by some staff officers of Gen. Torbot [*sic*] should be stopped otherwise I requested at once a Court of Inquiry." One of Sheridan's commanding officers confirmed Cesnola's statement, saying the Fourth had "fought splendidly" and merited "great praise" rather than criticism. Sheridan was sorry that jealousies disturbed Torbert and Cesnola and said he had only the "highest esteem" for the Fourth New York Cavalry "and its behavior both days" of the engagement.[9]

Cesnola, writing Hitchcock, then poured out his disdain of the raid, saying it failed in its aim "due to the horrible mismanagement of our Cavy. by Generals Sheridan, Torbot, Gregg etc. etc."[10]

To him, the fight at Trevilan's Station was a disaster, though most historians look on it as simply an inconclusive engagement. Cesnola, as usual, was without doubt. "Whoever says the contrary," he wrote, "he *lies* most awfully."[11] Four thousand horses and their equipment were lost, not by capture but by "hard marching, left on the road worn out by fatigue."[12]

Through ineptness of command the men had been sent on the raid with only two days' forage and three days' rations. So it was necessary to let the troopers fend for themselves. The result was harrowing.

I assure you that since then I have been ashamed of being an officer of this command, houses burnt, all pillaged, deprived of everything even clothing & furniture. The first party would arrive at a farm & take ¾ of what they had; the 2d party the other ¼; the third party would break into every receptacle of the house and take all what was not found by the other parties; then perhaps fifty more parties would visit that same house and damn the women because they could find nothing to plunder at and insults were added. The officers had no control on their men, and my Lt. Col. & myself were in several cases obliged to draw our revolvers after using without effect our sabers, not against the men of my regiment (thank God) but against others —oh, I must stop this narrative. I shall never be able to picture you [*sic*] the horrible things I saw.

The Fourth, he told Hitchcock, was due to finish its term of duty on August 29, having refused to re-enlist while Cesnola was a prisoner. "Now that I am again with them, they would re-enlist but it is too late."[13]

Cesnola hoped his "little regiment of veterans" would be well received when it arrived in New York in September. New York's Seventh Regiment, its frayed banners rosetted, had been greeted with bands and cheers, but there is no record of the reception the Fourth received later.

As Cesnola finished writing, he could hear the pickets skirmishing and knew he and his troops "shall probably open the ball again before night." He ended with a worried "Goodby."[14] But he came through the constant forays well.

However, he grew even more dismayed with the steady looting and burning by the battle-hardened troops and, as his days in the Army were coming to a close his mind turned with some relief to the practical and difficult matter of what he would do when he got out of the Union cavalry. When it came right down to it, he didn't really know what to do. "I have an idea . . . to put up a Military School and get the State Authorities to patronize it," he told Hitchcock. "What do you think of it—Do you think it will pay?"[15]

Cesnola's departure from the Army was not solely a question of the completion of his term of enlistment. Underneath, it was the familiar story, but with an added twist. Cesnola was not getting along with General Torbert, one of his commanders. Torbert, as Cesnola learned months after leaving the Army, had resolved to "crush Cesnola" for deeply personal reasons.

The Colonel heard the story at a dinner party in Washington in June 1865, an affair at which the champagne flowed freely and the tongues of Cesnola's old comrades, generals all, loosed upon him a torrent of news about Torbert's private life.

Cesnola had begun the exchange by saying he planned to write about Torbert in a book. The chapter would be headed "Great Heroic Deeds by a Very Small General."[16] As soon as the guests "had more Champagne in their stomack," Cesnola recalled later, "they began to tell every word they heard" of Torbert's similar feelings. Much of it was old news to the Colonel. But the crucial reason "not a little surprised" him.

The history of Torbert's antipathy went back to Cesnola's days as commander of the brigade when Cesnola had dismissed one Colonel Sackett of the Ninth New York Cavalry after courts martial. The Colonel, under arrest in his tent, had whiled the time away with a prostitute, a "very pretty" young woman who, at that moment, was the mistress of an unidentified "Amadio."

The officers of the Ninth complained to Cesnola after their personal objections at Sackett's tent were unavailing. Cesnola ordered Sackett "to have that woman out of camp at once," and sent a pass for her to Washington.[17] But a few days later, he heard she was still in the camp. He then took matters in hand, sent a provost marshall and a guard around to the offensive tent, had the woman arrested and removed to Washington.

In due course, Sackett was dismissed, then reinstated by Lincoln and when Cesnola reported for duty to Torbert after his release from prison, he found that Sackett was in the same camp and that the pretty prostitute had become his wife. She had also become friendly with the General, and for this kindness, as Cesnola told the story, General Torbert promised Sackett a Brigadier General's rank. But the husband was unlucky enough to die in battle. His widow became the General's wife. She had a long and delicately involved story to tell him about how Colonel Cesnola, in the distant past, had offended her most painfully, and the new husband vowed to the lady that he would revenge her and crush Cesnola "if it cost me a year's time!"[18]

Cesnola, of course, was out of the Army in less than that time, but before he left the service, he had another raid of eight days with Sheridan, Gregg and the privately vexed Torbert. It was a searing experience in which his troops crossed the Appomatox and crossed and recrossed the James three times. "No matter what the papers say," he told Hitchcock, "we were badly whipped."[19]

Cesnola saw the rout as promoting the return to power of his favorite general, McClellan: "Everybody seems confident here that nothing can be done and even the black Republican officers begin to see the necessity of having General McClellan at the head of this Army once again. . . . Since our nearly daily disasters McClellan has gained immense popularity here in the Army. Here it is even already said that he will in a few days replace Meade. Rumor says Meade has been or is going to be relieved. God grant it may be so."[20]

If McClellan again assumed top leadership, Cesnola told Hitchcock, "I shall continue in the service even as a private; but as things go now I like better to go home."[21]

It was not McClellan but Ulysses S. Grant, hero of Vicksburg, the battle that opened up the Mississippi to the Union—taciturn, more than slightly shabby, a heavy jaw beneath his light brown whiskers, his blue eyes tired but resolute—who took command. . . . As the news of the appointment spread, there was enormous pressure on the Democrats, now that war satiated the country, to nominate McClellan for the presidency. He would be a fit representative of those who had complaints about the handling of the war. Grant had lost 6000 men in a single hour's fighting at Cold Harbor. His prestige sank to the point where his enemies in the North called him "Grant the Butcher." For months, in almost every letter Hitchcock wrote Cesnola from his politically alive hotel in New York, he had asked how the Army would react to McClellan's being placed again in charge of the war. If this did not come to pass, Hitchcock hinted, perhaps McClellan could be drawn into making the political race. The forces of power were on the move.

At the end of June, Cesnola, who knew these forces well and knew in his Piedmont bones the advantage of powerful friends, wrote a long hymn of praise for "Little Mac" to Hitchcock. The hotelier marked the letter "Col. Cesnola's letter—Read to Gen. McClellan July 7, 1864."

"It must be a real consolation to his friends and a personal satisfaction to General McClellan to see that Grant"—who had all the supplies any general could ask for to take Richmond—"was obliged to come to Genl. McClellan's old plans," Cesnola wrote, "the plans which were by him and other aspiring Napoleonic geniuses considered and declared impracticable. Today McC has more popularity with the masses of the army than he ever had yet. General Grant has made a Grand failure you will see it soon or late confessed."[22]

In truth, Grant's forward leaders had failed to take the brash, quick action that would have smashed Lee's army. But the Southerner was, in fact, locked within south Virginia where the violent Grant harried him almost at will. The fine, proud leader of the Army of Northern Virginia was never to fight in his home territory again.

In the north, McClellan, under the impact of inactivity and the prod of politicians, was beginning to accept the idea, in that grim June of 1864 that he should challenge Lincoln for the Presidency. First-hand knowledge of how the army felt was valuable and someone as thoroughly committed as the Savoyard cavalier was a welcome partisan. Cesnola's grumblings were but one more instance of the complaints of many in the nation concerning the progress of the war and it was chiefly this widening dissatisfaction that encouraged McClellan to enter the political race.

In Virginia, Cesnola was preparing to leave the army. He was departing, however, in the flush of a grand and well-recognized feat of arms.

By this time, he had as little use for General Torbert as he had had for Colonel Swain. Torbert, to him, was a "very poor inefficient cavalry officer," and the generals around him were hardly much better. When Cesnola was sent on a reconnaissance from Deep Bottom to Charles City Court House and surrounded by a massive force of Rebels, whom he estimated to reach some 40,000, both Torbert and Gregg "were repulsed and in falling back closed all chances for me to reach safely our lines." It seemed the Fourth New York Cavalry was done for, and General Sheridan gave it up as lost.

"But to the surprise of every body I struck the rear of Malvern

Hill and formed line of battle with my little regiment 217 men strong, charged the rebels and cut through my way to Deep Bottom without losing a man except those who were killed. I even brought away my wounded."

The feat brought the miracle of a commendation from Torbert. "He was compelled to give me praise," Cesnola wrote with satisfaction.

This was his last major engagement in the Civil War. He was mustered out of service at Harper's Ferry on September 4, 1864.[23]

Cesnola, for all his difficulties with his commanders, had fought hard and suffered ten months' imprisonment. He had not hesitated to risk forfeiting release from imprisonment by warning the starving enlisted captives not to make shoes for the Confederates. With a cavalier-aristocrat's feeling of being above ordinary rules of conduct, he had felt himself badly mistreated in the pistol episode. On leaving the army he was practically destitute and chose to revenge himself by striking at its supreme leader. As the Presidential campaign got under way that fall, Cesnola sent Hitchcock three photographs of enlisted prisoners at Belle Isle in the last, numbing stages of starvation. Each man, his shoulders, elbows and knees knobby on emaciated limbs, looked wanly forward. All had since died. It was Cesnola's suggestion that copies be circulated with the legend: "This is how your government takes care of its fighting men." It was a cruel suggestion, to use the prisoners in southern camps against the man whose face had become engraved with the agony of war. The pictures were never used and are now in the archives of Dartmouth College.

Going north, Cesnola took with him the torn flag of his regiment, once lost and then recaptured, "the dearest thing I possess."

At Christmas that year he sent it as a present to Hitchcock, "It has led proudly to victory my men in forty seven battles and though now staffless (the present one is a rebel one captured at Front Royal Aug. 16, 1864) and ragged it is dear to the old men of my regiment and to their Colonel your friend. I have no person in the world whom I esteem more dearly than I do you; and when years have rolled on our heads & we are no more, your infant son now, a grown man then, may with pride show this memento of the great American Struggle as a gift to his father from a friend who fought not without distinction for his country."[24]

New York was tearing down its small buildings, its stables, its venerable inns and taverns that still stood among the newer structures along the narrow streets of downtown Manhattan. During the war, the impact of its financial district had vaulted over the parochial interests of Manhattan. Now it was the money: lender to the nation, the financier of expansion, the backer of the empires of coal and oil and copper and of the railroads that were pushing West. Many humble individuals had moved with profit from a small business to one that served a neighborhood or community and found a fortune to hand on to their sons. Now the growth—under the hands of brokers such as the war's financier, Jay Cooke—was on such a scale that it forecast a great complex nation of widely disparate peoples spread clear across the continent.

New York, as the central financial fountain that would nurture the country's growth, showed its confidence and its spunk. In Manhattan, men walked with a new gait. Cornelius Van Derbilt, who preferred the ancient spelling, had himself sculpted in his furred great-coat between panels of the ships and railroads he had developed. The sense of well-being that marked the city at the end of 1864 revealed itself most surely in small and intimate luxuries. On the ground floor of the Fifth Avenue Hotel, the Caswell, Mack & Co. drug store, "the finest and most spacious establishment of the kind in the world,"[25] offered the celebrated spring waters of Europe, from Kissengen, Vichy and Prymont. They were drawn from a marble tank that maintained the same temperature of the springs they came from.

Uptown, the Central Park had been carved from craggy land that had once been the home of squatters. Now, Harper's Weekly reported, "the scene between the hours of 3 and 5 P.M. is magnificent. The Drive is thronged with vehicles of every variety known to fashion and some which are not. Of late, a great feature had been the large number of female charioteers."[26] The Park, established only eight years earlier, had been developed by 1865 to the point where, according to Harper's, it was "more than twice the size of either Regent's or Hyde Park in London."[27]

America was just beginning to stand up to Europe, to compete with its public facilities, to attempt to match its cultural centers.

And there was a man, Andrew Haswell Green, a lawyer and a farsighted city planner, who had grand designs for the Central Park.

Green had been a member of the park's original board. He wanted the park to be the center of education and pleasure for the people. He envisioned museums of natural history and art, zoological gardens, an aquarium and astronomical and meteorological observatories.

As the dream took shape, the New-York Historical Society was offered first the old arsenal at 66th Street, now the headquarters of the Parks Department, and finally, because that was hardly large enough for future expansion, the land between 81st and 84th Streets on the westside of Fifth Avenue—precisely where the Metropolitan Museum of Art stands today.

The Society was founded in 1804. By the mid-1860s it possessed the largest and finest collection of art in America and called on Richard Morris Hunt to draw plans for the proposed building. Hunt, a Vermont native who had studied art in Switzerland as a youth, had been admitted to the atelier of Hector Lefuel in Paris, spent ten years at the Ecole des Beaux Arts, the first American to do so, and had shown such flair that he had been put in charge of the new work on the Louvre itself. He came home to help with the extension of the Capitol.

Now he unfurled for the Society's Building Committee headed by Frederic de Peyster, a socially faultless lawyer of Flemish forbears, a plan of princely proportions.[28]

It called for:

1. Picture galleries more spacious than those of the Louvre.
2. Sculpture galleries like those of the Vatican.
3. Apartments for the exhibition of specimens of Natural History and Antiquities as extensive as those of the British Museum, and
4. A Library to contain 500,000 books.[29]

The whole was contained in a structure that stretched along Fifth Avenue and would have been, quite literally, the Louvre of the Americas. The plan proposed Mansard roofs with baroque decorations that towered over restrained connecting halls, and the whole had the elegance of classical control and the splendor of rich detail.

The men of de Peyster's Special Committee on Subscriptions began to gather funds. They had not the slightest doubt of their success. They knew success well. They were Alexander T. Stewart, an Irish Protestant who had come from Belfast a poor man and had amassed millions in his department store; John T. Johnston, a railroad consolidator who had a fine art collection; Hamilton Fish, eventually Grant's Secretary of State; William H. Aspinwall, who had bought Murillo's *Madonna* from the King of Belgium with the fortune he made, during the gold rush days, from his ship and railroad route through Panama; and William E. Dodge of Phelps, Dodge & Co., dealers in copper and other metals. They had no doubt they could easily do what the men of the National Academy of Design had just done for themselves, that is, raise the money for a Venetian Gothic building of grey and white marble and bluestone, an exotic temple to conformity that was now being constructed at Fourth Avenue and 23rd Street.

These endeavors were emblematic of others in all pursuits who were blocking out the future with a bravura that was joyful and contagious. Museums, sporting clubs and social organizations sprang up in the city, taking a national lead in their fields. The atmosphere was one of an expected jubilant return to peace.

But not for Cesnola.

He was home from the War, and he was poorer than when he left. He was now thirty-four years old with a family to support. He had to do something about an income.

His first move was to try to get back in the Army by applying for admission in the First Veteran Corps that was then being organized.[30] He wanted command of a division but would settle for a brigade. He pointed out that he had served under Stoneman and Pleasanton and had taken part in "*all* the *raids* and engagements of the cavalry corps of the Army of the Potomac." He wrote Brigadier General E. D. Townsend that he could supply recommendations from a brace of politicians and no fewer than eight generals. More to the point, he promised to enlist a "large number of veterans in New York City" if he was authorized to do so. He professed himself and many veterans of the Fourth New York Cavalry ready to enlist in the infantry.[31]

"It is superfluous for me to say," he wrote, "that I am ready to undergo examination in regard to Infantry Tactics, etc. at any moment's notice as I have taught infantry tactics in this city for a long time."[32]

When this attempt did not work out, Cesnola wrote the Adjutant General's office for a transcript of his service record. He had been asked to open a military school in New York, he reported, and presently, in March, 1865, he did so, setting up a "Military Academy" at 907 Broadway.[33] He had caught the tempo of the times and suggested that every state should have its own West Point "for were this long struggle to give, at the end, no other good result, it will certainly render the American people a military nation equal to any in Europe."[34]

At this time, just before his second inauguration, Lincoln held a huge reception at the White House, one that was so big the guests overflowed the mansion. Peace seemed closer in those days as Grant hammered Lee and Sheridan's troopers cut a corridor of destruction toward the sea. The people clustered around the tall, shambling, awkward President whose inner strength they prized.

Office seekers went to the Capitol in such numbers that Lincoln spent a week with Grant, riding the General's big horse, talking of the close of the war and what would follow. Just before his inauguration, the President spent a few days in bed because of influenza, according to one account. Another account, however, said the President was "suffering from the exhausting attentions of office hunters."

The President, an agnostic who expressed himself in profound, Biblical terms, took the oath to uphold the Union for a second time and gave an inaugural address in which he spoke of malice toward none. The *Herald* described it as "characteristically simple and solemn."[35]

Less than a month later, Grant took Richmond. Lee surrendered the Army of Northern Virginia, and guns boomed all day in New York despite heavy rain.

Washington still teemed with would-be office holders, the throng swelled by ex-soldiers, when the President was shot. The country sorrowed for the man whose "kindliness and singleness of purpose," as George Templeton Strong put it, "had united the North and secured the suppression of rebellion."[36] Many men took the loss as a personal bereavement.

Ever the soldier-of-fortune and now more in need of fortune than at any time in his career, Cesnola began to claim that Lincoln had promised him both the rank of general and the post of consul. He let it be known in the proper places that he had seen Lincoln just a few days before the assassination and that Senator Ira Harris of New York, who he said accompanied him to Lincoln's office, had heard the pledge of military and private advancement.

Cesnola was a voluble man and his preference for McClellan over Lincoln in the 1864 campaign had been clearly articulated. There is not a shred of evidence in the National Archives or the Library of Congress that the alleged interview with the President ever took place, much less Lincoln's backing of a political adversary. On March 6, Congress confirmed a total of six hundred military nominations made by the President. Cesnola was not among them.

At the end of March, Cesnola wrote the Adjutant General's Office in Washington for an "official certificate" of satisfactory service in the Union forces.

Giving the Adjutant General an account of his service in the two regiments, he omitted the pistol charge and the dismissal that flowed from it. "It is of great importance to me," Cesnola wrote, "to possess an official document showing that I have served faithfully my adopted Country etc. I hope you will be so kind as to give me such a certificate knowing as I do that I have done my duty well and to the full satisfaction of my Commanding Generals under whom I have served."[37]

The Army sent him a perfunctory letter: "I am directed to inform you that the records of this office show you mustered into the service of the United States as Lieutenant Colonel, 11th N. Y. Cavalry February 22, 1862, to serve three years and resigned June 1862.

"September 25, 1862, you were mustered into service as Colonel 4th New York Cavalry. Taken Prisoner of War June 17, 1863, and honorably mustered out September 4, 1864."[38]

Breathing a sigh of relief at his spotless public official record,

Cesnola then began a different campaign. In June he went to Washington to see Secretary of State Seward, a vivid conversationalist with a more than usual fund of anecdotes, a liking for a good glass of wine and a good cigar. This time Cesnola did not stay in "Willard's Hotel" but at a boarding house on Pennsylvania Avenue. He cooled his heels in Seward's waiting room.

Then, finally, after three weeks of waiting, "bound to secure some office or other," Cesnola wrote Hitchcock that he was "pretty sure I have succeeded. I was offered temporarily a 1st Class Clerkship until the Consulship of Cyprus be vacated which will be in next October or at the beginning of Nov."[39]

It annoyed him that he was "obliged to beg for a position which my services in the Army still unrewarded ought to give me at once."[40] The State Department, however, was not like the ruling and indulgent Sardinian power of Piedmont with its Cesnola strongholds to dispense for services. It could not be cajoled into rewarding every foreign cavalier who had fought for the Union. Cesnola soon discovered it required political pull to turn the trick. He got it.

"Morgan & Harris [the two senators from New York] are strongly urging Seward on my behalf—the Consulship of Cyprus is yours Colonel [so said the Secretary],"[41] Cesnola reported, as he turned his mind once more to the nagging and constant problem, the need of cash.

His financial troubles were so intense that he had "written home" to Rivarolo Canavese for some money to pay Hitchcock, his "most generous friend" and relieve him of a "heavy load."

Although he tried to get the Army to reimburse him for the horse he left in the service, he was realistic enough to see that he wasn't going to get very far with a horse claim during the disbanding of the armies.

In another claim, he persuaded Senator Ira Harris to forward to the Union Agent of Prisoner Exchange, Brigadier General J.E. Mulford, a bid for $745 which he said the Southerners took from him when he was captured. Harris wrote: "I have no doubt of the entire truthfulness of the written statements of Col. Cesnola. He is an honorable man and a well educated and most accomplished soldier. He leaves the service penniless."[42]

Cesnola reinforced the appeal by writing to Secretary of War Edwin M. Stanton that he was not reimbursed when exchanged. He had a family to support, he reminded Stanton, and the money, representing four months' pay, "would be of the greatest value to me as I am very poor indeed and in great want of it."[43]

The Army had no heart. It carefully scrutinized the claim and pored over records of the Confederate prison. Lieutenant General Grant signed the report. It was brief: "Col. Cesnola seems to have no special right to the funds."[44]

Cesnola could splutter in anger, but he could do little else. He went about the business of becoming consul. It was hardly a prime appointment. Cyprus was no diplomatic prize. It had been an on-again, off-again consulate for forty years, and politicians had certainly not sought its dry ancient hills and long, shallow coastline for a favored constituent.

The current consul, a Virginian, had asked Seward in June of 1864 to move him to a vacancy in the American consulate at Alexandria in Egypt. But when Lincoln was killed on April 14 of the next year, J. Judson Barclay was still at his Cyprus post. He was quite willing to give up the consulate since he had become convinced, he told Seward, that a reply to his complaint about the $1000 a year salary "leaves me no hope that the present salary will be increased." He came home on leave and when he learned in September that Cesnola had been appointed to the post at Larnaca, he had no objections whatever.

In itself, the somnolent island in the far reaches of an inland sea held no special appeal for Cesnola. But it happened to be a good deal closer to his beloved Italy than another post he was offered, an unspecified one in Asia.

The State Department's experience with the consulate in Cyprus had been remarkably checkered. President Jackson had commissioned the first American consul there in 1835. Five years later, the position was canceled. Then in 1846, President Polk recommissioned the former consul, Mario de Mattey, a merchant who lived on the island, and he held the position, presumably profitable for a merchant, until his death. At this point, William Ledyard Ellsworth of New York arrived one day and "left without assuming charge eighteen days later." To fill the gap his quick retreat caused, Barclay received a recess appointment and was on leave when Cesnola acquired the station.

Moving quickly to become a citizen, Luigi Palma di Cesnola signed his papers in the Superior Court of New York on August 16, 1865 and took his oath with a neighbor, J. G. Sinclair, as witness. He gave his occupation as "soldier."[45] Officially he dropped the title of Count, which he had found expedient to use. But he kept the distinction in the name "di Cesnola," and he was not at all ready to renounce the Palma crest, that sparkling and impressive badge of status. It appears again and again, in salmon and in blue, on his personal stationery and on the calling cards he used in Europe.

With his wife and baby daughter, Cesnola sailed for Genoa on September 25, 1865.

By November 30, he wrote Hitchcock from Rivarolo Canavese that he was stopping at his mother's home to "recruit" the health of his "wife and babe who had suffered so much the voyage."[46] The little family had had a rousing reception in his homeland. It was at about this time that Cesnola began to call himself "General," a title he probably assumed on the stormy Atlantic.

His reception, he told Hitchcock, "was so grand, so general, that my wife *cried* of pleasure. Even the church bells were ringing! Processions, dinners, etc. Decorations from the King etc. But all this did not make me forget that I have left in the other side of the Ocean after my mother my best and most generous friends of whom you are the foremost forever."[47]

He was truly again on his own, badgered by his constant problem, lack of money, and burdened with thoughts of the future. His stay in Italy was longer than he had expected, chiefly because an outbreak of cholera had forced one steamship line to cancel stops at Larnaca in Cyprus and he was compelled to make other travel arrangements.

He took his time and used it to practical advantage. He had made some business arrangements "which ought to help me to make money," he wrote Hitchcock. A check on prices of wines that sold well in Delmonico's and Maison D'Or in New York convinced him it would be a good arrangement both for him and his friend if he arranged to import wine for the Fifth Avenue Hotel. He had discovered he could obtain wines of the first quality—Lacryma Christi, Capri bianco, Vermouth, and the like—at $5.25 for a case of twelve. Such wine, he well knew, then sold for $1.50 or $2 a bottle in New York. If Hitchcock's guests liked the wine, of which Cesnola had not the slightest doubt, he could order 500 to 600 cases at a time. In this volume, Cesnola told him, the cost per case would be $5. As an exchange operation, Cesnola thought also it might be profitable to market newly designed sewing machines in Europe.[48]

Having outlined these plans, Cesnola and his family left Italy for Cyprus.

Six

The ancients, seeing gods and beasts in the sky at night and the earth by day, felt that Nature, in making Cyprus, had flung an ox hide of an island on the wine-dark rug of the inner sea. Two promontories on the northern range of mountains, two on the southern range, formed end joints of its limbs. Between them, on both long coasts, arced the coastal bays of the belly. A huge tail of narrow mountains on the east pointed toward Issus on the Asia Minor shore where Alexander the Great in his youth had won his first battle.

Cesnola and his family arrived in the Bay of Larnaca on Christmas Day, 1865,[1] after a fifteen-day passage from Italy. In his book, Cesnola said that when they arrived the sea was rough under leaden skies, and because the port was an open bay without piers the ship had to anchor more than a mile from shore. At that distance, the town "looked the very picture of desolation; no sign of life, no vegetation anywhere visible except a few solitary palm trees, with their long leaves drooping, as if in sign of mourning."

His first reaction was like that of the consul William Ledyard Ellsworth, who years before had left without taking his post. Cesnola's first thought was not to go ashore at all but to remain aboard, "and not to land on such a forlorn-looking island."

The American flag had been raised on the steamer, a mark of respect for Cesnola, the new American consul, and, presently, as he mulled over a landing, there appeared on a row of stone buildings along the shore the flags of other nations. The representatives of Great Britain and France and other countries represented in the island were welcoming their new colleague. The flapping banners gave a new aspect to the town.

Then a large lighter flying the American flag arrived at the ship with some twenty men, all with the red fez commonly used in the island, then ruled by Turkey. They scrambled aboard the steamer, a motley armed crowd, some bearing ancient pistols, others with native weapons or carrying silver-headed batons six feet long. They pushed their way to Cesnola's quarters, and he went out to meet these men of his staff. He stood erect and steady after the fortnight of rough passage. His mind was made up. There was no turning back.

After tolerating the kissing of his fingertips, Cesnola and his family were on their way ashore in the lighter. The looks of Larnaca seemed increasingly forbidding the closer they came. Finally, the lighter lurched to a stop in the shallow water some four to five yards from shore. By now, a large crowd had gathered to watch the arrival. They heard the boatmen give "wild and deafening yells" of encouragement to each other as they tried to free the lighter. But it was stuck fast.

Immediately, a boatman jumped into the water and signaled to Cesnola to sit on his shoulders. Other boatmen did the same for the staff, and the group was carried to the beach, their feet wet from the uneven ride. It was a most undignified and undiplomatic entrance, and Mary Cesnola, who was six months pregnant, would have none of it. She stood looking at the shore suspiciously, with her daughter Genie at her side, an adamant expression on her face.

One of the consular staff suggested a chair be held for her by two strong boatmen and one was brought by scampering attendants, eager to please their new consul. But his wife would not leave the lighter in such a manner.

Eventually, when all the luggage and most of the men were ashore, the ship again floated. It was pushed ashore and Madame, "refusing all aid, sprang lightly to the beach."[2]

The Cesnolas were surprised to find there were no hotels in Larnaca. They were forced to accept the hospitality of the Italian consul, Cavaliere Candido Negri, and his wife.

At the end of the first week, the Cesnolas had found a large stone house which they were to occupy during the length of their stay. It stood, as did those of other consuls, along the beach and was reached through a broad and long passageway. An empty outbuilding of fair size rose near the main building.[3]

Cesnola moved headlong, then, into the consular colony at the capital. Besides Negri and his talented wife, there was the French consul Giorgio Colonna-Ceccaldi and his brother, an aide, one Simondetti who had just brought his young bride to Larnaca, and several others. Although ruled by Turkey, the island felt the power of the British in the heydey of their imperial strength, and the greatest commerce to and from Cyprus fell to the British. The Italians, at the time of Cesnola's arrival, were under Austrian control. French power was fast fading, and, in the eyes of the English the "European colony [in Cyprus] was utterly decadent."[4]

In 1866 the head of the British mission, the leading consular force in the island, was R. Hamilton Lang, a young diplomat who had come to Cyprus five years earlier at the age of twenty-five. He spoke French fluently, had a knowledge of Arabic that enabled him to read *The Thousand and One Nights* in the original and was studying modern Greek. One of his closest friends, Demetrius Pierides, fanned his interest in the Grecian language and also in antiquities. Even more stimulating was his purchase of a gold coin, turned up at Salamis in the sock of a plough. He bought it for five pounds and sold it to an English collector almost immediately. Identified as a head of Pnytagoras, King of Salamis around 350 B.C., it brought Lang 70 pounds.[5]

Lang was a product of stringent English upper-class education: self-reliant and cheerful. He lent the Cesnolas some furniture, told them stories of life on the island and pointed out where ancient relics had been found. A few months later, Lang accepted the position of head of the Ottoman Imperial Bank, a ranking post in the island, and his position as consul was filled by Thomas B. Sandwich, who had been vice-consul.

In but a few weeks Cesnola was well into his consular stride. His first request of the State Department was for a strongly made U. S. flag, and in less than a month's time he was asking permission to dress his consular employees in uniform and charge the expense of seventy dollars for the four uniforms to Washington.[6] It well may have been about this time that he had made for himself the general's uniform, rich with epaulettes of gold braid. The American post in the Near East, under Cesnola, was surely going to keep up appearances with and edify the Turks.

Keeping up appearances was an especial concern for Cesnola, still in the throes of the constant problem of money.

He had rejected the idea presented by his mother's influential family that he rejoin the Italian army. Though his Civil War record now made this possible, it was unacceptable to him after he learned, on a secret trip to London, that Italians were at the time regarded internationally with disdain.

As a possible expedient, Cesnola expanded on an earlier idea— selling American sewing machines abroad—to the entire range of "articles more properly known as *Yankee notions*." He wanted "somebody"—he did not ask Hitchcock directly—to send "some boxes of those things" by the ship of Mr. Dabney (Charles M. of Boston). He could then sell them on commission.[7] That would require no cash outlay.

In the meantime, Cesnola settled down to learning what it was to be a consul. He found the task repetitive and dull. He made quarterly reports on ship traffic in Larnaca, on imports and exports and, very occasionally, on the building of a carriage road.

He wasted no time in getting to see the island itself, going across from Larnaca on the south coast through the treeless, chalky midland plain that the ancients called "the happy land" for its fertility and the richness of its flowers, vegetables and fruits. Now, for lack of irrigation to channel and store its winter rain, it was a parched, sundried, barren stretch of flatland and infrequent hills between the verdant coasts. He saw the northern limestone mountains that fell precipitously into the sea only forty miles from Asia Minor.

Most of the western and about half of the southern shores were of arable land, the pebbled soil suited for vines outlining the hills as they did in the Piedmont of Italy. Above them stood the ancient peaks of Olympus and Troodos from which the flanks of the southern slopes descended to the dazzling, blue Mediterranean in gentle, indented bays. It was there, in the soil that flowed along the streams down the mountain, that man had found the most hospitable land in Cyprus, and it was there that the most ancient of the towns existed, the old Paphos, Amathus, and Curium.

On a tour Cesnola talked to the old residents and heard the ancient tales; of Richard the Lion-Hearted marrying Berengaria of Navarre in Limassol while on crusade; of Paul and Barnabas coming ashore at the fabulous port of Famagousta on the east coast to preach to the Jews, of the long, panoplied concourse of Greeks and Persians and Arabs and Egyptians that raided and conquered the ultimately complacent natives.

But in his report to Secretary of State Seward on the tour, Cesnola concentrated not on scenery or background but on cotton and the British Empire. He pointed out that a British company had set up a "ginning factory" the previous year and would likely build others soon. They were much more productive than those run by mule power, and the English were transporting the cotton by camels to the coast from where it was shipped to Trieste or Marseilles. Cesnola thought the U. S. government should get into the field "since individuals don't have the means or knowledge."[8]

Soon he was honing his principal objective: on January 20, 1866, twenty-five days after shoulder-riding into Larnaca, he asked Seward for a raise. The consulate's archives were in great confusion, its letters in Greek, French, Italian, even Arabic. "This state of things," he complained, "is doubtless owing to the consul being occupied chiefly in endeavoring to eke out the expenses of his official position by engaging in commercial pursuits."

Cesnola's main complaint was that the other governments in Larnaca paid their dragomen or translators, and kavasses, or guards, but the United States left that expense to the consul. After deducting that expense from his $1000 annual salary, Cesnola figured his own income at $480 a year.[9]

He appealed to the pride of the State Department. The Cyprians were paying a great deal of attention to the American consul after the

Civil War, "and it's often the cause of humiliation to the American Consul that he finds himself in an inferior position to even the vice consuls of other nations."

He had explained this all to Hitchcock at some length, and the New York hotelier advised him to build up his reputation, to have a biography of himself prepared. By using it judiciously, Hitchcock would try to get him a "more lucrative position." This moved Cesnola to call him a "dear and generous friend. . . . God ought to bestow upon you every kind of blessing for you are the best man of the world." He managed to be the first in a series of biographies of eminent Italians called "A Necklace of Illustrious Italian Contemporaries."[10] Both friends recognized that as an advocate of the Democratic McClellan, Cesnola could hardly expect more than he had received already from the Republican Johnson. It would plainly require special effort to get him a well-paying position from the government.

In line with this aim, Cesnola was acutely aware of the importance of politics. He considered President Johnson "the very man to reconcile both sects" and feared that when Senator Ira Harris, his political benefactor, voted against the President at the impeachment proceedings, Harris would lose his influence.

At the same time, Cesnola was exploring two other routes out of his financial dilemma. He had already bought antiquities and had begun to pick up pieces of ancient terra cotta and now started to dig in fields near the consulate. In addition, he indulged himself in "commercial pursuits," sending off samples of the local wine to Hitchcock and to Park & Tilford in New York in the hope that each would order some.

Hitchcock's baby son, Maynard, had died, and Mary, soon to give birth, was sure she would have a boy. She planned to name him Hiram. But when the baby came, born in the consulate March 14, it was a girl, and, though they enjoyed both their children, the Cesnolas were sorry they could not name the infant after their friend whose health was troubling him again.[11]

The couple was now settled into "one of the very best houses in Larnaca," and it had been comfortably furnished. Life moved along smoothly with consular dinners, tours across the large island and

Cesnola's growing interest in his collecting.

A happy break in the routine came with the visit of Hiram Hitchcock and his wife in 1867. At thirty-four, Hitchcock had been forced to retire because of his health. He came abroad, making with his wife the Grand Tour through the principal states of Europe and the Near East, Egypt and Palestine and, because of his friend, Cyprus. The four had a very pleasant fortnight together. Cesnola, who had "doubted whether a man like Hiram Hitchcock would ever be able to find a wife worthy of him," was completely taken by Mary Maynard Hitchcock.[12] She played the piano gracefully and had brought along duets for piano and flute, Cesnola's instrument from boyhood.

Her husband brought news of New York. The Atlantic Cable had finally been put in order and was bringing news daily from the continent. The spacious new Albany boats on the Hudson, the *Dean Richmond* and the *St. John*, were like four stories of the Fifth Avenue Hotel set afloat on the river. More men, impelled by their wives, seemed to be going *to* Europe these days than were emigrating *from* it. And the wealth that was mulching the luxuriant atmosphere of the expanding metropolis was throwing up such exotic personages as Daniel Drew, Jim Fisk and Jay Gould, financial adventurers of new dimensions. New York, which had passed from a second-rate seaport to America's leading metropolis during the Civil War, was now well on its way to becoming one of the leading cities of the world. It was a fresh and gargantuan picture that Hitchcock painted, and Cesnola, who knew the great cities of Europe, listened in unaccustomed silence.

It was shortly after the Hitchcocks left that Cesnola's mother, at the age of fifty-nine, died in Rivarolo Canavese. The consul, in telling Hitchcock of the death, called it "the hardest blow that a man can receive in his life. My dearest and best of mothers is dead!"[13]

He went to Piedmont by the next Austrian steamer to settle family affairs with his brothers. It was arranged that the brothers would sell the lands that fell to Luigi in the will, and Cesnola immediately wrote to Hitchcock that as soon as this was done he would "settle my dear good friend my debt."[14] He owed Hitchcock $1000, a year's salary.

His hope of meeting this crushing obligation through selling his

inheritance in Piedmont fell when the Italian government put cleri-
cal lands on sale at low prices with provision for payment over ten
years. As a stopgap, Cesnola pushed Italian and Cyprian wine in
America. But that did not work either. Finally, he told Hitchcock to
tell Park & Tilford to get whatever it could for his shipment and send
him the money.[15] What hope he had now resided in his efforts to get
a better post from the State Department. It was an endeavor that
called on all his Italian persuasiveness and guile and all Hitchcock's
skill and suavity in handling important people.

Still, he pushed ahead with his collection of medieval and ancient finds, hiring workers among the humble but shrewd natives.
They were glad of the work as they knew that foreigners sought such
relics with a curious passion and a loosened purse. Through long,
dismal seasons they scratched the earth into which old mud-made
buildings had fallen, excavating for finds they could sell to one or
another of the consuls. Eventually, Cesnola joined with the two Englishmen, Lang and Sandwich, both knowing and solvent, in hiring a
single group of workers to dig for them alone. This arrangement gave
the energetic, strapping American consul of thirty-six the liberty to
concentrate on building his friendships with the Turks, a delicate and
painstaking process, and on maneuvering at long distance to get a
better paying diplomatic position in a "more civilized" area of
Europe.

In the fall of 1868, Cesnola had his doubts about his prospects.
Ulysses S. Grant, the great war hero, was running for the Presidency
and the consul expected nothing from him or his party. The situation
was a simple one: Cesnola "never liked that man," feeling he had
reaped the rewards of McClellan's carefully planned tactics.[16]

To make matters worse, the consul had heard rumors that Congress might pass a bill that would make the foreign service one of
tenure, and also allow the Secretary of State to abolish some posts and
create new ones. As Cesnola saw it, Cyprus, Candia and Scio in the
Turkish Empire quite likely faced abolition or downgrading to unpaid agencies because of their scant commerce with the States.

It was time to promote himself, and he encouraged an Italian
editor to include him in a group of biographies of "Illustrious Italians
serving Foreign Governments,"[17] and arranged for some New York

missionaries at Beyrouth to print a catalogue for travelers of his small collection of antiquities.[18]

For his own part, he took on the work of consul for three other nations, Greece, Russia and one he never named.[19] He found himself swamped with work as he handled the civil and criminal affairs of more than three hundred Greeks in twenty days, issuing as well more than five hundred passports to the Greeks who were quitting the Turkish island. It looked as though war might break out between the two foreign nations. If it did, the Greeks wanted this brilliant horseman to be commander in chief of the Hellenic Cavalry. Cesnola took the bid as he had taken the lavish praise of retainers in his Rivarolo home. He received the offer as a tribute not to him but to the "memory of the great deeds done for that country" by his uncle, Alerino.[20]

Now he had other offers to be weighed, largely the harvest of the heroic tone of the two biographies that had appeared in Italy. The offers were very tempting, but involved his resuming Italian citizenship. He talked them over with his wife, but, though she would have liked the title of Countess, she vetoed the move unless he was made Consul General of Italy in New York.[21] She knew what she wanted. Home.

So did he. The better future, Cesnola wrote, would be for him to be appointed consul of the United States at Turin with a salary of $2000 a year. Senator Harris had promised to work for him, and the prospect seemed promising.[22]

But now his other avenue to solvency, the antiquities, intruded. He knew very well he would never sell his "Phoenician Museum" to the United States, as he called the varied group of crusaders' and ancients' relics he had put in the outbuilding at Larnaca.

Cesnola had reason for his view. Earlier, kept up-to-date on New York affairs by Hitchcock, Cesnola had offered his "Museum," then of about 1600 pieces valued at $15,000—fifteen years' salary—to the lawyer Hamilton Fish, head of the New-York Historical Society. He told Fish that the English consul at Larnaca (his friend Sandwich) had informed the British Museum about their finds and that that museum was to send an agent to the island to buy them. Since he, Cesnola, was "one of the largest stockholders," he could enforce his decision not to allow the collection to be sold until he heard from Fish. The offer the consul made was detailed, complete with an agreement to accept the same price that he fully expected to be offered by the British Museum, payable over "any length of time" if the Society would pay unspecified interest. He signed himself "L.P. di Cesnola, late Bt. Brig. Genl. U.S.V. Cavy., U.S. Consul."[23] Fish didn't answer him.

The Society, a favorite institution of the old landed gentry of New York and the Hudson River Valley, had not only a priceless treasure of national historic documents but still had an equally priceless offer from the Board of Commissioners of the Central Park to give the Society the old arsenal and land around it in the park for a museum. Before the Civil War—on August 14, 1860—the Society's executive committee had appointed five of its officers and members to look at the arsenal and its surrounding ground as the location "for a grand Museum of Antiquities, Science & Art."[24]

The men looked over the arsenal and its adjoining lands and found them "the amplest accommodation for its Museum and Gallery in their greatest imaginable expansion."

The Society's art holdings demanded ever increasing space, the five held, reporting: "So forcibly does the future already press upon the present that some immediate measure to meet this exigency has become an urgent necessity."[25]

They needed a law authorizing the Park Commission to deed the Society the land and, in March 1862, they got it. They then took another look at the arsenal—which more than one hundred years later is still in use—and decided that, though it was "substantially built," it should be razed in favor of a fireproof building, preferably one designed by one of society's leading architects, Richard Morris Hunt. The Society decided to follow conservative custom and operate on a pay-as-you-go basis. To do so, it set up a formidable Committee on Subscriptions to the Arsenal Improvement Fund with Frederick De Peyster as chairman. The committee had fifteen subcommittees, each with its own chairman and two associates. The architectural plan was one of a romantic Gothic nature with a deepset entrance opening on its southern facade. But it was planned in brick, and the park commissioners had rejected it, ruling out such a plebian material.

With that first plan shelved, both parties took a closer look at the arsenal site and its four adjoining acres. The park commissioners had other objections beyond the use of brick, and for several years wrangled with the Historical Society over them.

While they were doing so, Cesnola, now adept at casting off such slights as Fish handed him, concentrated on selling his pieces in Europe. He didn't fail, however, to seize a chance of interesting the Historical Society when one of its leaders, the artist Frederick Church, stopped in Cyprus on his way home from Jerusalem. He implored Church to get the Society to consider buying his collection but, once the American sailed, Cesnola pushed his antiquities nearer at hand.

A good many European papers had written about his discoveries, and the notices had prompted the eminent American historian and at the time a diplomat in Berlin, George Bancroft, to inquire about them. Through Bancroft, Cesnola hoped to sell his finds to the Berlin Museum. The institution, he wrote in 1868, "very likely will buy the entire collection *if I give it cheap.*"[26]

The consul had already sent off to Paris, to the leading dealers in ancient coins and artifacts, Rollin & Feuardent, a group of finds. The income from them made it possible for him to pay for Parisian winter clothes that Mary Hitchcock, on the tour, had bought for Mary Cesnola.

Soon his finds were so numerous that he could send extras on to his homeland, the museum in Turin, and to Hitchcock. As he did so, Cesnola reminded Hitchcock to keep trying to get him a better post in Europe, suggesting the New Yorker might use a new preface to one of his Italian biographies. The preface was most flattering to the new President Grant, not precisely one of Cesnola's enthusiasms a short time before. He confided to his friend that it would be perfect if Grant would be magnanimous and appoint his old rival McClellan as minister to either England or France, "and then I would apply for a consulate under him."[27]

By June 1869, Cesnola's two routes out of penury met at a crossroad when Hitchcock told him the "right" backing might bring him a consulate in the Piedmont capital of Turin. He immediately wrote his friend that if he thought "some antiquities could be apreciated [*sic*] by some of your influential friends and would *make them work with more activity for our cause*," the consul would send a box for each.[28] His men at the digs were doing well.

There was a slight hitch, however: there *was* no Turin consulate. Hence Cesnola needed a lobby of impressive American travelers who would write Hamilton Fish, now Secretary of State and Cesnola's superior, to say they had passed through Turin and were struck by the urgent need for an able American diplomat there.[29] Cesnola wrote his senator, Ira Harris, that friends of his in America, headed by Hiram Hitchcock of New York, were working to get an American consulate set up in Turin "with a salary of $2000 per annum for my benefit." The new Kingdom of Italy, was now a fact acknowledged by the creation of many European consulates there, and America should follow their example. A petition presented to Fish by the Senator would be the "best mode" of working it out, Cesnola told Harris, saying Hitchcock would do the work on the petition.

Harris went to work without any further lengthy petition. Cesnola backed him up by dedicating one of his Italian biographies to the Italian Secretary of War and, drawing on his own experience in the Civil War, composed, as he called it, "a *panegiric* of Grant (diplomatically done.) " If that preface of praise for the leader he so recently abhored was translated "and put before the eyes of proper influential persons at Washington," Cesnola pointed out, it might be of "great help to obtain what we want."[30]

Cesnola's antiquities project was also proceeding apace. Bancroft in Berlin promised a visit from one of Europe's most prestigious experts in antiquities, Dr. Carl Friederichs of the Berlin Museum.

Dr. Friederichs came, took a very close look, said little and bought carefully, choosing pieces that were not duplicates of those in his own museum. The German did not like the collector's wife. She objected to men smoking in the parlor and enforced her objection. Not limiting herself to household matters, she also took part in the conversation, a practice that Dr. Friederichs found deplorable. He continued on his way to Suez leaving Cesnola with the encouraging notion that a major European museum had a buying interest in his collection of ancient terra cottas and figures.

This upturn in his affairs confirmed Cesnola's determination to use all his tremendous energy, resolve, and connections in Europe and the new world to wrest a secure future for himself and his family.

Seven

The great stone head was heavy. It was solid limestone three feet long and almost a foot wide. Its stone eyes stared impassively at the diggers who saw in this strange huge head, with its curled stylized beard and peaked cap, a mute and prehistoric forebear. Dug from the ancient site of Golgos in early March 1870, it had proved too heavy for the diggers to raise without help. In calling for help, they called also for trouble.

Andrea Vondiziano ordered one of his workers to find some idle men in the streets of the nearby village of Athieno who could lift the head and other sculptures taken from the old soil onto two carts. Vondiziano wanted all to be in readiness when his superior, Cesnola, arrived.

In Athieno, word spread quickly among the owners of the earth-brick houses that a great find had been made in the fields where the barley grew at Aghios Photios, the current name of Golgos.

These mild poor folk, keen in worldly matters, well knew that men from other lands paid well for their antiquities. The French consul, Comte Melchior de Vogüé, now at his new post in Constantinople, had in that same locality found some fine stone heads and statues and had rewarded his workers handsomely. Other consuls were eager for news of productive sites. They would also pay for the information. As night began to fall, the populace moved out of town and swirled around the new find.

When these crowds began to gather, Vondiziano dispatched two couriers on muleback to his chief, some fifteen miles away at Larnaca.

It was midnight before they arrived. Cesnola, tired from a long, wearisome general meeting of consuls that day, was sleeping soundly. He woke to the pair's loud quarreling with guards in the consulate yard. Each wanted to be the first to tell the general what was going on at the dig.

From them Cesnola learned, "the peasantry had rushed in large numbers to Aghios Photios with spades and pickaxes, all eager to participate in the diggings, and that the owner of the ground and his relations were also at work upon it, that wonderful things were discovered and that the greatest confusion prevailed."

As Cesnola and the first messengers spoke, another messenger arrived. Vondiziano, powerless before such a crowd, was sending a plea to Larnaca for the police. He told Cesnola that the local police at Golgos were claiming all the finds in the name of the sultan himself. The imperial order covered even the sculptures some peasants had carried off "hoping to be protected by declaring themselves in the service of this or that consul."

"I saw there was not a moment to be lost," Cesnola recalled later, and, mounting at once, he sped off on his mule, *"ventre a terre,"* its belly to the ground, as he put it, in his flat-out rush for Golgos.

It was soon obvious that speed was crucial. Not far from Larnaca, center of all the consulates, he stopped some men galloping toward him. Perhaps, he thought, they were more messengers from Vondiziano.

He found otherwise. Some in the group had been directed by the police to report to the *caimakam* or Governor of Larnaca, and others, even more of a threat, were peasants who sometimes worked for other consuls. They were taking news of the find to these rival-colleagues of Cesnola's. In later days Cesnola learned that two of his associates had already, in fact, gotten the news by the time of the encounter and, reacting as he had, were by then mounted. The messengers, then, not only confirmed the find: they brought word that the American consul had gotten there first.

The scene, as Cesnola later described it, was "wild and weird."

All Athieno was bivouacked on the desert-like plain of Aghios Photios. The moon had not yet risen and large fires were lit at different points, throwing fantastic shadows as men moved about, eagerly gesticulating and conversing. The light falling upon their swarthy faces and parti-coloured dress, gave them the appearance of a band of brigands, which in some measure they were.

More than a hundred milled about, shouting, fighting, their acts rousing their mules and oxen, who jerked to their feet snorting and braying. As the din subsided periodically, an infrequent snatch of a man's song sounded on the dark rim of the gathering. In the center, silhouetted against the glow of fires, lying on its side, was the colossal head of stone.

As Cesnola approached, word spread that the American consul had arrived, "and the uproar and confusion instantly ceased." Cesnola, who had been in Cyprus more than three years, had only recently won a test of strength with the governor at Larnaca. The crowd knew his spirit. They were also imbued with the spirit of an old Turkish saying: One must kiss the hand he can't cut off." They had long been accustomed to hearing Cesnola called "General" and to respect the fiery cavalry officer who had moved across battlefields in his native Italy as a boy and had controlled large groups of men in the American Civil War.

Cesnola knew this, too. As an officer, he knew precisely what to do.

As he drew near, he saw that a pair of Turkish policemen were guarding the sculptures.

I at once rode toward them [he wrote], dismounted, and ordered one of them to take my foaming animal in charge and walk it about, which he did without question. I then called the other *zaptih* and motioned to him to disperse the crowd and clear a space around the sculptures. He obeyed as promptly as his companion and these steps had due effect upon the peasants.

Then, "by the fitful gleams of the fire-lights," Cesnola looked for the first time at the massive stone head, its capped skull above the mysterious face, its stiff, long beard with four curls turned like fronds of primeval fern. It was a countenance of elemental force.

It was not, however, a moment for contemplation. Cesnola ordered the sculptures lifted to the ox-drawn carts, and, giving his mules to Vondiziano, asked him to escort the little caravan on the road to Larnaca. When he met Cesnola's servant, who was bringing the consul's bed and clothing, Vondiziano was then to exchange supervision of the sculpture for that of Cesnola's personal things and return to Golgos to aid in an extensive dig at the site.

"Thus, I may say," wrote Cesnola, "that I rather captured than discovered these stone treasures."[1]

In making what amounted to a military *coup*, Cesnola joined the company of adventurers and diplomats who for more than a hundred years had opened up the tombs and capitol buildings of the ancient world; of men who roamed the earth on diverse missions—priests and scholars, merchants and government officials in far lands—who had felt the appeal of exotic artifacts; men who had been led to search for the relics of their own spiritual beginnings, for those mementoes beyond price that attested to the realities of the days when the Bible came into being.

It was in the Holy Land and beyond, in the sacred Land between the Two Waters, the Mesopotamia where life itself was said to have begun, that many searched and dug and found. In the seventeenth and eighteenth centuries, the self-reliant British traveler led the way for others among them, Frenchmen and Scandinavians, religious and secular officials. They studied the land and the languages and came to feel at ease in the strange communities where the Greco-Roman, the Assyrian and Egyptian cultures had flourished long ago.

All the while, at home in western Europe, the appreciation of ancient art, particularly that of Greece and Rome, spread from the secluded intelligence of a seventeenth-century Roman cardinal, who collected three hundred Greek and Roman originals in one year's time, to the more general love of ancient pieces in the eighteenth century that allowed Sir William Hamilton to sell his collection of vases to the British Museum. More and more, the interest in the arts of old summoned the devotion of the modern man and when, after the disturbances of 1848, the Louvre was opened to the public as a state museum, it displayed some 117 objects of antiquity. The Louvre's interest in such works remained constant, and it was one of Cesnola's first memories of Cyprus that a French warship had been sent to carry home a huge and ancient vase discovered at Amathus.

With his discovery at Golgos, Cesnola became one with a various band of looters and protectors, men of different aims and methods who lived and worked at the same time and whose intentions were often difficult to distinguish.

At the beginning of the nineteenth century, Lord Elgin took to England the most striking parts of the Parthenon's friezes. He snatched them from the acropolis that rose like a mesa, steep-cliffed and barren, above the clustered, white honeycombs of Athens and, in effect, saved them from almost certain destruction in war.

Both Lord Elgin and Cesnola had obtained from Turkey, which then ruled Greece and Cyprus, *firmans* or licenses, to dig; this permit, a rarity, Cesnola guarded well, with a careful cultivation of the Turks on Cyprus. Another searcher, Heinrich Schliemann, a German who had retired at forty-one years of age, wealthy and convinced he could unearth the legendary Troy, had run into trouble seeking such a permit in 1868. Repulsed by the Turks, he had gone back to Athens with his young Greek wife and put himself to the task of learning Turkish in three weeks.

Cesnola had managed the Turks more directly and with greater sophistication, thanks to his experience during and immediately following the Crimean War. Now that experience was paying off. The commerce he did on the side at the consulate would change abruptly. Cesnola, in effect, had for some time been handling the articles in his museum as he might have handled the Yankee notions. Now, with the Golgos find, he would deal with museums.

When the American missionaries had made the 1869 catalogue for him, it was to let travelers know that the pieces were "For Sale to suit Amateurs." It noted that they "may be seen at the American Consulate in Larnaca," and added, in a conspicuous note, "Only the Austrian Lloyd Steamers Touch at Larnaca regularly." Presumably, the catalogue, in fact a throwaway sales brochure, was distributed by Cesnola's consular and Italian friends in the Near East and Europe.

The American consul, through sales in this fashion and in the Parisian headquarters of Rollin & Feuardent, had supplemented his income to the point where he had long ago bought out the shares in his collecting concern from the two Englishmen. He had worked out an effective method of operation by putting natives of proven trustworthiness in charge of various digs, and, by rushing from one to the other, he had been able to amass the greatest horde of antiquities ever gathered in the island. He had thus learned how to make massive and speedy aggrandizement from the ancient world, and he had no hesitation whatever in criticizing the work of other archaeologists and collectors.

Of Queen Victoria's private archaeologist, an army captain who worked in Jerusalem, he wrote Hitchcock on February 16, 1870: Warren "had spent some 6 thousand pounds already [$24,000] and what he found was worth nothing." Cesnola suggested that Hitchcock caution a "Mr. Prim" of America not to follow the captain's lead in digging in Jerusalem, as the American minister at Constantinople had advised. He thought Mr. Prim "has better to come on to Cyprus and I will show him the place of ancient historical cities where he can spend more profitably his money in digging." He had drawn a map of Cyprus with its new cities marked in green, its old in red.

Cesnola had now a virtual monopoly on Cyprian antiquities. Lang, intrigued at first, had finally dropped any concerted work in the field after the first novelty passed. He was busy, moreover, with his position as leading banker in the island, though he kept some Cyprians looking out for important ancient pieces. After all, he wrote, "Our houses became like earthenware shops. The pieces found might be counted by tens of thousands and the tombs opened by thousands." He relinquished the field, but for an occasional, interesting relic, to Cesnola.

The consul-cavalier took full advantage of the lack of interest and, once Dr. Friederichs departed, prepared to increase the sale of his antiquities. No longer would he bother with the troops of tourists who came to his house from ships. He saw no reason why, once the Royal Berlin Museum, one of Europe's finest, had bought some of his antiquities, and the Vienna Museum had done the same, that the continent's other major museums shouldn't follow their lead.

Early in 1870 Cesnola began to deal with both the Louvre, which reflected Napoleon III's keen interest in antiquities, and with the Imperial Hermitage Museum in St. Petersburg. The walls of both these splendid Italianate palaces on the river banks of their nations' capitals were hung with the treasures of the Italian Renaissance, with Flemish and English masterpieces gathered by the Bourbons or by Catherine the Great in the art auctions of the years of revolution.

To the magnificent building that stretched along the Neva from whose carpeted and colonnaded chambers Catherine of Russia had kept in touch with Voltaire and the French Enlightenment, Cesnola wrote in French on crested paper. For the first time the coroneted Palma coat of arms appeared on his personal stationery. On January 2, 1870, he wrote Stephani Alexandrovich Gedeonov, Keeper of Antiquities there, suggesting—this was before the find at Golgos— that the Hermitage buy his complete collection of some five thousand objects. "I believe Your Excellency has heard in the scientific papers," he wrote Gedeonov, "how by chance I discovered a Phoenician necropolis containing more than 4000 tombs and that in every tomb I discovered ancient art objects."

He wanted to sell the terra cottas, vases, statuettes, stone objects, bronzes, copper and glass ornaments *en bloc* and sent forty-four photographs to show the work. Both the Berlin and London museums, he told Gedeonov, had already purchased a set of Phoenician vases, and he hoped the Hermitage "would also buy a portion of my collection."[2]

Thus the consul canceled out in one paragraph what he had set as a requirement—purchase *en bloc*—in the previous one. It was a measure of his uncertainty as well as his desire to sell. He also failed to label the pictures with prices, an oversight that swelled his correspondence.

Gedeonov notified the Director-General of the Imperial Hermitage Museum, His Excellency General Hofmeister of the Court of His Majesty the Emperor (Alexander II), that the consul of North American United States "has discovered in Cyprus very vast, ancient graves and excavated them very successfully." The most important of Cesnola's discoveries, he told his superior, had already been acquired by the Berlin and British Museums; though the objects were not in themselves beautiful, he felt the Imperial Hermitage Museum would "lose its standing among other museums" should it fail to make a purchase. He sought, and received, permission to spend 6000 francs [$1200] for three painted vases, two male heads, two limestone statues and two terra cotta statues.[3]

By the time his letter reached Cesnola, however, Golgos had been discovered and Cesnola exulted in this sweet combination of glorious find and imperial patron.

He described the trove in numbered paragraphs: "Ten colossal statues and limestones more or less in good condition with bearded heads and pointed hats and with heads of a battering ram," down through "sixty heads mostly colossal and several magnificently well-preserved," a "statue of a nine-foot Hercules with a lion skin on his head," and, finally, "a monstrously big head, intact, that measures more than a meter. It was necessary for me to get a chariot with two bulls to bring it here. This head is perhaps unique in the world."

"I will be very happy if the Museum of the Hermitage would decide to buy these magnificent objects found all together in earth of 100 square meters," he told Gedeonov. For payment, the museum could take "all the time it desires, even a year," he wrote, the need for cash coming in second to the urge to sell.

The Italian of noble family well knew the appeal to the powerful of special treatment, and he made a point of telling the official of Imperial Russia that he wanted him to "be the first" to know of the Golgos find although he recognized that the museums of Berlin, the Louvre and London "would be happy to acquire these objects when they know about their existence. But I propose them to you first and I will not decide anything until I hear from Your Excellency."

The Hermitage, he told Gedeonov, should send an agent "to acquire these objects and those still to be discovered."

He proferred still another suggestion: "A warship could take all these objects without difficulty."[4] Cesnola liked that tale about the vase of Amathus.

Gedeonov pressed this advantage immediately. He asked that the General's proposition "be agreed to as quickly as possible." His

Assistant Keeper, Johannes Doell, he informed Hofmeister, should be sent to Cyprus posthaste to buy 25,000 francs ($5000) worth of the finds.[5]

Hofmeister passed on Gedeonov's proposal with great enthusiasm to the Minister of the Imperial Court, Count Vladimir Theodorovich Adlerberg: "Indeed, compared with foreign museums, the Hermitage is foremost in its holdings of ancient vases and gold objects and it is precisely for this reason that the museum is worthy of being enriched with these antiquities of a new kind." He was so sure of the desirability of the objects that he told the court that insurance, packing and shipping charges could be paid for first by Cesnola who would be reimbursed with the first regular payment of purchase. [6]

Before the decision ran its slow and even way from the count to the museum and down to Cyprus, the consul had received from the State Department a letter that was a mortal blow to his position and all his aspirations.

The consulate was to be closed in three months.

The news, Cesnola told Hamilton Fish on March 30, "has brought desolation in my household as well as utter ruin to my private affairs!"

It was "very poor reward" for his service in the war and at the consulate in Cyprus, and left four hundred to five hundred "of our wealthiest American citizens" without a representative there, he complained; but, beyond that, the move affected his "archaeological researches and successful discoveries" that were the talk of "all the Savants of Europe."

Cesnola had failed to interest either his own government through the Smithsonian Institution and America's leading museum, the New-York Historical Society, in his work. He did not want to take financial support offered by England and Prussia. He had invested "all the money I had in the world (some $20,000) in these excavations; and now by the decision of the Dept. am utterly ruined."

This would follow, he explained, because, once the consulate was abolished, "the fruit of so much labor, study and expense will never be allowed by these semibarbarous Turks to leave this island as the Firman granted to me by the Sultan is in my possession as Consul not as a private citizen."

He pleaded with Washington to postpone the consulate's closing for at least a year to give him time to dispose of his collection and raise money to leave Cyprus. If the government's decision to close the Cyprus post was considered absolutely necessary, he would not ask the State Department to act against its own interests. But, in that case, he told Fish, "I only beg that I may retain my present position as U.S. Consul, though without emoluments, until my affairs can be arranged."[7]

He had spanked Fish for ignoring his bid to the New-York Historical Society; and he had also left Fish an alternative through which the U.S. Consul, paid or unpaid, would operate under the American flag in Cyprus.

As Cesnola waited for a reply from Washington, it was more necessary for him than ever to see that his antiquities should find a respectable and financially appreciative haven.

Before the end of April, as the ice in the Neva still enclosed Russia's "window on the west," word came from Cesnola's French consular colleague, Colonna-Cecealdi, that Melchior de Vogüé, who had first uncovered a small corner of the temple at Golgos, had shown pictures of Cesnola's finds to the Comte Alfred-Emilien de Nieuwerkerke, superintendent of the Louvre and other imperial museums. The count, who had a suite of seventeen rooms in the museum palace, offered "a great hall at the Louvre" in which the museum's officials could inspect the antiquities. Vogüé (whose archaeological explorations in the Near East had been sponsored by the government) had pronounced one statue bearing Cyprian inscriptions so fine that "only Paris could know how to appreciate it at its true value."

Colonna-Cecealdi warned Cesnola on two points: he cautioned against such "merchants" as Rollin & Feuardent and against showing even photographs of his finds to other museums if he wanted to deal with the Louvre.[8] (Curiously, this letter from Paris to Cyprus is in Leningrad, the old St. Petersburg.)

But Cesnola was not to be bound. He had not only sent more photographs to St. Petersburg but told Gedeonov at the end of May that the Louvre had offered him a room for those very pieces and stressed the urgency of the occasion by adding that he would probably be transferred to a consular post in Canada before July.

He would have liked to sell his collection in America, he confided, "but my compatriots in general have not yet enough taste for archaeology." After America he preferred Russia "to all other governments," he wrote, "and I am completely persuaded that other museums would be very jealous to see my entire collection in St. Petersburg."

He was inclined, finally, "to make sacrifices if the Hermitage decides quickly to buy it at a price altogether reasonable." He did not fix one.[9]

The appeal to pride, with a bargain to boot, proved irresistible.

Gedeonov sent a wire to the American consulate in Beirut to be passed on to Cesnola: "Avoid negotiations with Paris. Agent for the Hermitage leaves immediately."[10]

Doell, a young man who traveled with a pleasing and pretty companion, "Mademoiselle S." brought with him the blessings of Alexander II who had read the reports of Hofmeister and Count Adlerberg, and an order "to acquire the objects." The assistant curator would have four months' time to make a catalogue and 1200 rubles ($1200) expense money above his salary.[11]

To Cesnola, in stifling Cyprus, this meant a compounding of good news. He had just heard from Washington that, surprisingly, the government would keep the Larnaca post active until he was "ready to quit it, that is to say, in several years."[12] He was looking forward to digging in the luxuriant southwest, at Old Paphos, about which Homer had written:

But laughter-loving Aphrodite went to Cyprus
To Paphos, where is her precinct and fragrant altar.

Prospects for Cesnola in this hot and arid summer bubbled like a mountain spring of Piedmont. He told Gedeonov that he was besieged with offers: the Louvre was willing to pay 250,000 francs ($50,000) for the very group of pieces, the Golgos collection, that Doell was about to catalogue. Cesnola claimed to prefer the Hermitage to the Louvre and Boston over Berlin. Actually, he had already sold to Berlin, and there was no new offer from the Germans. At any rate, with such a wealth of offers, he had come to the conclusion that he should sell the whole as a group or nothing.[13]

France was now taking a close look at Cesnola's photographs and the Comte de Nieuwerkerke, a sculptor and protégé of the Princess Mathilde, pronounced his discovery, Cesnola told Gedeonov, "the most beautiful" found in Cyprus.[14]

The consul and the Russian were now getting down to a subject Cesnola had been scrupulously avoiding: the actual price. He had told the curator in April that he was "not a merchant of antiquities" and it was "somewhat difficult" for him to arrive at a figure. Now he wrote with what he termed his "habitual frankness and loyalty" that he had no idea what his collection was worth. Estimates had ranged from 270,000 to 400,000 francs ($54,000 to $80,000) and he estimated he had spent 100,000 francs ($20,000) on the diggings. Cesnola stated he would be willing to accept 300,000 francs ($60,000).[15]

What Cesnola really wanted was to have St. Petersburg give Doell "full powers to buy all the collection" at a price set and agreed upon between him and the agent. He pressed the point by saying he expected the Louvre to send a representative to Larnaca soon with *carte blanche* to do just that. Not only the Louvre but Boston also wanted everything he had gathered. It was not the first time that he mentioned the Boston museum's trustee, Charles C. Perkins, who, to Cesnola's delight, telegraphed him from America about the Cyprian finds. Perkins, a careful, meticulously educated New Englander, had entrée to the executive offices of Europe's museums.

Cesnola told Gedeonov he would also require that his antiquities be known as the "Cesnola Collection." A "little vanity" on his part, the designation would serve "to repay me for all the work I've done."[16] The whole sale could be settled "with a few words," he felt, and he hoped they would come by telegraph since he would not want to keep a Parisian with *carte blanche* waiting too long.

The Parisians, at the moment, were having other, weightier problems. Their ruler, the president-prince and emperor, Louis Napoleon (son of the Corsican's brother and stepdaughter, Hortense de Beauharnais), a cold, polite, subtle man who had spent a solitary youth of exile dreaming in the mountains of Switzerland, had finally reached power and meant to maintain it. For the task, at a time when Bismarck's Germany was moving toward dominion over Europe, Napoleon III, victim of another generation's vast disorders, needed more strength than he had.

The emperor eventually became the dupe of the strong men of his day, Cavour in Italy and Bismarck in Germany. It was in dealing with Bismarck in that summer of 1870 that his character signaled his fate.

When the vacant throne of Spain was offered to a Hohenzollern prince, France, frightened at the prospect of having that family on two borders, demanded that William I of Prussia, the ranking Hohenzollern of the day, refuse the offer. The king agreed to all that was asked by the French foreign minister, the Duc de Gramont. However, when France demanded that he see to it that no other Hohenzollern be named to the Spanish throne, William took personal offense and refused. He telegraphed Bismarck an account of the meeting.

Bismarck edited the agreement to make it appear that William had refused to grant the French demands. The rumor spread that William had actually declined even to see the French envoy and had given his reply through an aide-de-camp.

Napoleon III and the rest of France were wild with anger. The day after Bastille Day, on July 15, 1870, they sang the *Marseillaise* outside the Chamber of Deputies as it endorsed war with Prussia, and they greeted the announcement with shouts of "A Berlin!"

In far-off Larnaca, Cesnola knew that the imminent war could jeopardize the negotiations he was engaged in with the Louvre. He turned his mind toward the marble-embanked Neva with its palaces of opulent nobles flanking the massive Winter Palace of the Emperor of all the Russias.

Just a month after France declared war on Prussia, Cesnola entered into final negotiations with Director-General Hofmeister. His "Conditions of Sale" of August 16, 1870, listed five points: (1) The Cesnola collection was sold to the Imperial Museum. (2) It was to bear the name "Cesnola" in perpetuity. (3) The price for the entire collection was 80,000 rubles ($80,000); for the Golgos finds alone, 68,000 rubles ($68,000). (4) The museum would pay for packing and delivery and Cesnola would advance up to 7800 rubles ($7800) for this purpose. (5) Cesnola agreed not to "deal definitely" with any other museum for thirty days.

The collector wanted his money right away, for, claiming poverty, he said that though he was glad to do so, he would have to borrow the shipping costs from a Turkish bank at 12 percent interest. He itemized the shipping charges by sailboat at 3800 rubles ($3800) down to 200 rubles ($200) for food and pay for workers and packers.

Hofmeister had told him that he had only to advise the Emperor of the sale and the money would be forthcoming from the Imperial Treasury. Cesnola, then, while admitting that the sale had not actually been closed, besought the Director-General to pay him with a check he could cash in Constantinople. It could be drawn on a bank in London, Paris or Turin. Cesnola preferred that the Piedmont town be used.

He hoped Doell had told the director that he truly wanted the Cesnola Collection to go to "High Highness Your August Sovereign," and he reminded Hofmeister that he had other offers. France, he told the Russian, wanted to pay for the antiquities immediately, to have the trophies packed and held at the French consulate until the war ended. Then a warship would be sent to carry them to France.

Doell went off to Beirut and its telegraph staion, his tedious work of cataloguing completed at last. It was the work, precise and orderly, of a dedicated assistant curator.

His loyalty to the museum is obvious to this day. Sewn into the file of correspondence about the Cesnola antiquities in the archives of the Hermitage is an undated, torn letter. In the file, it follows Cesnola's long letter of August 16, and is addressed not to anyone in St. Petersburg but is, rather, from Dr. Friederichs of the Berlin Museum to Cesnola. After congratulating the consul on the Golgos find, Friederichs told him that Perkins of Boston had inquired about the value of the Cyprian finds.

"I told him," Dr. Friederichs wrote, "that I cannot recommend the acquisition."

The rest of the letter is cut off, leaving a half-sheet in the file. Did the German give Perkins his reasons? Did he express himself on a purchase by Russia? Was this missing fragment shown to Gedeonov, then to Hofmeister, then to Count Adlerberg and, ultimately, to the Emperor Alexander?

Whatever unfathomable event occasioned it, reluctance quickly succeeded to rejection from the enormously rich Russian court. It all came as a swift, complete disaster.

Not only did Russia after practically certain acceptance refuse him, it dropped its offer to 3000 rubles ($3000) for "some good pieces."

France fell. On September 3, 1870, the Emperor Napoleon III, with 80,000 troops, surrendered to the Prussians at Sedan and was imprisoned. The Comte de Nieuwerkerke was dismissed. The warship never came.

Eight

In America the post-Civil War boom had steadily increased. The new order and center of the greatest energy was summed up in the telling word "rails."

The New York market had given two clear signs of unusual strength, one, in 1866, when it maintained price levels despite the fall of stocks in London on a broad scale, and the second when it survived the shabby and flamboyant cornering of gold by Jay Gould, Jim Fisk and President Grant's brother-in-law, Abel Corbin, and the maniacal doings of the day of its denouement, Black Friday, September 24, 1869. The price of gold—already at 145—had soared to 160 on the belief that the three men had a gold monopoly and that the federal government would not sell any of its vast store. As the rising price of gold affected all other investors, brokers pleaded with Jubilee Jim Fisk and with Gould to sell. The pair remained determined and untouched. Brokers collapsed on the floor of the Exchange. Some were taken to hospitals. One, almost unnoticed in the frenzy, committed suicide.

As a desperate measure, the government sent James A. Garfield to Wall Street to shout the news to brokers from the Subtreasury steps that the government had decided to put on the market $10 million worth of gold. Immediately prices catapulted twenty points and kept falling. Many were ruined and forced to go bankrupt. Gould divided more than $11 million with Fisk.

Soon the market was back to its previous concern with rails. The lines of rights-of-way, aided by government from local to federal levels, cast a grid over the whole country and blocked out a tic-tac-toe on which countless Americans, humble and rich, placed their pieces of money on this and on that and on still another line in the almost sure game of winning.

Between 1866 and 1870, the prices of railroad stock soared. Thirty-three hundred miles of track bound one coast to the other. With this meteoric increase in personal wealth came an optimism and assurance that found outward expression in elaborate clothing and gourmandizing.

New York society was centered around the tree-shaded square, Madison Square, where James Stokes, insurance man and broker, and the Jerome brothers, Addison G. and Leonard W., brokers, had built large private homes. (Leonard W. Jerome's daughter, Jennie, was to be the mother of Sir Winston Churchill.) Schieffelins lived in the vicinity, as did John David Wolfe. His daughter, Catharine Lorillard Wolfe, was to give her superb art collection and $200,000 for its upkeep and increase to the Metropolitan Museum of Art. The Fifth Avenue Hotel faced directly onto the square and the entrance provided a stage for display of the most fashionable activity.

On most afternoons, the plaza between the hotel and the square offered a scene that would have caught the imagination of the new and ridiculed Impressionist painters in Paris. Open carriages, piled with the fur robes that covered the occupants, wheeled over the Belgian paving blocks, free-running dogs looping around them as they headed up the avenue. On the horizon, the spires of St. Patrick's Cathedral, still being built, towered above the brownstones and the classic palaces in the fashion of European cathedrals. The first Plaza Hotel, restrained and quiet, stood just south of the great park where the driveways were crowded with the vehicles of those who loved leisure, spankingly fresh air and gossip. There were those who whispered of William M. Tweed, boss of the city, who managed to increase the city's debt from $36 million in 1868 to $97 million in 1871. On occasion, the socially prominent would enter their carriages and wend their way to a private art collection, after having obtained written permission for the privilege. More and more of these private galleries stood behind the brownstone or marble facades of the homes on Fifth Avenue since August Belmont in the middle 1800s had installed the first sky-lit picture gallery in New York. In his home at Eighteenth Street, visitors could see oils by Rosa Bonheur or the meticulous every-blade-of-grass military scenes of Meissonier or Bouguereau's ponderous nudes. Nowhere in sight was the work of Manet and other Impressionists. Such collections, however, evoked public interest and when *Putnam's Magazine* published a series of articles on the art galleries in the city, it included that of John Taylor Johnston, considered the best in New York. Johnston's pictures were all "wholly modern" for the period, and the collection spanned senti-mental, mid-European, anecdotal oils such as the "Old Beau" by Kraus, a picture of an aging cavalier with two German peasant girls, and some fairly recent paintings by the affable but solitary New Yorker, John Kensett. There were a number of American painters represented in Johnston's collection. Frederick Church's first paint-ing of "Niagara" rated higher praise from the *Putnam's Magazine* writer than Thomas Cole's allegorical series on the "Voyage of Life." Europeans in the group other than a woodland scene by Corot, a canvas the writer disdained, ran heavily to peasant girls, Oriental girls, military scenes (two by Meissonier) and church interiors. Easily the best picture of the lot, the writer felt, was one of a "sensual, brutal Turkish patrolman with armed foot-runners" by Decamps. "Per-haps," he concluded, "there is no such piece of mellow, rich and harmonious color in any gallery in New York."

Copies of the magazine moved slowly to the far corners of the world, and one eventually reached Cyprus.

From there, a year after it was published—in July 1871—Cesnola wrote to "John T. Johnston Esq., New York," telling him of his "most valuable and richest private collection of antiquities existing in the *world.*" He had no fewer than *ten thousand* pieces and "every object was *found by me.*"[1] This wasn't precisely the truth but was close enough to it, he felt, since his diggers presented him with the finds.

The consul made a solid attempt to sell the collection to the new museum that Johnston headed, one that Cesnola referred to as "The New York Art Museum."

The joint project of the New-York Historical Society and the Parks Department for a museum in Central Park had foundered after the city offered a seven acre plot between 80th and 84th Streets along Fifth Avenue. The Society, unable to put up the building on its own, was forced eventually to abandon the project.

The usual account of the founding of the Metropolitan Museum owes much to inter-institution courtesy, as it is customary to omit details of the Society's well-polished plans for just such a museum. Credit for suggesting that it was time to found a national museum of art has regularly gone to John Jay, namesake-grandson of the first Chief Justice. On July 4, 1866 (when the Park's Tammany men were wrangling with the Society), Jay, then minister to Austria, pushed the idea in a speech in Paris. He well knew the Society's plan. He was one of its life members.

Jay, who became president of the Union League Club, had its art committee look into his suggestion. It did so with a flourish.

Three hundred of the city's most important men, clergy, lawyers, artists, educators, and publishers, headed by William Cullen Bryant, met at the Society's theater in 26th Street in late November 1869 and heard George Fiske Comfort, the poet-publisher and a Princeton professor, promote and expound the idea. Cesnola's collection, relatively small at this time, came in for discussion but quickly faded from the scene, as the group was low in cash. They decided instead to follow the approach of the South Kensington Museum in London and assemble a show of loaned works of art and locate a place to hang them.

It was agreed that the new museum of art in New York should be "on a scale worthy of this metropolis and of a great nation." To make it such, the group appointed a committee of fifty men to do the basic legal work in setting up the museum. On this committee were William T. Blodgett, Joseph H. Choate, Andrew H. Green, Robert Hoe Jr., John Taylor Johnston, Henry G. Marquand, W.C. Prime and Russell Sturgis Jr. In a few months' time, the organization was settled and the first slate of officers, with Johnston as president, was chosen.

The eight trustees, who included the artist Kensett, the collector Aspinwall and the civil servant Green, decided to raise $250,000 by public subscription. After a fifteen-month fund-raising drive, however, they had collected only $106,000. Johnston, the president, gave the top donation, $10,000. The rest came from 105 other donors, only one of them, Miss Wolfe, a woman. Ultimately, the city paid for the museum building and its upkeep. But as late as 1870 the Historical Society tried on its own to establish a museum at the Metropolitan's present site.

In Cyprus the consul-cavalier took the news of the lack of interest in his funds realistically. Refused by St. Petersburg and thwarted by Paris, he embarked on a campaign of build-up that would make his rejected collection a sought-after prize.

First, however, he pressed a point he had raised before with Hitchcock: the two should team up in some "sure, honest & pleasant" business.[2] Hitchcock, though still in retirement in New Hampshire, was very much in touch with the world of affairs in New York and Washington and gave Cesnola no encouragement. Actually, the future was a huge guessing game. Hitchcock himself was off to Colorado to do a little prospecting. Was it for gold? In their letters, Cesnola joked about this. But, beyond suggesting that Colorado was a healthy and sometimes profitable place to be, Hitchcock never made clear what he sought there with his mining gear.

Cesnola now began to promote his antiquities, starting, of course, in his homeland, Piedmont, amid a growing cloud of envy. The very quantity of his finds roused critics. As he was reporting in January 1871 to the Royal Academy of Sciences in Turin, the Turks controlling Cyprus began to raise objections to Cesnola's very active digs. In fact, they got an order from the Sultan banning all further excavations in Cyprus. Cesnola could not even dig in land he had bought in Paphos and wrote Hitchcock that "in spite of all the steps taken by our Minister at Constantinople to obtain permission, for me to dig in my own ground was refused!" The ruling forced him to face the probability that he would have to give up the hope "to make hereafter any new collection for New York."[3] What he had in mind, it seems, was to sell his first collection in Europe, and make a second collection for the new world.

The Parisian firm he had been dealing with, Rollin & Feuardent, had sent a son of the house, Gaston L. Feuardent, to London, and the young dealer had rapidly become the "man of business of the British Museum." In that position, he had written Cesnola saying that he was ready to buy the whole collection for the British Museum on a commission basis since he could hold the pieces until the museum, momentarily out of funds, could purchase them.

Cesnola told Hitchcock he thought this explanation "all humbug. The Englishmen like to make commission money as much as the Americans. Now, it seems, the British Museum intends to purchase my entire collection but doesn't want to deal *directly with me*. Why? It is easy to understand."[4]

The consul withheld his feelings from Feuardent, merely suggesting the dealer pack up and come to Cyprus to inspect the collection and then make his offer. Feuardent did no such thing. He apparently told Cesnola, in turn, to bring his antiquities to London.

At this juncture, such a trip proved difficut. Cesnola who must have disliked being told by a junior what to do, was soon embroiled in a conflict with the Turkish Empire over the exportation of the antiquities. He had already sent one boatload of antiquities away on the ship *Napried* but that vessel, taking fire shortly after sailing, sank within sight of the Levant.

In his book on Cyprus, published in 1878, Cesnola gave this account of his big shipment:

The Governor-General of Cyprus for the Turks had informed Cesnola that his license, although it permitted him to excavate, did not allow him to export his finds. In fact, the Governor told the collector he had been instructed to block any such exportation.

Cesnola, at this point, had assurance of the American Squadron in the Mediterranean to "convey the collection to thc United States." But, before any of the fleet dropped anchor in the broad bay of Larnaca, Cesnola, always aggressive and pressed by events, had found it possible to charter a private vessel. He now had packed all of his antiquities in 360 large cases, and he was ready to move.

Then, as his hired vessel was discharging her incoming cargo, a Turkish ship-of-war moved into the bay with political prisoners. The prisoners disembarked. Then the corvette anchored practically in front of Cesnola's residence. It did nothing, just rested there, armed. Ominous.

Cesnola sent his personal dragoman Besbes to the Custom House for an export order for his cases. The Customs Director showed Besbes two orders specifically banning just such a shipment. He reminded the Turk of the Governor-General's protest.

The consul sat on his porch, pondering the news moodily, the corvette in full view. Besbes looked at him "through his great blue spectacles with his red-rimmed eyes and impassible aspect (he is one of the ugliest men I think I ever saw, but at the same time one of the most faithful).

" 'Besbes,' said I, 'these antiquities must and shall go on board the schooner this day! Suddenly I saw a sort of twinkle in his eyes, and a curious expression dawned on his lips as he said, looking very meekly at me, 'Effendi, those telegrams are to prevent the American Consul from shipping antiquities,' and then he stopped. I replied with some heat, 'You seem to take pleasure in repeating the information to me—I should think I ought to be aware of it by this time.' Besbes did not lose a particle of his equanimity, but only said still more meekly, 'There was nothing in those orders about the *Russian Consul.*' I understood then what he meant, though my Western civilization would never have arrived at this truly oriental solution of the difficulty. 'Right,' I cried, 'go quickly to the Custom House and tell the Director that I wish to see his two telegrans.' " Having confirmed the fact that the ban was on exportation by the *American* consul, Cesnola then shipped his finds out of Cyprus as the Russian consul.

That was the public recital of the events. But what he privately told Hitchcock was quite another tale.

After Cesnola had enjoyed four full years of complete freedom to dig and export all "free from Custom House duty," the new Grand Vizier wrote the American representative in Constantinople, one J. P. Brown, "only a Dragoman who acts as U. S. Minister and who is more *Turc* than the *Turcs* themselves," telling him to advise Cesnola that his firman called for the sending of all the duplicates in his collection to the Turkish Court. The Empire, just becoming aware of its native treasures, was organizing the Ottoman Museum in Constantinople.

THE GLITTER AND THE GOLD

Cesnola had one of his own Turkish employees translate the firman for him carefully. It dealt with "*all statues which* are *duplicates*," he told Hitchcock. Not a single duplicate of a statue had been found Cesnola decided, so the ruling did not apply.

But, to his horror, the Turks then ruled that seeing that the Consul only sent two boxes of vases to the Turkish Court, the Porte, controlling commerce, ordered "the American Consul *through* his Legation to SEND and DELIVER in Constantinople to the Porte, the HALF OF HIS COLLECTION OF ANTIQUITIES!!!!"[5] Cesnola practically ran out of punctuation capable of expressing his astonishment. The consul was not to export "*one single piece!*" until he had complied with the order.

A copy had been sent to the Governor of Cyprus, a Turk whom Cesnola, astute enough not to have overplayed the friendliness of the Greeks on the island, had long cultivated at dinners and trips around the island in easy companionship. Far from acting to impose the order, as Cesnola's book would state, the governor, hearing of the forthcoming order before it was sent, gave his friend forewarning of its arrival.

Thus Cesnola "was enabled to pack up nearly 200 cases with the *most* and *best* of my collection; and to freight a vessel and send them away before the order came to Cyprus. Everybody is astonished here, at the gigantic work I performed in less than two weeks, and I must confess I am astonished myself."[6]

It had been a most satisfactory accomplishment.

The order, however ineffectual, still rankled. "Think that the Porte claims half of my collection as a *Royaulty* for my discoveries!!!!"[7] he shouted-in-writing to Hitchcock, his English sliding into half-French under the pressure.

It was at that moment, without any doubt, that he first decided he should himself be the Minister to Constantinople. In this same letter to Hitchcock, he said, "It is a great disgrace to our government to have such a dirty individual as Brown is to represent the United States."[8]

Within three months' time—by January 17, 1872—Cesnola shipped out of the island "the whole of my *Statues, glass* and *Vases* worth sending away." Not only that. His men were still digging "but

without leave. . . . The Governor here being my friend *shuts his eyes*
and let [*sic*] them dig."⁹

When he had finally received Brown's peremptory order from
the Porte to surrender half his collection to the nascent Ottoman
Museum, he played for time by whipping off to Brown in Constantinople "a most *saucy* letter asking if he *ordered* me to obey such
insane orders." While the slow mails gave him the needed time,
Cesnola got off the rest of his collection. In Brown's meek and "jes-
uitical" reply, he offered to transmit any of Cesnola's objections to
the Turkish Government. Cesnola sent off a long list of objections to
the ruling, acting as if the dispatched antiquities were, in fact, still
in Cyprus.¹⁰

He kept his men at the digs, and they made considerable discoveries, including a beautiful but broken Venus. Cesnola was sanguine.
He told Hitchcock that he had real hope of finding a work by Prax-
itiles at Paphos but did not expect to find a Phidias there. All the
latter's works were accounted for. He had checked the list personally
the last time he was at the Vatican Museum.¹¹

Having gotten his treasures where they would remain his, Cesnola now wanted to build up his own reputation and that of his
collection. He now had a promise from Hitchcock that he would write
a full account of the discoveries for a major American magazine. What
Hitchcock put together must be one of the first and surely one of the
great examples of personal promotion. It was impressive, a fifteen-
page spread in a leading monthly.

Harper's New Monthly Magazine, one found on the parlor side
tables in most well-to-do homes, was selected. The magazine ranked
countless notches above the more mundane and newsy *Harper's
Weekly* which dealt with such matters as P.T. Barnum's fires and the
deaths of prominent figures.

The monthly had standing. It concerned itself with truths as
timeless and values as imperishable as only mid-Victorians could
relish. It was run by Joseph Wesley Harper who was mayor of New
York in 1847 when Madison Square was opened and he, presumably,
visited Hitchcock's hotel there.

Through this influential outlet, news of the General's great finds
in Cyprus was disclosed to Americans. The article ran in the July

1872 issue, complete with a half-page engraving of Cesnola in the gold-epauleted uniform of a brigadier general. No matter that he had been a colonel in the Civil War. *Harper's* printed the picture with assurance on Hitchcock's say-so. Cesnola, his hair parted down the middle, his walrus mustache ending in twirls, obviously a man who enjoyed eating, looked the part of a capable commander. He had an air of authority about him. In short, he looked splendid.

So did his antiquities.

The frontispiece showed Cesnola's faithful dragoman leaning against the ear of the Colossus of Golgos. His large, Mediterranean eyes filled with awe, the Cyprian looked squarely at the reader, one hand cupping the helmet-shaped, Assyrian-looking cap of the massive head.

With this introduction, Hitchcock got right down to business. "The importance of General Di Cesnola's discoveries in the island of Cyprus and the archeological and artistic value of the collection which he had made can hardly be overestimated." [12]

To reinforce the importance of Cesnola's discoveries, Hitchcock then mentioned Stonehenge, Pompeii and the Bible. The Colonel was traveling in high company.

Hitchcock saw that he stayed there. In discussing inscriptions the consul unearthed and about which a specialist on the staff of the British Museum cautioned against premature disclosure, the writer turned to cuneiform-marked tablets found by Layard in legendary Nineveh. These latter conformed to Jewish scripture and sent archeologists scouting down a rich avenue of research.

By this time the reader was quite ready to accept mention of the Rosetta Stone. It seemed only natural to hear about the two marble fragments found in the Roman forum in 1817 that fortuitously completed the Capitoline Tables. Hitchcock was quick to point out that "with certain other manuscript discoveries they enabled Niebuhr to write the most reliable history of Rome." [13]

Hitchcock was rhapsodic:

"There are islands of the sea—sepulchres of the ages—which can unfold the history of ancient civilization to one who searches the dark recesses with a heart for classic memory and who can read their language of death; and Cyprus from its history and position is preeminently one." [14]

And indeed this island forty miles from the coast of Asia Minor and sixty miles from Syria was awash with tides of history. Hitchcock enjoyed the surging spectacle of Israel, Assyria, Phoenicia, Greece, Carthage and Persia coming ashore on the mountainous, 3500 square miles in succeeding waves of dominance.

It was conquered by Artaxerxes, son of the great fifth century Persian warrior Xerxes (and Hitchcock did not identify him for his culturally elect audience), by the Great Alexander and by Rome. Here "Titus made a pilgrimage to the shrines on his way to the capture of Judaea" and was accompanied by Tacitus. In the annals of the early church, Cyprus was the "field of the first great mission to the Gentiles, the scene of the first great triumph when Saul (Paul) converted the Roman governor."[15]

"Here," and Hitchcock indulged his resources of imagination, "must have been a grand Christian church which knew the presence of Mark and cherished the birthplace and home and grave of Barnabas."

The Turks receded "before the mailed form of Richard-the-Lion-Hearted" and, on his departure, reappeared. "The vines still yielded the classic wine of Strabo and Pliny" and at Famagousta were "magazines of the arms of chivalry stained with the blood of followers of Baldwin, Tancred and Saladin."[16]

After five full pages one could hardly wait to scratch this earth with Cesnola and bring the artifacts and art of this most heterogeneous of ancient lands into the light of modern day.

The suspense was quickly closed. Cyprian digs were few. A ninth-century codex was taken to Paris in 1673. No organized research followed except at one location. That failed.

Hitchcock then waved the General on stage.

"To Di Cesnola, therefore, the field was in reality new and it is certainly a subject of congratulation that an explorer so able as he was proved was led to enter it."[17]

The first thing he told his readers about "Count Luigi Palma di Cesnola, of an old Italian family" was not the peaks of his discoveries, not their significance in illustrating this rich history, not the variety or value of his finds. In the hills overlooking the busy diggers, Hitchcock on his grand tour listened well to his host. His first attention was to Cesnola's military record in the Civil War. In sum, Cesnola was a hero and his reward was his rank of General and his position as consul.[18]

It was becoming clear, after the long linking of his name with the greats of history and the strategic placement of his own war record, that the Italian cavalier himself and not the writer was one of the most adroit promoters of all time. Surely the emphasis was placed where the forceful cavalryman called for it. The pliant writer followed the claims of his subject.

Hitchcock recounted Cesnola's quick and thorough success in digging. The General located the sites of the dozen most ancient cities in his consulate and, digging at a place that had been tried before, he uncovered the burial ground of the ancient Phoenician city of Citium, "the Kittim of the Scriptures." His reward: the yield of several hundred tombs, tiny figurines of the crowned Venus, the "hugh, bearded giant of Assyria, the sphinx of Egypt, the woman of Phoenicia playing the lute and the many illustrations of busy life, normal and grotesque."

It was only then, seeing the finds laid out upon the parched ground, Hitchcock wrote, that Cesnola "realized as never before the similarity of ancient Eastern art; and he foresaw that by patient research in the island an additional light might be thrown upon the Ethnography, history, religion and art of the East."[19] Curiously, it should be said here, Cesnola's failure in this very field of archaeology, linking the finds with the facts of ancient life, undermined the value of his art.

Hitchcock described the personal, "never-to-be-forgotten" tour when the discoverer took him over the district around Larnaca, site of the first digs. He showed the New Englander the "stupendous Roman aqueduct" that still worked and the "columns, cornices, mosaics and tombs the men had dug up with iron and wooden bars, with the use of hoe and basket or with their bare hands." The visitor, captivated, did not question whether bars, both iron and wood, could damage, could even break, ancient statues.

Hitchcock and his readers were looking on a world of wondrous age and beauty. The Greek glass was "positively wonderful." Gold jewelry, silver spoons and daggers, copper mirrors and battle axes gleamed through his prose.

European museums, he reported, were eyeing the collection carefully. In August 1870, the Russian Imperial Museum had sent a representative to examine the thirteen thousand pieces Cesnola collected. This was just a month after the Emperor Napoleon III offered to buy the lot for the Louvre. But by the time Cesnola had accepted the offer, Napoleon was no more, having lost his throne at Sedan.

Hitchcock hoped that "America, of which the discoverer is a worthy and honored citizen, will anticipate the action of London, Berlin and St. Petersburg." Berlin, of course, had all it wanted. St. Petersburg had bowed out entirely. Hitchcock didn't mention Boston.

It was an article clearly intended for the eyes of the founders of the Metropolitan Museum of Art.

Nine

In 1872 Manhattan broiled in the summer and then shivered as the winds of winter funneled through the streets. Fully half the population lived in tenement warrens, some seven hundred in a single five-story house crammed among others between City Hall and 14th Street. A sewing girl who worked at home earned six cents apiece for making blue cotton shirts or "hickories." She had to furnish her own thread.

The slums bred not violence but deep disorder, the banding-together of cronies to best the city. The Irish disgraced their own in the Tweed Ring that plundered New York, twisting its government into a tool of illegal trafficking in public funds. In 1861 Tweed went into court as a bankrupt. Ten years later, his wealth was estimated at $20 million. And by that time, the new County Court House behind City Hall, still unfinished, had cost the taxpayers $12,500,000. On it had been spent sums greater than those expended for the Capitol Building in Washington. Yet, despite the general dismay at the scandal, its after-effects were those that led men to hope and even expect better times. The market continued ebullient. Society softened its rigid manners of pre-war days. Archibald Gracie King gave his daughter's debut ball not in his own home but in Delmonico's at 14th Street and Fifth Avenue, its mirrored ballroom reflecting the white-gloved, formally dressed couples in the cotillion that was society's favorite dance. The waltz was not considered respectable.

To the wealthy of New York, planning had proved it could change the face of one part of the city. The squatters' area uptown, beyond the city's gas lights, which in 1870 reached to 59th Street, had not long before been a shambles of makeshift huts, half wood found in foraging downtown, half-flattened tin cans. Now, in the early 70s, much of the Central Park had been blasted, terraced, planted, its footpaths smoothed, its carriage roads paved, its lake filled with swans. Most of its 843 acres, particularly that in its south-ern part were "a miracle of exquisite landscape gardening." Every-one knew the Mall, the Terrace, the Ramble, the Museum of Natural History. It had been a wondrous achievement and, hung with gonfa-lons and resounding to long Sunday band concerts, had proved a great and often lively pleasure. The skating there was more tangy than anywhere in the city. Men could push women sitting in chairs fitted with runners across the pond, that was burnished with torches, murmuring with its throng of people. In the late summer, top-hatted men and hoop-rolling children moved on a vine-covered walk over-looking the Mall. From there they watched the promenaders below, sheltered by four rows of American elms.

The American Museum of Natural History had fallen heir to the stately armory in the park which the city had bought from the state in 1856. Now its first three stories were given over to the "magnifi-cent collection of the American Museum Association," some 12,000 birds, 1,000 mammals and 3,000 reptiles and fishes. On the top floor, Professor Daniel Draper ran the Meteorological Observatory of the Central Park.

With this space taken, the new Metropolitan Museum of Art, exulting over purchase of two art collections in Europe at the out-break of the Franco-Prussian War, had leased 681 Fifth Avenue near the Vanderbilt homes in the Fifties for two years. The one-time Dodworth Dancing School cost the trustees $9000 a year and pro-vided a place where they could show their friends at private soirees and the public in general their vaunted paintings. They were so valuable and so celebrated, the museum's report said in 1872, "that the mere announcement of the purchase in America had caused excited comment throughout Europe." Among them were Francesco Guardi's luminous "Rialto," Frans Hals' vibrant "Malle Babbe," and one of Giovanni Battista Tiepolo's mural studies.

Cesnola was busy seeing to it that the trustees were talking about him as well as their paintings and about his collection "rescued" from the Turks. On February 8, 1872, the New York *Observer* ran an editorial following a speech by Hitchcock on the "wonderful excavations of Cesnola in Cyprus" and praising the consul for getting thirteen thousand antiquities out of the island before "an order from the stupid Government of Turkey put a stop to his work." The editorial sounded as though it had been written by Cesnola himself.

Johnston, the museum's president, told the trustees at their February meeting that Cesnola's pieces were now in the hands of Rollin & Feuardent and if not sold as a unit to a museum within a year, they would be auctioned off by the dealers. He reported on Cesnola's being agreeable to arbitrate the price. The consul had, of course, carefully pointed out that the Louvre had been willing to pay 360,-000 francs or $90,000, exclusive of duplicates, and that the Russians had valued the group at $70,000 without the ancient glass which he termed "the handsomest in the world." The collector gave no reason for the Russian disenchantment. It well may be that he did not know it himself.[1]

A month later, on March 18, 1872, when the executive committee gathered in the large 23rd Street studio of the landscapist Kensett, Johnston assured them that Cesnola was set on selling his collection *en bloc* and would not consider for a moment selling separate portions of it. He said the collection was "unbroken."

It was at this point that Cesnola began exaggerating the condition of his treasure. Far from being intact, it had been broken from the very beginning by private sales, gifts and formal auctions. The latter had been held in London in 1867, 1869, 1870 and 1871. He had, in fact, sold some four thousand pieces of sculpture, glass, pottery, jewelry and the like in the previous fourteen months.[2]

The items sold were not, as Cesnola kept saying, mere duplicates. In January of 1871, the consul sold what the superlative London auction house, Sotheby's, described as "excessively rare" finds made at Dali, the Cesnola summer home, and a "unique example in quite perfect form" of a Greek bottle decorated with serpentine reliefs. He had disposed as well of ancient jewelry, gold rings of plain design or set with sapphire; a red jasper intaglio of Mercury; Mars in garnet; earrings of gold hoops of twisted wire terminated in calves' heads. Other precious pieces the Sotheby sale took out of the collection were gold ornaments for the dead, "thin plates of pure gold which were placed on the brow of the dead, usually six inches long, a broad flat band pressed in low relief with designs of acanthus leaves, rosettes and scrolls."[3]

He had learned how to get the most from his finds. When Cesnola sent Hitchcock a couple of baskets of antiquities in 1871, he was so busy he had no time to clean them. But he advised the New Englander to do it. What he did was to soak the encrusted vases and lamps in water for a full day, then make a solution of muriatic acid and water and "with an old toothbrush. . . . rub the vase with it gently and you will see it smoking. If the solution applied to the vase smokes *too freely* add more water to it; if it does not remove the crust add more acid." After cleaning, the piece was to be soaked in water for a couple of hours. It was all very easy, Cesnola said. He had cleaned as many as three hundred vases himself in that way "in a few hours only."

It was a strange thing, but in London "they prefer the vases dirty as they were found in the tombs; while in Paris at an auction sale, those I had cleaned sold *three times* more than the identical ones which I left uncleaned."[4]

The reaction of the public to his finds and what that could mean to him made Cesnola whistle. "If my entire collection was in Paris, London or even in New York and exposed to the public, what amount of money would be made in that way!" While he wanted to make as much money as he could, he added, "But I have no desire to emulate Mr. Barnum in any way indeed."[5] However, he wanted to do it in a manner that would not offend those who had the funds to buy his finds.

His promotional activities now included having Hitchcock send the *Harper's* article to a score of prominent Europeans from London and Turin to Constantinople[6] and giving personal gifts to Secretary of State William H. Seward, who visited him in Cyprus earlier.

In addition, he had presented gifts to the Museum of Antiquities in Turin and to other museums and learned societies in Athens, Rome, Dresden, Berlin, Paris, Perugia and Florence.[7] He was made an honorary member of each of these societies and, moreover, received decorations from the kings of Italy, Bavaria and Greece.[8]

He was now, in fact, an international figure, and when he went to Turin in July 1872, his arrival on leave from his consular post was announced in the Piedmont papers. In Paris, that August, he and his family stayed on the Champs Elysees and the director of the Louvre visited his suite there to look at some of the antiquities.[9]

The New York Museum, as Cesnola then called the Metropolitan, was hesitant about buying his whole collection, undoubtedly because of limited financial resources and, though Hitchcock was putting "extraordinary efforts . . . a brother would not give him so much trouble" into getting the collection bought by the struggling museum, the consul was setting up a whole panorama of courses of action to dispose of it in Europe.

Cesnola had by this time recognized the value of unearthing still more Cyprian finds. He told Hitchcock on August 14 that he had already gotten in touch with an Army officer with political power, Major General John Love (a "friend of Pres. Grant and Senator Morton") who had agreed to "use all his influence in my behalf to obtain the post of Minister Resident at Constantinople." Then he added, "I am disposed to spend *ten thousand* dollars to secure that appointment." He wanted it not for the salary but for the *honor*.[10] He would also be more in a position to influence the granting by the Turkish regime to its outlying provinces of licenses to dig and of orders to donate to the Ottoman Museum.

Meanwhile, he kept sending Hitchcock boxes of the terra cottas and jewelry, telling him to dispose of them "precisely as if the antiquities were your own. Whatever you do with them I shall always be satisfied—recollect this—Dispose of them as if you would of things belonging to yourself—You may need them to make presents to some influential friends to obtain the post at Constantinople. Do whatever you like and you will always have my thanks whatever you do."[11]

Cesnola then moved on to London where, for all his position and seeming authority, he listened most carefully to advice. But it had to come only from Hitchcock, his proven friend. Cesnola's contact in London, also a friend of Hitchcock, was Captain John Vine Hall, a ship commander and a man who appreciated the General's talents. As others were to recognize much later, Hall saw that Cesnola was one of the most acquisitive collectors of all time. He also knew that for him to advise Cesnola to concentrate on collecting would do no good. So he asked Hitchcock to tell their friend to sell his present collection "and then go and [dig again and] make further discoveries."[12]

People at the British Museum had suggested that the collector get bids from each interested museum and let the highest take his pick, the other museums following in the order of their bids. At one point, Cesnola thought he would sell the Golgos collection separately. Then he toyed with the idea—not liking it very much—of having a full auction. By doing that, he would lose on commission 33 to 40 percent of the amount realized.

As it happened, he settled into a charming little house and garden near Captain Hall's and arranged to have the most impressive of his finds at Golgos displayed in a private gallery at 61 Great Russell Street opposite the British Museum.

Cesnola and his wife, who had been troubled in Cyprus with the fever prevalent there, enjoyed an active social life in England and looked forward even more to that of New York.

Their ease would have been troubled had they known that Gaston Feuardent, the proficient, thoroughly trained antiquarian, had written the head of the Imperial Hermitage a full year earlier for "aid in my researches on the authenticity of the objects in the Cesnola Collection." His only aim, he wrote August 8, 1871, was "to find the truth" by which to "render service to the archaeologists of the old world."[13] He did not express concern for those of the new. Although there was no attempt to deceive, the letter was signed "General Cesnola" in Feuardent's handwriting. On the company's paper, it was sent from New York where Feuardent was setting up a branch of the Parisian firm. A postscript, saying he would be "most appreciative" of the help was signed "Your devoted servant, Gaston L. Feuardent," and it is reasonable to assume that the dealer and his family were acquainted with the museum director. Feuardent wanted a set of photographs that Doell had taken in Larnaca in the summer of 1870 and listed eleven that he especially sought.

Cesnola himself had been contacting the Hermitage, but this time he had written not to His Excellency General Hofmeister but to Doell, the young assistant curator who had gone to Larnaca and catalogued his finds. In January 1871, Cesnola had been surprised to learn the catalogue would be published. He objected because his entire collection, his many finds since Doell was in Cyprus, were not included.[14] Half a year later, however, he was only too glad that the catalogue existed and wanted a French translation of it. Fast.

By that time, a catalogue, "drawn up scientifically" was vital to him as he confronted knowing curators. Never having prepared one of his own, Cesnola proposed to have Doell's translated from French to English and published in New York.[15] Such a move would protect his shaky reputation as an archaeologist.

In October 1872, with a sale imminent, he definitely needed the catalogue "so well edited . . . [it] will be of great value to me right now." He guessed at the reason for his not having received it before, and he told Doell he would publish it under the Russian's name.

As a parting thought, he wondered if it were "possible that the Museum of St. Petersburg has renounced for all time buying at least a portion of this unique and very important archaeological discovery."[16] Doell's reply is not bound into the Hermitage file.

The consul was now facing difficulties on other fronts. It looked as though both the British Museum and the Louvre would be extremely selective in any possible purchase. Had Feuardent, dealer in antiquities for both museums, played the role that Dr. Friederichs had with the Berlin and Boston sales? Had he warned them that the wisest course would be to choose most carefully from the Golgos finds, pieces whose provenance, or source, was clear?

Cesnola told Hitchcock in late September that he had "assurances from the British and from *three* others that they will make important selections out of my collection,"[17] which certainly makes them sound as if they were listening to the cautious and doubting Feuardent. The situation was so uncertain that, seeing it, Cesnola knew he faced a general, open and expensive auction in Europe that winter if matters did not come to fruition soon.

Across the Atlantic the New York museum had its own doubts without advice from any expert. Johnston wrote Hitchcock in late July that there was a "lack of confidence" in Cesnola and that he could not tell what prospect there was of the museum purchasing the Cesnola collection. "First, there is the very great difficulty of saying what the collection really consists of after all its vicissitudes, and then there is the uncertainty that as high a price as the collection will warrant will be put on it." Furthermore, he went on, the large number of duplicates and the very real question of whether the collection would come "within the purview" of the museum compounded the problem.[18] Throughout Europe, much of the material of this kind then being found eventually appeared in archaeological or natural history museums.

Hitchcock responded with the stock political answer, I'm-glad-you-asked-that-question: "I am much gratified that you should have written me, in confidence, what has been said unfavorably of General Di Cesnola and his collection. It enables me to more fully appreciate the difficulties you encounter with reference to the matter and gives me an opportunity to speak *confidentially* to you, of one or two things."

The New Englander, writing from Hanover, said he had been working "very industriously and faithfully" with a number of people at the museum, then run by its bustling trustees, and had been contacting officials directly and indirectly. He had lectured and promoted his friend's interests. He reminisced about his "sojourn in Cyprus and a fond desire that these works should come to America." He assured Johnston that he had absolutely no financial interest "and never will have" in the sale of the collection.

"This being so," he went on, "you can judge of the *pain* it has given me, to find an undercurrent adverse to the General and his collection, without being able to get points enough to call the parties here in America, who are in that current, to account."

He was entirely certain that the origin of the doubts came from "conspirators" in the Near East. He had been told this, he wrote, by a former and two present U. S. ministers to Turkey.

As for the consul's personal character: "If General Di Cesnola's life is not a sufficienty [*sic*] character," he concluded, "I could exhibit a correspondence embracing a number of the most honored men in Europe that would set at rest any suspicion that he was capable of doing other than right."[19]

That disposed, for all time, of the New Yorker's worries about the collector. Johnston then asked the man who was undoubtedly the most respected American in the British Isles to examine the collection. That man was fifty-nine-year-old Junius Spencer Morgan—head of the international banking firm. He was quick-minded, aware, emphatically and unabashedly patriotic. Morgan presented himself at Cesnola's door at 1 Finchley New Road on September 23, and the minute he left the consul wrote Hitchcock:

Today Morgan came here at 3 o'clock to visit my small private collection, and he seemed to be admiring everything *too much;* to convince me that he is a *great connoisseur* in *antiquities.* When a person admires everything on about the *same scale,* there is reason to doubt, of his knowledge; however he declared himself very much satisfied, and perfectly enchanted at what he had seen.[20]

Morgan said he would wait to see the gallery pieces until William T. Blodgett, the trustee whom the Metropolitan had appointed to view the entire collection, arrived from New York. Captain Hall's sister, an elderly and wealthy widow, Mrs. Mark, who had an income of $30,000 a year, was, happily, a great friend of Blodgett. She described him as a "good connoisseur of objects of art, and a millionaire." She had promised to get the trustee and the collector together at a fashionable dinner in her country seat. Her "generous thought," Cesnola told his friend, was prompted by the idea "that perhaps it may help to decide him to purchase my collection!"[21]

The consul's interest in the post at Constantinople was still active. The U. S. Minister there, George Boker, now had decided he wanted to remain there with Cesnola joining him as secretary of legation or in some other position. The important thing was that he had offered to pay for Cesnola's digging expenses in Cyprus in return for "a very small portion of the objects found there! What do you think to form a society composed of *Boker you* and *I* and dig the whole island?" Cesnola asked Hitchcock. He would become Secretary at the Turkish capitol. "Then we must have you appointed Consul at Cyprus in my place, and afterwards Boker gives me as many *French leaves of absence* as I want, and I come to Cyprus with you, and show you all the spots where to dig, and organize everything like I used to have before—my own house would be taken by you, and we would make a great name no doubt—What do you think of this wild plan eh?" He didn't want Boker to pay the entire digging expenses. It would be better, he thought, if each of the trio would put in $2000 and Hitchcock would act as "disburser and treasurer of the society." He was "still the *KING* of Cyprus," able, under a compliant governor, to do what he wanted "in spite of all opposition."[22]

There was a postscript. Morgan had returned.

Just as I was finishing this letter, the bell rang and who came in but Mr. Morgan *again* with Sir Somebody I forgot the name. He begged me to allow to look again at the Collection for a few minutes longer with his friend. I said yes and the English gentleman is a *real connoisseur.* He was enthusiastic about the glass and said *to me* he never saw anything so beautiful. Then he said to Morgan, "Of course you Americans must buy this splendid collection," and Morgan added—"I think such is the intention of the Art Museum."[23]

Morgan then revealed that "from what Johnston writes, the Art Museum intends buying it in block."

The banker told Cesnola "very candidly: you know, General, I know very little about antiquities, and I really cannot guess why Johnston wants *me* to look at it, except perhaps he intends to make me share toward buying the collection!"

The consul had been through many near-sales before. He was trying to keep his feet solidly set on fact. "I believe the Americans will buy my collection," he wrote Hitchcock, "when it has really been bought by them and not before."[24]

But he could not resist feeling, for the very first time, the unalloyed, pristine joy of success. Within two days he had spurned the Duke of Edinburgh and lorded it over one of his many brothers-in-law.

Feuardent had begged him to escort Victoria's second son, the

duke, through his collection at the gallery "and explain to his Royal
Highness all the particulars about its discovery, etc. etc.," Cesnola
wrote Hitchcock September 25, "But as H. H. only goes out of curi-
osity I declined to be present."[25]

With the probability of the sale almost assurred, Cesnola asked
Hitchcock to send $300 to his wife's brother, William Reid, as soon
as he could, as the latter, having lost the fortune he made in the Civil
War, needed the funds badly. Reid had always treated Cesnola
poorly since his marriage. But now: "How God is good, toward me!
I was cast away by my wife's relations, because I *was poor*. Very soon
I shall be *richer* than all of them *together!*"[26]

It was important that he be as rich as possible. Johnston had
heard the reports accurately. Neither the solemn thanks of the Russian Foreign Office, expressed through N. Ignatiew, for the "zeal and
ability" with which Cesnola performed his consular duties for that
country, "so well answering to those friendly relations which so happily connect our two countries,"[27] nor his mounting social *élan*
turned the once-poor cavalier's mind from his pursuit of cash.

All the vigor and forthrightness of a man making his first fortune
at forty years of age went into the showing of his Golgos collection
in the gallery opposite the British Museum. He worked from 9 A.M.
to 5 P.M. "to put the collection in order," he wrote Hitchcock October
18, "and I do not know what I would give to have you here to see
it. It looks magnificently."[28]

The ancient, grainy, white limestone statues stood in four large
rooms, raised on dark red pedestals, their forms clearly outlined
against the wall of the same dark red. The works revealed the inner
nature of the much-conquered Cyprians, the influences of their
stronger invaders apparent in the massive figures. These rounded,
gentle, semi-Assyrian, semi-Egyptian, semi-Greek sculptures spoke,
actually, of a regularly semi-captive people. It was only in an occasional grave marker, or in archaic smaller pieces that the sharp thrust
of the individual Cyprian made itself felt.

Englishmen poured into the exhibit, but the most important
visitor was an American. William T. Blodgett, then forty-nine years
old, a self-made multi-millionaire, manufacturer of varnishes, a man
now able to indulge his taste for art, came to look en route to his

Italian villa. It was he who, as first chairman of the Metropolitan Museum of Art's original executive committee, had joined with Johnston to spend $116,000 to buy the "famous Belgian and French collection" later purchased by the Museum, and, in fact, its greatest drawing card at its first show in December 1871. Blodgett had invested in real estate on New York's Fifth Avenue and in society's increasingly popular watering place, Newport. But he enjoyed Europe and particularly liked Italians. He had, in fact, helped so many Italian emigres who had come to New York that he was decorated by the Italian government. He had written already to his fellow trustees from the upper reaches of Egypt when he heard of the Italian's remarkable finds, urging that the Cesnola collection be acquired.[29] It had been Hitchcock's idea to have him, then a museum vice-president, examine the collection with Morgan.

The New Yorker was impressed. But, knowing the difficulties the young museum was encountering in raising funds, he suggested that a $15,000 advance be paid to the insolvent Cesnola and that the final decision on the purchase of the entire collection be deferred until after it was shown in New York. This plan, Cesnola told Hitchcock, "does not suit me at all; the Museum as I said to Blodgett must buy it in *London* advancing me the sum I need and then for the remainder I shall give the Museum all the time they desire."[30]

It would probably take him a month to repack the collection and then cost him $6000 "and more" to ship it to New York and, if expenses in Manhattan were what they had just been in London, $500 to have the pedestals and shelves made.

Faced with the Feuardent deadline, the agreement by which the dealer, at the end of the year, would have the right to auction off the entire collection. Cesnola pressed hard, then and thereafter, for outright purchase by the New York museum.

Once again, he thought publicity would help. He wanted a copy of the July *Harper's*, "marked to attract attention," sent to the editors of the *Athenaeum Art Journal,* the *Pall Mall Gazette,* the *Illustrated London News* and the *Graphic.*[31]

Doell had sent on several copies of his catalogue, about to be published, with a friendly letter, and now Cesnola sought to have him add to his book as a "great favor" a preface telling how important the

Russian curator thought the Golgos finds were.

"It is not impossible that the Museum of New York will buy the entire lot," he pointed out to Doell, "but the Americans don't pay much attention to art." If Doell would add the opinion he had—which conformed to that of the renowned Sir Austen Henry Layard who had unearthed Nineveh—that the "unique collection of Golgos" should not be broken up, then "perhaps by your authority [it will] make these men appreciate it."³² Doell agreed to do it, and he immediately entered the special category of friend and confidant.

In early November, Cesnola wrote him that the museum offered $50,000 by telegraph "and I have decided to accept it." The catalogue would be of *"great help"* to him "for the Directors of the Museum of New York would like naturally that I do a catalogue raisonné of my entire collection and there your work would be my business." He added that the museum had asked if he would "accept the post of Director" if the Metropolitan bought his collection. The collector asked: "What would your counsel be?"³³

The sale was not to be concluded so quickly, however, and Cesnola owed the final purchase to the auction clause in his agreement with Rollin & Feuardent. Blodgett got a telegraphed approval of purchase from Johnston and Morgan, used it in the museum president's name personally in mid-November, with little more than a month remaining in which the collection could be sold privately. Then the banker went aboard his yacht and wrote Johnston:

I must say that I think you have thrown rather too much care and responsibility upon me in this matter. I have neither knowledge or information upon the subject, and to have called in experts would have jeopardized the purchase as the necessities of Genl. Cesnola were such, owing to his agreement with the parties who had advanced him money to bring them here, that a public auction would have been the result, and then the British, and other Museums would have stepped in, and taken what they wanted, and thus the collection, as a *whole,* would cease to exist.³⁴

Once Cesnola, now hard pressed by his contract, agreed to void the sale if Johnston was not satisfied with the collection's value, Morgan signed a contract with the collector. He gave Cesnola

$20,000, promising $15,000 in one year's time and another $15,000 in two years.[35]

Cesnola now put his mind to getting himself a job, and he wrote Johnston that "the important thing, once the collection is in New York, is to classify it correctly and to arrange it properly." He told Johnston he had three hundred pages of notes about the discoveries, thereby making himself the indispensable expert to do the job. Cesnola said nothing about having Doell's catalogue but went on: "Here in London the Savans already say, that the collection by going to America will be lost to the scientific world! It must be the pride of the Trustees of the New York Museum, to prove to them the contrary."

If the collection was properly handled, in a year or two "the archaeologists of Europe" would be "obliged and forced to cross the Atlantic and go to New York to study it there."[36]

Cesnola then settled down to a cheerfully exultant month as a lionized celebrity of the winter season. He saw John Jay, whose suggested museum was now being built in Central Park, on a visit to the gallery. He met Prime Minister Gladstone, long an *aficionado* of archaeology and Sir Henry Rawlinson, the politician-archaeologist who had gained fame in Persia. He had become a favorite of the wealthy American, Cyrus W. Field, promoter of the Atlantic Cable that was now carrying word to Johnston about the purchase of the Cyprian finds.

On Thanksgiving Day, Field entertained Cesnola and others at a "princely dinner" in Buckingham Palace Hotel. Gladstone had the seat of honor among the eighty to a hundred guests, "several dozens of Lords, some Cabinet & Foreign Ministers, etc. etc.," Cesnola told Hitchcock. Field had given Cesnola the second place of honor, at the right of Gladstone.

"You may believe me when I tell you that most of the guests were looking at me and asking to each other who could be that lucky fellow who was monopolazing [*sic*] the entire conversation of the Premier of England during the whole dinner. It is the second time I am invited at dinner by Mr. Field and both times I have been placed next to Gladstone. It seems everybody in London wants to make me a *notorious* person if not a person of note."[37]

It was all very wonderful, but it did leave him with a headache, and he was forced to make his account a short one.

Now he told his friend that Dr. Samuel Birch of the British Museum felt that "if the Trustees of the New York Museum know what is to their best advantage, they will secure my services as the Director of their embryo Museum and send me back to Cyprus to dig for them. I would like it very much."[38]

He would never ask for the post though. He would wait to be asked. Through his close friend, in effect, he was setting the wheels in motion. "Mr. J. S. Morgan, Cyrus, Gordon and many other *big guns* here, think also the same."[39] That ought to get Hitchcock off to a good start.

For himself, Cesnola switched vessels to sail with Field's party for America aboard the "Java," a paneled palace of a ship.

Johnston wanted the museum to buy the collection with funds raised by public subscription. But he was realist enough to know that the young museum, settled into the dancing academy uptown, had no suitable place to exhibit the heavy Golgos statues and an "equal impossibility of raising the money to pay for the collection unless we show it to advantage." It was a real dilemma. He wondered if Cesnola's family should come to New York at all.[40]

But asking Mary Reid Cesnola to remain in London at that point would have been like asking a Snow Goose to stay in Egg Island Point, New Jersey, for the summer. It wasn't even tried.

On Christmas Day, 1872, seven years exactly from the day he took a piggyback into Larnaca, Cesnola wrote on crested paper to Doell in St. Petersburg. His entire collection had been bought by the new museum in New York. The Cesnolas were leaving the next morning.

He asked that a copy of Doell's catalogue, presumably with the new, praising preface, be sent to him at the New York Fifth Avenue Hotel.[41]

Ten

Grant had been reelected, his first term one of unlimited prosperity. It had been a postwar period in which a mounting population surged across the nation. Men at war had learned from others, the length and breadth of the land, just how big their country was. George Templeton Strong told a story he heard at dinner during the war years. A huge, six-foot Kentuckian lolled about a bar, just returned from a trip to Europe. "How did you like it?" he was asked.

"Well, I liked it pretty well," he said, "all except England. Didn't like England at all."

"Why not?"

"Why, I didn't dare to go out of the house nights for fear I'd step off."

Rigid forms of etiquette maintained the old order, and as wealth increased from one generation to the next, slipped into even more formal and more European modes of conduct. The new barons of America, postwar profiteers rougher than their earlier exemplars, snatched in aching insecurity at the manners of the traditional leisure class of France and England. The nation's leading artists studied in Rome.

At home, women at the great resorts of Saratoga and Long

Branch wore clusters of diamonds as they watched fast horses. A fashionable woman required eight to a dozen trunks for her clothes. It was not just to rest—a lady of the day did little else—but to be seen, to be appreciated, to flirt, to enjoy herself, that she went to a watering place each summer with all the accoutrements of a full winter season in the city.

Now, in the winter, her skirts so wide that her husband followed in a second carriage, she swept up marble stairs of the new Fifth Avenue palaces in a blaze of gaslight, two dressing maids lifting the train of her satin dress, her lace fan of mother-of-pearl inlaid in gold fluttering like a tropical bird. Not for her the powderless simplicity of old. She was an enameled figurine.

The talk of the soirées at the end of the Christmas holidays in 1872 was of European royalty. Napoleon the Third had died and the papers were full of his operation, his first few days of seeming recovery, his decline and the loving smile he gave the former empress as she leaned over him before he died.

In New York, the center of interest was William Marcy Tweed whom the *Herald* described January 4, when it sent a man to the Tweed office in Duane Street, as "looking as bright, as beaming and as bucolic as in the best days of his Boss-ship." He wanted to be left alone. He was on the eve of his trial that in January riveted attention on the court of Oyer and Terminez.

Despite local scandals, the country's sense of growth was paramount. Americans, with the new railroads giving them a feeling of the country's magnitude, moved around to see their land. Having left their homes for war, men left now for the pleasures of peace, and, though looking to Europe as the arbiter of conduct and fashion, began to build great institutions of their own.

The Art Museum in New York, barely three years old, was on its way to becoming the Louvre of the Americas. Behind it and fully aware of what they were doing, was a coterie of comrades, wealthy, politically powerful and socially distinguished. In its annual report of 1873, the Metropolitan Museum of Art commented: "The Museum is now completely established as the leading institution of the kind in the country; and its permanence and future success are entirely assured."

Long accustomed to managing railroads and mammoth manufacturing outlets, they took over Johnston's dilemma about the Cesnola antiquities and resolved to display them in a style that would spur subscriptions. With these, the trustees could buy the entire collection.

And when, finally, after seventeen days at sea, the steamship *Java* sailed past the villas of Staten Island and skirted the Battery with its Immigration Depot, it was to a new world of position that Cesnola, once the solitary immigrant, arrived. The Cyrus Field party was among only 142 passengers on whom the British line lavished their mid-Victorian attentions.

The travelers found New York dirty, its streets clogged with unshoveled snow. The *Herald* complained of this editorially, saying that, as usual, only Broadway was cleaned up after a snowstorm. It was enough to make one despair of even a reform government.

The "General," as everyone called Cesnola, had sent his antiquities from London in five different ships. They had been packed into 275 chests, some of them nine feet long, and the bill, which Johnston apparently paid, was about $11,000.[1]

It was not long before the country heard about the archaeologist-general, of whom, as the *Herald* of January 29 wrote, "everyone who has a reverence for archaeology has heard with admiration." With him, the paper reported inaccurately, "came the numberless Cyprian antiquities which he disentombed."

The article, more than two close-packed columns, was a font of biographical misinformation, the most graphic of which was the statement, obviously from Cesnola's personal account, that his "commission [as general] was on Lincoln's table on the evening of the President's assassination and was later signed by Johnson." A year or so later Cesnola said Lincoln gave him the rank orally.

The unnamed journalist lauded the collector for his "physical courage and prowess, his practical shrewdness, the kind of acumen known as 'mother wit,' " and deprecated the work of Cesnola's English and French contemporaries, Lang and de Vogüé, who had made merely "some trifling excavations. . . ."

Actually, as the Oxford scholar, Dr. John Myers, pointed out later, Cesnola's British contemporary in Cyprus, T.B. Sandwich, published a paper "of fundamental importance" on the styles of ancient

Cyprian pottery, and R. H. Lang "laid the foundations for our knowledge" of Cyprian sculpture.[2] In the dim first years of archaeology, the Englishmen had trained themselves by minute comparisons of form and style to be scholars rather than mere collectors.

In the *Herald*'s opinion, the general "had managed to raise the corner of the Homeric veil and had unmasked 40 centuries." This sounded like the fulfillment of the dream of Heinrich Schliemann, resting in Athens that January from his work in searching for Troy. The *Herald* passed the German by to concentrate on Cesnola. The collector, John Taylor Johnston, the Metropolitan Museum of Art, the City of New York and the United States were to be congratulated "on the fortunate series of events which have placed so invaluable a collection permanently in the midst of us."[3]

For Cesnola, it was a most satisfying reintroduction to the city where he had passed the worst days of his life. Almost at once, he met Johnston, a self-made millionaire and art patron, as were many of the museum's board. He found the president "a very nice man in every way." Even more important, Cesnola told Hitchcock, "He said he *wants to satisfy me in everything.*"[4]

Johnston called a meeting of his executive committee to introduce the collector. W.C. Prime was there, chatting about the days he dug in Cyprus. But the formality of meeting did not last long. "After discussing several things," Cesnola told Hitchcock, "the meeting adjourned to a nice little champagne supper, etc. etc." In those days, such "etceteras" invariably meant lobster and hot breads. In the course of the evening, Johnston revealed he would give a "grand reception etc. etc."—again meaning a fine meal—to introduce Cesnola to the trustees.[5]

In the natural first order of things, however, Cesnola checked in at the State Department in Washington, calling on Hamilton Fish who "offered [him] quite unexpectedly the post of Secretary of Legation to Constantinople."[6] He refused it.

By this time, he had seen Hitchcock and had undoubtedly heard the New Englander say he wanted to get back in the hotel business. This would automatically make it less desirable for the collector to go into business with Boker. He had already spent a good deal of effort in untwining himself from his partnership, enforced by poverty, with

Lang and Sandwich. This had been a move he had accomplished only after getting his inheritance and selling some of his first antiquities.

Since then he had worked alone, most successfully, and he saw no reason now to ruffle the future. He already had the money he needed. It would be well if Boker worked to obtain a *firman* and export permits for him. Then he could go back to Cyprus and dig on his own.

In early February, Johnston, at a reception at his home, introduced Cesnola not only to the trustees but to other leading figures of New York society and politics. He had his own red carpet which was unrolled to the curb on such occasions, and on it that Monday evening walked Governor Edwin D. Morgan, General McClellan, Chancellor Corsby, Prime and "princes of industry," board members of the new museum.

As they entered, each was introduced to Cesnola and when all had met him, the party moved into Johnston's unrivaled picture gallery, hung, European fashion, with four or five rows of canvases, one above the other. There, Cesnola made what the *Herald* called a "brief and graceful address in perfect English."

He began: "Coming as I do from a land which has been called the land of art, it is with a peculiar satisfaction that I find myself tonight the occasion of this elegant gathering—not as an acknowledgment of any humble efforts of mine in the path of science, but as an evidence that the country of my adoption has awoke to the one thing needful to place her at the head of nations—namely, a fervent interest in art." The hall reminded him of the galleries of the Princes Doria and Borghese.

Already there were "some munificent patrons" of art in America. But, since their collections represented but individual effort, it was not enough. The arrival of the news of the purchase of his collection by telegraph was to him "eminently American," and he was proud to be able to place in the hands of the founders of the first great museum of art in America a collection "believed to form a link between Assyro-Egyptian and Greek art." He hoped the New-York Historical Society's famed Egyptian collection would eventually be joined with that of the Metropolitan to form a complete history of ancient art "from the cradle to the times of Pericles."[7] The Society held it during Cesnola's lifetime and sold it to the Brooklyn Museum, where it is today.

Cesnola ended with a promise he could hardly have expected to fulfill. If he found works by Phidias, Praxiteles or Lysippus, "they shall adorn no other museum but of my adopted country."[8]

Two weeks later, the trustees voted to hire Cesnola to unpack, arrange and classify his collection. They would pay him up to $500 a month and appropriated $10,000 for repairs, purchases and salaries, including Cesnola's.[9] And, as Johnston moved to rent a mansion on West 14th Street, not far from the uptown Delmonico's, Cesnola and his family went off to Hanover to visit the Hitchcocks. He wrote ahead to tell Mary Hitchcock that though he had not played his flute since she was in Cyprus, and was "entirely out of practice, I shall take it with me at Hanover nevertheless and will try what we can do together."[10]

There, for more than a month in the depth of winter, as the snow sifted through the venerable goblet elms arching Main Street and the bells of horse-drawn sleighs sounded over the white hills, the Cesnolas visited their closest friends.

As they left New York, the General's plumb-straight figure, thickened now at forty years of age, was clad in a furred greatcoat, his wife was plumed and veiled, his daughters warmed their hands in muffs. They went by train to Lewiston, a slow journey of two days, then took a sleigh that jingled over the covered Ledyard Bridge up the steep-hilled River Street to where the Dartmouth Hotel stood at the main crossing in the old town, a four-story brick building with green shutters. Its five Doric columns echoed the classic buildings of the old commodious eighteenth-century square on which it stood. Hanover was a town set in the foothills of high mountains that, in winter, exhaled a pervading fragrance of wood smoke. There, standing on a hill, was the "Old Row," the white austere buildings, green-roofed against the pale February sky, of Dartmouth College.

Already a hundred years old, the college had been the dream of the poor farmer's son, Hiram Hitchcock. Now, wealthy from his hotel days and later work as a banker in Hanover, respected, donor of a fine set of Cyprian antiquities to the college, a gift to him originally from

Cesnola, Hitchcock and his wife lived in a large clapboard mansion. Three stories high, it had a steep mansard roof and a tower and stood just off North Main Street, within sight of the square. To it came the professors who were their neighbors and the friends who visited from New York.

The town had a young air. Most of the students were Yankees who studied by the light of kerosene lamps, bought wood from the farmers and heated water on an iron stove to use in their large tin bathtubs. When in funds, they ate at the inn, to be told, if they complained of the fare: "You got to take just what we got; we ain't no Fifth Avenue Hotel."[11]

Inside Hitchcock's fine home stood one of the most impressive private collections of antiquities in America. Perhaps he preferred crusaders' weapons, but what he had was what his close friend had collected and had sent him. Writing in *The Dartmouth* of November, 1872, a commentator noted, "We hardly know of another collection so extensive, held by a private person, as that of Mr. Hiram Hitchcock of Hanover," and Dartmouth itself was one of only five or six, including Harvard and Yale, who could show "anything of any consequence in the line of antiquities."

The college paper introduced the collector in a long rhapsodic article that appeared in March, after Cesnola had returned to New York. He had been "in our own little Hanover as the guest of one of our Art-loving citizens. . . . An American we are proud to own him, yet thanks to an Italian sky for the warm enthusiasm, the charm of manner, so glowing, so magnetic. He is delightful in the social circle, plays the flute to perfection, speaks English well, with an agreeable foreign accent, and is a wide-awake, ready talker."

Some of his antiquities had arrived broken, and the article warded off criticism. Cesnola's workers, the paper declared, gathered terra cottas from the "pulverized earth of Cyprus as careful housewives took eggs from the bran in which they had carefully packed them." The writer thus turned a bright simile but one that was hardly apt in view of the hard, sunbaked soil of Cyprus in summer.

Otherwise, the paper caught the competitive nature of the collector and his aggressive foresight in securing title to land in Cyprus.

It was in the name, as it had to be, of a Turk, in this case his faithful dragoman to whom he was to credit the Russian-envoy-ploy in getting his antiquities out of the country.

He was, then, as he had been, "master of the situation, a sovereign in his own right." The independent city-state in Piedmont was enjoying rebirth in Cyprus.

Cesnola sounded eager to go back to the island. "The Pasha of Cyprus uneasily turns on his pillow and dreams of mines of gold and precious stones being secretly conveyed by subterranean passages to ships far-off and out at sea and wakes with a start to ask if still the fair Isle be his or not?" Cesnola, it concluded, hopes "yet to out-rival in the future all that now so astonishes and bewilders us."[12]

Perhaps, as he turned in his bed in America, he was reveling in dreams of "mines of gold."

Refreshed and glad to go back to the thick of things, Cesnola returned to New York where he rented a house at 173 West 47th Street. It was a three-story building in a row of similar single-family homes between Sixth and Seventh Avenues. Within two blocks were four marble works where he might find artisans to help him prepare his important first exhibition.

He felt he needed "about a year" to do the job, and he sought a leave of that length from the State Department.[13] He did not get it.

Johnston was sympathetic, if the department was not. He was willing for Cesnola to stay as long as necessary to do the work and name his own price.[14] It was an era of expansiveness. As Grant went through his second inaugural that March, it was recalled that during his first term, $368 million in public debt had been canceled and the country's finances had shown a steady and consistent rise.[15] It looked as though in this golden country, where George Inness had not long before painted "Peace and Plenty," that well-being was a preordained and natural state of affairs.

In such an atmosphere, Cesnola went at the task of preparing his show with all the ardor that his success and his new associations bred. He faced, however, one compelling problem: time.

Originally, when he found he would not have a year in which to do the job, he expected to take six months, maybe five months at the very least. When he unpacked the treasure March 7 in a part of the Douglas Mansion not occupied by the family, he told a reporter for the *Herald* that a mere three-month lapse between unpacking and opening would be "impossible." Actually, the show was in the hall and on the walls in a brisk two-and-a-half months.

The General could be as brusque with a reporter as with a private. As the antiquities were delivered, he sat at a desk, a "chaotic sea of Cyprian antiquities, surging and frothing at his feet," and he refused "to give any clew [*sic*] as to what was being or would be done." To the writer, the scene looked "bewildering."[16]

It well may be that the collector himself didn't know just what would be done. There he was with this chaotic clutter, and he had to make a fine exhibition, $60,000 worth of one, in less time than it took to repair, restore, reassemble and arrange these stone personages, faintly smiling as though aware of the depth of the task. It was not easy. Indeed, many of them lacked their heads, and in many instances it was a primary question of just which head went with which torso. In a great many cases, the tips of noses, the ends of fingers had fallen prey to rough passage—in being dug out of the hard ancient soil in which they had been found, in being carted to Larnaca on the backs of camels that sank to the ground from time to time for an unexpected rest, or in being hoisted to and from ships which took them great distances over the moving sea.

The general had been provided with help. One of these assistants was Theodore Gehlen, a German cabinetmaker, expert at mending broken furniture and willing to try his skill with broken statues. With this and other help, Cesnola fashioned order out of the disarray. The effect did not always go just as it should; there was so much material and so much to do and so little time. A large sarcophagus, found intact and delivered to 14th Street in pieces, was eventually put together in the basement of the Douglas Mansion. The only trouble was that the pieces were not reunited in their original order.[17] No matter. The large, sculptured stone coffin proved an impressive display.

A number of the figures, happily, were intact and required only a wash of stone emulsion, it was judged, to fit them for the eyes of the men who would support the General's future digs. Many of the statues, however, had their heads glued on, limbs added, gaping joints filled in and noses and fingers joined. When all was done and in place, they made a splendid silent assemblage, a visitation in the bustling new world of a quiet, if vacuous, set of envoys from the ancient Near East.

When the audience went to see the show at the end of March 1873, they felt the warmth of recognition at the exhibits of their friends: Samuel P. Avery's pottery, and faïence, long a familiar collecting hobby of the New York art dealer, Robert Hoe's rare books, Prime's Sèvres ware, the remote and solitary scenes of John F. Kensett, and loans by "numerous millionaires of the city."

The new, the unexpected, the exciting display, it immediately appeared, was the great treasure from the legendary East, the missing link between Egypt and Greece. As their carriages rumbled away in empty clatter, it was this that stirred the cloaked visitors. They were in the presence of deities from the morning of the civilized world, strangers draped and armed, some bearing votive offerings of birds and fruits. The silent sculptures were smooth as egg shells.

Around his treasures walked the famous general moving among them as among time-tested troops, courteously attentive to the guests, speaking about the great find at Golgos, in short, giving a continual lecture.

Some visitors were startled. Some saw "the gem of the collection," in a bearded figure with three closely curled tresses falling over each shoulder. Was this solemn figure, eight-feet-two-inches tall, a dish in one hand, a dove in the other, the two-sexed embodiment of all procreative power? Was this a bearded Venus?

Hitchcock, in his introduction to the collection, was not one to stifle such speculation. "The savans [sic] of Europe," he wrote, were "still divided in their opinion whether it represented a high priest of Venus or the Goddess herself." Actually, it was later revealed that the body had been found separately at Golgos, with the head, arms and feet missing.[18] These had been carried away, Cesnola said, by acquisitive peasants on the night the Golgos find roused the crowd gathered on the desert-like plain of Aghios Photios.

Cesnola made use of a simple ruse to get them back. He had a

Above: The sight of Curium evoked in Cesnola dreams of romantic adventure. (From L. P. di Cesnola, Cyprus. Courtesy, The Metropolitan Museum of Art.) *Below: With a row of guards protecting his dig, Cesnola directed the work from a hilltop. (From* Harper's Weekly. Courtesy, Dartmouth College.)

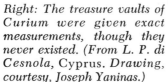

Left: In introducing Cesnola's finds to America, Harper's Monthly *pictured him as a gold-epauletted general. (*Harper's Monthly, *July 1872. Courtesy, The New-York Historical Society, New York City.)*

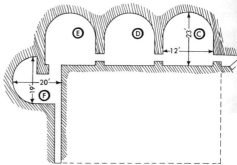

Right: The treasure vaults of Curium were given exact measurements, though they never existed. (From L. P. di Cesnola, Cyprus. *Drawing, courtesy, Joseph Yaninas.)*

The new museum in the park featured a "Long Branch" entrance. (Courtesy, The Metropolitan Museum of Art.)

Above: Additions to the original building sandwiched the original structure of The Metropolitan Museum. (Courtesy, The New-York Historical Society, New York City.)

Right: The opening of the Metropolitan Museum at Central Park in 1880. (The New York Times, April 4, 1880. Courtesy, The Metropolitan Museum of Art.)

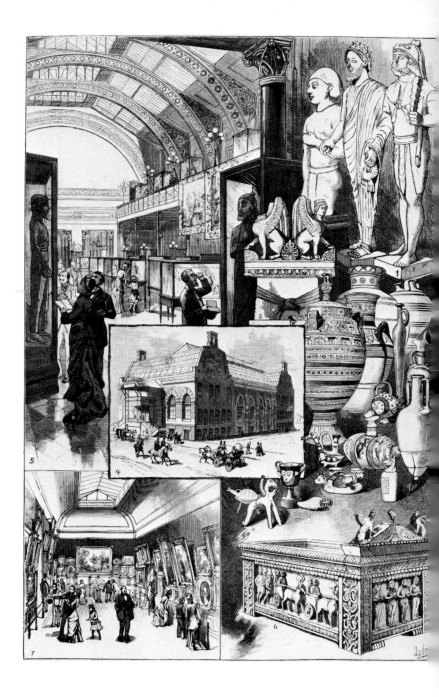

Left: Some critics thought the girders in the new museum made it look like a railroad station. Most were enchanted with Cesnola's finds. (Frank Leslie's Illustrated Newspaper, April 10, 1880. Courtesy, The New-York Historical Society, New York City.)

Right: Main Hall. (Courtesy, The Metropolitan Museum of Art.)

Below: Heads and torsos and other Cyprian figures stand in spotless cases in a sun-shaded gallery. (Courtesy, The Metropolitan Museum of Art.)

Above: Ancient glass from Cesnola and Marquand collections was a prominent display in early days at the museum. (Courtesy, The Metropolitan Museum of Art.) Below: Cesnola's Cyprian sculpture stood in glass cases in the park building. (Courtesy, The Metropolitan Museum of Art.)

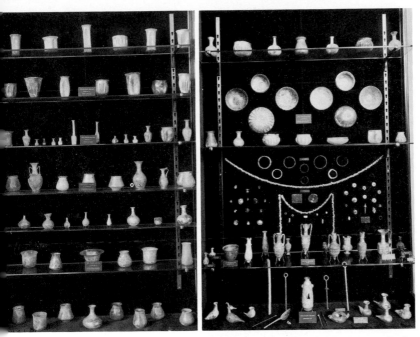

Above: Classical glass that Cesnola brought back from Cyprus includes Greek and Roman pieces. (Courtesy, The Metropolitan Museum of Art.) Below left: That little circle in her hand, was it a mirror, a dish or a button? (Art Amateur, August 1880. Courtesy, The Metropolitan Museum of Art.) Below right: Pottery of the Cyprians was imaginative, evocative and alive. (Courtesy, The Metropolitan Museum of Art.)

Above left: The massive stone head had a stiff, long beard with four curls turned like primeval fern. (L. P. di Cesnola, Cyprus. Courtesy, The Metropolitan Museum of Art.) Above right: L. P. di Cesnola in the early days of his directorship. (Courtesy, The New York Public Library.) Below: A good many journals lampooned the charges against Cesnola. (Courtesy, The Metropolitan Museum of Art.)

Statue No. 23.

In England as the "Bearded Venus," in France as the "Venus Barbue,"
and in Italy as the "Venere Barbuta."

of head which originally belonged to Statue No. 23. (See | *No. 4.—Another head, of the same class as that which now adorns No.*
and Cesnola Collection No. 601.) | *No. 23. (See Cabiat's plate 29, and Cesnola Collection No. 604.)*

—As it stands in the Museum in Central Park. (See | **Statue No. 23.**—With proper style of head on to cut No. 8.

Was this solemn figure, with a dish in one hand and a dove in the other, the two-sexed embodiment of all procreative power? Was this a Bearded Venus? (Card prepared by G. L. Feuardent. The New York Times, May 29, 1881. Courtesy, The Metropolitan Museum of Art.)

" *Look here, upon this picture, and on this.*"—HAMLET.
I.   II.

Charge No. 22.—Statue of a Priest, as it stands
in the Museum in Central Park; artotype from
a photograph now on sale at the Museum.

Charge No. 22.—Statue of a Priest, as it stoo
in the Museum in Fourteenth Street; artotyp
from a photograph published by the Museum
but no longer on sale.

A controversial statue acquires an arm somewhere between 14th Street and the uptown museum. (Card prepared by G. L. Feuardent. Courtesy, The New-York Historical Society, New York City.)

Detail, showing the mortise-hole A, into which
the dowel was inserted that held the right hand
and patera.

" My answer is : In the entire collection I
object in stone. . . . !"—

1
STATUE No. 39.

As described by Mr. Hiram Hitchcock in *Harper's Magazine* for July, 1872. The head alone, with its "benignant face," to use the words of Mr. Hitchcock, is figured in the *Magazine*.

2
STATUE No. 39.

As represented in Doell's *Sammlung Cesnola* published in 1873. This is an exact copy of Doell's lithograph which, he says, he made "with great care" from Cesnola's own photograph of the statue.

S
As exhibite
from a photo,

Remark the feet, legs, and base, and the absence of the head. When Hitchcock describes the statue from the photograph sent him by Cesnola, he places most emphasis on the head with its "benignant face." When Doell sees the statue, the head is no longer attached to the body, nor does he know that they were ever supposed to belong to one another. Doell places the body of this statue in the "good Greek" group. The head he calls "archaic." In the text, he says the statue was found at Golgoï, but in the preface, having probably read in Mr. Hitchcock's article in *Harper's Magazine*, that it was found at Salamis, he cautiously says that the responsibility for the information regarding the localities quoted in this book, rests solely with General di Cesnola.

Remark t
In the *Guic*
by the Trus
without he
just seen, i
and is clas
period—no
period—an
"archaic."
the statue i

The body of this statue is made up of unrelated fragments : as a partial test, let the reader endeavor to connect the broken right arm with the portion of a hand attached to the thigh. This cannot be done without bending the arm. But the arm is not bent, it hangs down straight. Mr. Hitchcock tells us that Cesnola, in writing to him about the discovery, says he found the statue at Salamis. In the description nothing is said about the *feet.*

a single restoration of any object or part of any
the Committee, January 5. 1881.

	4	**5**
o. 39.	**STATUE No. 39.**	**STATUE No. 39.**
in Fourteenth Street,	In this illustration the feet, legs, and base are seen as represented in Cesnola's *Cyprus* published in 1878.	Here we have the statue as it now stands in the Museum in Central Park. The illustration is from Mr. G. C. Cox's photograph on sale at the Museum.
ach in 1874-1878.		

head, feet and base.
Collection, published
in 1876, this statue
hough, as we have
—is numbered 336
the Græco-Roman
the "good Greek"
ed 217 is classed as
made of Salamis;
e Golgoï find.

Remark the absence of the head, and the difference between the feet, legs and base of this illustration, and the same parts as shown in No. 2 from Doell. Compare also with No. 3 showing the same statue in Fourteenth Street. Cesnola in his book says the statue came from Golgoï. Says nothing about Salamis, and describes the head separately with its "benignant face," as coming from Golgoï.

Remark the absence of the head and the addition of entirely new feet, legs, and base. This is the statue referred to by Mr. G. C. Cox in his unsought testimony before the "Committee." He said that he himself saw the new feet made by a stone-cutter, who came to the Museum for the purpose. He pointed out in Doell's illustration where the new pieces had been set in, and he told the Committee that if they would look at the photograph made by himself, and would go with him to the Museum, they could see the restoration for themselves. Mr. Cox's offer was not accepted. In the Museum Catalogue the statue is said to have been found at Golgoï.

(Courtesy, The Metropolitan Museum of Art.)

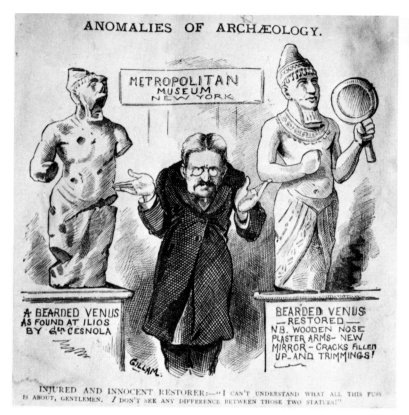

ANOMALIES OF ARCHÆOLOGY.

METROPOLITAN
MUSEUM
NEW YORK

A BEARDED VENUS
AS FOUND AT ILIOS
BY G.ᵗᵉ CESNOLA

BEARDED VENUS
—RESTORED—
N.B. WOODEN NOSE
PLASTER ARMS— NEW
MIRROR — CRACKS FILLED
UP AND TRIMMINGS!

GILLAM.

INJURED AND INNOCENT RESTORER:—"I CAN'T UNDERSTAND WHAT ALL THIS FUSS
IS ABOUT, GENTLEMEN. I DON'T SEE ANY DIFFERENCE BETWEEN THOSE TWO STATUES!"

Above: Puck *had fun with the trial.* (Puck, *November 28, 1883. Courtesy, The Metropolitan Museum of Art.*) Below left: Joseph H. Choate, Cesnola's attorney. Below right: Gaston Feuardent. (Courtesy, The Metropolitan Museum of Art.)

Litigants in the Feuardent-Cesnola case went each day for nine-and-a-half weeks to the Old Post Office Building in City Hall Park. (Frank Leslie's Illustrated Newspaper, *September 25, 1875. Courtesy, The New-York Historical Society, New York City.*)

U.S. District Court Room. The trial was as popular as an opera. (Frank Leslie's Illustrated Newspaper, *September 25, 1875. Courtesy, The New-York Historical Society, New York City.*)

Henry G. Marquand, the museum's president from 1889 to 1902. (The Daily Graphic, November 15, 1883. Courtesy, The Metropolitan Museum of Art.)

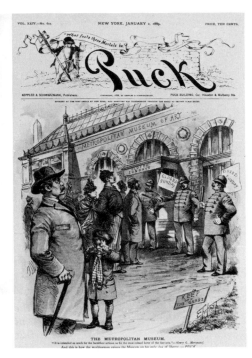

It took some doing to have the museum open to the general public on Sundays. (Puck, January 2, 1889. Courtesy, The New-York Historical Society, New York City.)

The Metropolitan Museum of Art in 1894. (The J. Clarence Davies Collection, Museum of the City of New York.)

Richard Morris Hunt used Rome as key to 1902 building along Fifth Avenue. (Courtesy, The Metropolitan Museum of Art.)

The Director worked at his desk in the museum until the last week of his life. (Courtesy, The New-York Historical Society, New York City.)

copy of Layard's 1853 *Discoveries in the Ruins of Nineveh and Baby-lon,* and, after checking with his peasant contacts about what others had taken, would go to the acquirer's house. He would tell the illiter-ate man that the book he held was one of divination. The collector would then select a page with an engraving resembling the piece taken, "then, boldly turning to the engraving," would point it out to him and demand its immediate restitution. Cesnola offered a reward if the arm, leg, head or whatever was given to him quickly.

"The amazed and convicted peasant would clap his hand on his head, or use some other sign of astonishment, calling out 'Panagia mou!' [my Blessed Mother!] 'He has a book telling him everything!'" and shortly after, "the missing object would be forthcoming."[19]

Today the statue, the intriguing controversy over it having sim-mered to a dead stop, is noncommitally labeled by the sexless title of "A Votary." Male, female or both at once, it is left up to the viewer.

All through the summer of 1873 visitors from across the country went to see the great Cyprian amphorae or wine vessels in the en-trance hall and to marvel at the famed Cesnola Collection of the new Metropolitan Museum of Art. Of all the articles written about it, Cesnola liked best the one by Clarence Cook in the *Herald.*[20] A poet and critic, Cook took the trouble to talk to the General at some length and, as a result, gave Hiram Hitchcock considerable credit for the collection being in New York at all. Cesnola probably liked least the New York *Times* piece of July 6, saying the show needed a good, cheap catalogue and the museum needed a director.[21]

The summer lazed along with but a few, faint clouds making only the financial experts among the carefree feel concern. Most of the New York merchants and bankers abandoned, as usual, the crowded gas-lit receptions for the resort watering places. But despite the gen-eral ease, it had been all too true that the Franco-Prussian War had resulted in a sharp decline in European eagerness, hitherto enor-mous, for American railroad paper. As early as the end of April, *The Chronicle* of New York warned that the condition of banks and the heavy increase in general credit called for caution "and foretokens danger."

Few listened.

As for Cesnola, he was concentrating on the many long articles in the city's ten daily newspapers, and others throughout the country, celebrating the grand acquisition of the new museum. Generally, the *Herald* was most appreciative, writing in July that two thousand visitors had enjoyed the show and that Cesnola, helped by a "corps of assistants" given him by the museum, continued to prepare "countless" exhibits and a general catalogue.[22] The *Times* was somewhat less ecstatic about the results, calling the statues of interest only from the archaeological standpoint.[23]

As summer waned, Cesnola prepared to return to Cyprus. Before he left, he wrote a report on his excavations for the museum trustees. It repeated, to a large extent, the rather vague historical passages of his paper for the Royal Academy of Science in Turin in 1871. However, it added specific dimensions, previously lacking, for the Temple of Golgos, and it attributed the generally broken state of most of the statues to Christian iconoclasm directed against heathen idols.

Pretty nearly every statue had been more or less mutilated which would go to prove that the Temple was violently destroyed either by an invading hord [*sic*] or by Christian fanaticism [*sic*]. I am led to believe that the last hypothesis is the correct one as in Cyprus the edict of the fanatic iconoclast Theodorius was carried out most scrupulously.

In another site apart from Golgos, he said, his diggers "exhumed a torso whose limbs and head had been found two days before [crossed out] afterwards [inserted] buried at a distance of 200 yards."

He then signed a six-point "Memorandum of Agreement" with the trustees which reads as though they were among the few who read the financial reports closely. The businessmen-trustees could sign it or not, at their discretion, up to December 1. If they did sign it, they could cancel it on three months' notice. The pact called for Cesnola to dig "for works of Art for the Museum."

"All that he may discover or cause to be discovered" would belong to the Museum and would be shipped to the Museum when it so ordered. In return, the museum agreed to pay Cesnola up to $5000 a year for the expenses of his digs, and he was to give the institution an accounting of such costs.

As to his personal salary, that was tied to the value of the objects found. And that value was to be set by the museum, not by Cesnola. His salary, under this formula, could reach $10,000 a year, provided the Metropolitan priced his finds in two years at $50,000.²⁴ Thus, if the museum trustees considered his excavations were worth the $50,-000 by 1875, Cesnola would receive $20,000 plus expenses of digging and presumably of shipping.

After a farewell dinner at Delmonico's, Cesnola, with his family, was on his way. His catalogue was still unfinished. But his exhibition was an enormous success, and his position in the world of archaeology one of the foremost of the time. From that point of view he existed in the aura of moving to a full-sunned noon.

From the reports that were rippling through the learned world, Cesnola knew that his work would eventually be measured against that of a determined, intelligent and tireless fellow amateur. Heinrich Schliemann, who had brought all his German persistence and linguistic skill into his search for the legendary Troy, had, by August 1872, cut a deep trench to the bedrock through the fortress hill of Hissarlik. In a tiered cross section, he had exposed the stony remains of no fewer than seven buried cities. Unlike Cesnola, he remained at the single site, exhorting the workers, examining their every find, improving methods of digging under the watchful guidance of learned men, many of them English. One, the famed pathologist, Dr. Rudolph Virchow of Berlin, made exact drawings of skulls found at different levels.

It was the third city from the rock bed that Schliemann identified as the real Troy of the Trojan myth. By the next August, that of 1873, faith and endurance were transforming the legend of Homer into a truth of ancient, actual existence, and the third city, its contents found in the ashes of a great fire, held not only the stones of walls and palaces but a primitive sacrificial altar and a great, unique treasure of gold.

The ocean cable carried the news. Priam's Gold, the most priceless ancient treasure ever found, gave the world two gold diadems, their many tiny links of delicate metal glinting in the news stories across the brow of Schliemann's young Greek wife and falling in long, decorated tassels to her collarbone. A double-spouted goblet in a boat shape seven-and-a-half inches long, of 23-carat gold, seemed the reality behind Homer's description of the vessel in which Achilles poured a libation to Zeus and then drank it himself. The very volume of the treasure was numbing: 8700 small gold rings, buttons and ornaments, a strange gold bottle, a goblet and a small cup of electrum, a metal four-parts gold to one of silver. This was proof, as Virchow wrote in his preface to Schliemann's *Ilios*: "*Here*, upon the site of the ruins of the Burnt City of Gold—*here was Ilium.*"[25]

Eleven

Cesnola had received the word. He knew now that exact details must underpin his reports on digs, and, as he excavated at Salamis on the island's east coast, he made drawings of the several types of tombs there. He was working still in the dawn-days of archaeology, and he must have felt that the exertion of drawing the tiny tombs exempted him from giving their dimensions. For whatever reason, he just did not do it.

But he missed no chance to run things, to give orders. He told the Archbishop of Cyprus that a mass grave containing petrified human bones, a place that attracted annual processions, held "antedeluvian beasts" and not the remains of humans. It "put a stop to such absurdity," the general told Johnston in a report in 1875.[1]

Though the account of his explorations on his return to Cyprus held scant archaeological information, it made good reading. He had dug for John Ruskin. The English critic, hearing that Cesnola was low on funds for his explorations, sent him $2500 and asked him to see what he could find. The result was not impressive. Somehow, Cesnola managed to do better for himself in his scouting and digging operations than for anyone else. Furthermore, Ruskin had promised Cesnola twice as much as he actually sent. Cesnola spent a few months digging for Ruskin at Soli but came up with only three or four "fine statuettes, some heads and several vases," a result which he considered "not brilliant."[2]

Then Cesnola moved on to Amathus on the southern coast. It was there that the huge stone vase had been found, the one that had so impressed the French Government that it had sent a warship to carry it back to the Louvre. It was plainly a proper place to search.

While Cesnola had been in London and New York, some of his diggers had found in Amathus a fragment of a colossal Assyrian-style statue of a "Phoenician Hercules" holding a headless lion by one of its hind legs. Cesnola told Johnston that the British counsul contended for it with the Turks but lost out. It wound up in the Imperial Ottoman Museum of St. Frene, "a dirty, small magazine of antiquities, without any order or classification."[3] The implication in his report was easy to read: if he had been there, the statue would have been his.

Then, this time giving dimensions carefully, Cesnola sketched the construction of tombs at Amathus, a prelude to his account of finding a unique, sculptured marble sarcophagus. It had lain for centuries in a tomb whose walls were decorated with drawings made by lamp smoke and, though "something like the one existing in the Museum at New York, it showed a difference" that made it "much finer in every way."

Getting the huge coffin out of the tomb without the aid of a pulley or other machinery took ten full hours. Then, many hands hoisted the sarcophagus to a low cart made for the purpose, and finally it was "dragged slowly by eight oxen and 26 men over rough fields strewn with stones."

The task of taking it to the shore, a half hour away by foot, required six full hours. Buckling under the great weight, the cart had to be repaired more than a dozen times. But at nightfall Cesnola, who had commanded every detail of the operation, "had the pleasure of seeing it safely conveyed on board a boat which was lying in wait for it"—his logistics were splendid—"and to see it set sail for Larnaca."[4]

Cesnola and some of his band of men then ate and rested, waiting until the cool of night to move on. Riding under a "brilliant moon," they passed easily over the sylvan alluvial plain that, fed by earth and water from the mountains beyond, bloomed with ane- mones, irises, poppies and marguerites.[5] In a five-hour ride, they skirted Limassol, the largest town on the south coast besides Larnaca and, passing the ancient villages of Kolossi and Episkopi, came at last to the western shore.

There stood the remains of the ancient royal city of Curium.

To Cesnola, three thousand miles from the broken aerie of Ces- nola in the Piedmont Alps, somehow this abandoned ruin by a genial sea became for him the embodiment of that symbol of his family's historic fame. It was a small plateau, a mesa, a mere few hundred feet above the wide sea and easily climbed, yet, when Cesnola described it in his book, *Cyprus*, it was "built like an eagle's nest, on the summit of a lofty elevation . . . and almost inaccessible on three sides."[6] This was a perfect description of Cesnola itself.

Cesnola sat in a campaign chair under a distant tree and exam- ined the hill through a glass while a Cyprian cooked a meal for him over a campfire. It was easy for Cesnola to imagine that the ancient kings of Cyprus, safeguarded on such an eminence, could withstand scores of enemies, whether armed with bow and arrows or with shield and spears. The very rock of the hill itself had been sheared off on the east and south into a natural fortification. Nothing in the ancient town remained standing. "Everything lay prostrate by time."[7] The whole scene evoked in Cesnola dreams of romantic ad- venture that colored the present as well as the past.

Around the whole huge mound ran a wide, moat-like ditch which served not only for defense but, with many thousands of rock- tombs carved into its sides, as Curium's "city of the dead." The ancients had honeycombed the one hill and then gone on to cut multi-roomed chambers for the dead into the neighboring hills.

Exploring the entire site, Cesnola found some unopened tombs between the hill-city and the sea, and it was in some of these, seven to forty feet below the surface and hermetically closed since the burials, that Cesnola made his first discovery of tomb objects in Curium. Removing a stone slab from the entrance of one of the tombs, he found lying at the doorway two earthenware lamps, coarsely yet curiously made. Inside were four large wine vessels, lettered in Phoenician, and farther inside, among some bones, a plain gold ring and two silver bracelets with asps' head finials, two very tarnished silver earrings and a short-handled bronze mirror.

It was enough to spur him to look further even though the Comte de Vogüé, in his thorough exploration of the island a decade earlier, had seen nothing worth mentioning. Cesnola found seven sites where shafts of columns, either of marble or of granite, were lying only half buried, recumbent where they had fallen in the heat and winds of centuries. He noted also a set of stone steps by a well, a large millstone to which a copper ring, now orchard green, had been riveted, and everywhere masses of broken pottery on the ground.

As Cesnola tramped over this ancient soil, his boots touched from time to time the hard surface of pieces of marble pavement which on close inspection showed ruts made by chariot wheels.

The consul was experienced enough by now to know that small mounds of clay were the debris of small homes and larger ones, often near fallen columns, were those of public buildings, even, perhaps, palaces. These latter he examined carefully. At one such site, whose eight shafts of granite attracted his attention, he found beneath the columns a mosaic pavement of marble and stone. Red, brown, white and blue pieces formed a flowering floor of large lotus flowers bordered by two coiled bands.

Cesnola called his workers together, and they pored over the fine, patterned area. It had been broken, they noticed, not just where the columns had crashed but in unexplained parts, in a section that Cesnola determined lay above the eastern wall of the building. The earth had been loosened there as deep as seven feet. To Cesnola, this was the work of treasure seekers. His account, in his book, reads like an adventure tale.[8]

Altogether, the hill of tombs, the palatial mosaic, the evidence of grave robbers, as Cesnola wrote later, combined "to fire the imagination."

As he told the story afterward, Cesnola, guiding men who worked in a crescendo of excitement, made a careful survey of the site. He found there a portion of the mosaic that sounded "quite hollow," and, digging a full "twenty feet deeper than the treasure hunter had gone, I discovered a gallery excavated in the rock, eleven feet four inches long, four feet ten inches wide, and scarcely four feet high." He was giving dimensions a great deal of attention.

A stone slab haphazardly closed a doorway. Within was an "oven-shaped cavity." The dry Cyprian soil had seeped through the roof and almost filled it. The men worked steadily, taking out, finally, no fewer than three thousand baskets of earth. As the first chamber was cleared another opening appeared ahead on the north wall. This led to another chamber, similarly filled with earth, and as his men began to empty the second of earth, Cesnola examined the first one with care.

Then it was "trimmed," all earth removed save for a foot and a half on the floor. It was at that level that bones and objects were found, and diggers had gradually arrived at this method of partial clearing to protect their finds. Some archaeologists searched their workers at the end of each workday. Cesnola never did. He followed the "trim" system, and now he poked into the earth remaining in the first chamber with a foot rule. It touched something hard, a something that turned out to be a bracelet of gold. It had rested there for eons, a circle in a small heap with other ornaments of gold.

The archaeologist ordered both chambers trimmed at once. As this was done a third chamber appeared, was trimmed, and exposed a fourth. Their work completed, the trimmers were ordered off to other work, much as Schliemann had given his workers a rest period as Priam's Gold began to emerge at Hissarlik.

It was then that Cesnola, accompanied by his foreman and a man to hold a lantern, undertook to examine all four chambers minutely. The work so far had taken weeks.

To the special cadre, it appeared that the vaults had been hewn out of the limestone by a copper or iron tool barely half an inch wide, its size indelibly imprinted on the walls of the four rooms and low passages between them.

Cesnola, proving how sensitive he was to the exacting demands of the developing discipline of archaeology, said that he first measured each room and vainly searched on their walls for inscriptions, before he went back to the first chamber to see if there was more gold there. He supervised his foreman as the latter poked around with a knife in the dirt on the floor and then ran the earth twice through his fingers as through a sieve. The lantern carrier repeated the examination.

Almost immediately a gold bracelet matching that found a month earlier came to the foreman's grasp, then two gold signet rings with scarabs of agate, four pairs of gold earrings and many gold beads. Before they reached the floor, inlaid with blue pebbles set in sand and plaster, the room had yielded up a treasure in gold. Cesnola was to describe it thereafter with classic simplicity: "the gold room."

No human bones or sepulchral urns turned up. As a result, Cesnola concluded happily, the chambers were, in truth, treasure vaults for the mosaic-floored temple above. It required several days to search the four floors of the treasury, and Cesnola "remained in it the whole time, and every object was discovered in [his] presence. Scarcely a moment passed without some gold ornament being brought to light." In his report to Johnston, he said that of the three men in the vault, he was the least excited, "though there was a good excuse for it."

Signet rings of pure, solid gold, one gold ring set with an amethyst, others mounted with nude statuettes wrought in gold and decorated with fine granulated goldwork, such were the pieces that made up the treasure. The earrings showed various styles for pierced ears, the delicate loops ending, often, in the head of a lion, bull, or goat. Bracelets of solid or hollow gold, being larger, gave the metalworker more scale in which to show his skill. The details of the beasts' heads that formed the ends of the ornaments were alive with vigor or calm with the placid grace of rosettes and other floral decorations. In gold necklaces, the artisan's skill exulted in fashioning ornamented beads, some in the shape of lotus flowers, some as tiny melons or acorns, the key link often being the head of a god in miniature.

The archaeologist felt that the finest of all the many necklaces was one of filaments entwined into a thick gold cord ending in exquisite lions' heads of the very fine, difficult granulated work. It was clasped with an intricately made gold knot.

Two bracelets, solid and weighing three pounds each, bore in Cyprian script the name of Eteander, King of Paphos. They were to be known the world over as the "royal bracelets of Cyprus."

But the literal crown of the "gold room" was, like the Treasure of Priam, a group of diadems. Here they had variety. Some were thick gold bands embossed with geometric designs. Others, thin gold leaves, had been stamped with outlines of animals and flowers.

Sifting the soil in each of the three remaining chambers, Cesnola found a treasure of silver jewelry and artifacts in the second cell, which he designated the "silver room." Then came one alternately called the "alabaster or bronze room," and finally, a very low compartment containing utensils, lamps, bowls and tripods of bronze, copper and iron.

Ever now the thorough archaeologist, Cesnola tried to explore a very narrow, long passage leading from this vault along the west wall. He went in with his chief trimmer, each holding a light; "but beyond 130 feet, the lights went out, and crab-like we were obliged to retreat, very lucky not to have remained suffocated inside." It was an adventure story he had to tell, as well as one of spying out the secrets of the ages, and there is final relief in the end of his tale that he managed to "return to Larnaca with all my treasures."

The entire group was known as the "Treasure of Curium," the priceless, unique collection that for years represented the summit of Cesnola's finds.[9]

The archaeologist-general was hardly shy about letting the world know of his treasure, and he was well aware that as a result his reputation in the intriguing and increasingly scientific field could be a major one. "My diggings at Curium have been still more successful than at Amathus," he declared, "and when I publish my last discoveries, they will throw forever into shade those of Schliemann."[10]

When the news became public, even before he published his book with its graphic diagrams of the four vaults and their exact measurements, many wrote him in ecstatic mood.

"You might have dug up the grandmother of Priam, or unearthed the most lovely Venus who ever felt her living charms harden into marble," one enthusiast rhapsodized, "and not have so caught the attention of the world by the act, as you will do by shaking in its face five pounds of gold actually dug out of an ancient pit. There is nothing so fascinating as 'buried treasure.' "[11] Cesnola had roused the interest of important figures half a world away.

The only trouble was that the treasure, as such, never existed. The precisely measured floor plans that Cesnola gave in his report of

1875 and in his book three years later—the versions differed slightly
—were of treasure vaults that simply had never existed. He had not,
in truth, dug the royal bracelets out of an ancient pit. This gold had
never lain on a blue-pebbled underground floor nor been screened
through the hands of chosen and trusted aides. All of this collection,
it was eventually determined, had been bought from native diggers,
found in separate tombs or gathered from the boundless riches of the
bazaars of the ancient land. Indeed, one of the few verifiable facts in
Cesnola's accounts is that the hill was there at Curium, standing
solemnly above the sea. The mosaic spread its formal, faded carpet
among the old, bleached and fallen columns. The place was pocked
with tombs.

But the vaults, for which some of the best archaeologists of the
succeeding generation sought in vain, were a hoax. They were not
there to be found. They had never been there. The account of the
vaults, even the vaults themselves, the supposed source of the
miraculous and brilliant treasure, were an invention of Cesnola's
fertile and desperate mind.

To meet the terms of his agreement with the new museum, the
collector had to grasp from this worn land an awesome horde of
antiquities. He now knew the powerful trustees of New York. He had
some idea of what it would take to inspire them to spend another
$60,000 or so for another "Cesnola Collection." Competitive to the
core, a trait many of his mentors in New York shared, Cesnola,
dreaming on the camp stool as he pondered far-off Curium, determined to match himself against the most renowned treasure seeker
—and finder—of the day, Heinrich Schliemann. He would present
the five-year-old museum of the new world with a trove that would
rival Priam's Gold. In the end, his writings about the Curium "expedition" bear comparison rather with an adventure tale than with
Schliemann's accounts, primitive though they were, of many-layered
Troy. However, for a brief and glorious time this fantastic treasure,
fretted with the splendor of the ancient Near East, carried the cavalier Cesnola on an arc of meteoric fame. He did, in fact, compete
successfully with Schliemann. He did, in fact, sell the collection to the
Metropolitan, the most promising museum in the world. He got the
job as its director.

Ironically, the fabled horde of Curium gold has for half a century been hidden in a vault. It is walled up. Immured. Imprisoned in a vault of the Metropolitan Museum of Art, it is beyond access even to researchers. For Cyprians, who have built their own archaeological museum and have called Cesnola "the looter," it is a collection, however uncatalogued, that is ancient and Cyprian and that carries with it in its metal tomb the poignancy of a lost national treasure.

Cesnola was hailed as one who had made a fabulous find. But the truth of the matter was that though Cesnola stayed in Cyprus until 1876, he never matched the Golgos find of six years earlier.[12] He had left his wife and daughters in Rivarolo Canavese where they would find schools and freedom from the fevers of the Levant. Taking his brother, Alexander, to Cyprus with him, he taught him his methods of handling Cyprian workmen and Turkish overseers, much as he might have tutored a more compatible Hitchcock. The younger Cesnola dug for another two years, amassing a quantity of not particularly noteworthy objects.

For the General, now known internationally because of the Metropolitan's acquisition of his first collection (which the museum had committed itself to in mid-1874),[13] it was a period in which he had crossed a bridge but had not yet found the land on which his life would at last take root and grow.

His position in the world was more secure than it had ever been before. It was not only the money he had made in disposing of his antiquities in America, although that was of fundamental importance to his family, but, having become famous in a new exciting field, it would be unthinkable for him to return to simpler days. He could not possibly think of selling Yankee notions. It was out of the question for him to spend more than occasional moments relishing the pull and tug of mediating differences in Cyprus between the Greeks and Turks. He was a general. It was the title he liked best and which he held over the longest span of his life. Yet it was a fact that now, in 1876, there were no wars of dimensions respectable enough to engage his interest. He found he had to be a soldier of fortune.

There was Victoria, thirty-eight years on her solid throne, governing an expanding empire through the stoic British envoys who could keep a sort of peace with a handful of men and a band. There was Italy, finally united under Victor Emmanuele, a country free from discordant fragmentation and internal war. There was America, its South salving its anguished past, its West rampaging on a course toward civility, its East financing changes through the entire land, and, of vital meaning to Cesnola, the leading, and only, center for the arts.

Not long after he had left New York, the Panic of 1873 had erupted. The vast expansion of credit, the enormous imports, the reckless development of rails of the postwar years had collapsed in a furious debacle. Everyone was hurt. On September 17, 1873, the New York & Oswego Midland Railroad failed to meet about one million dollars in debt. The next day, the signal failure of the monarch of finance, Jay Cooke & Co., broke all confidence in the money market. Pandemonium such as had never been seen before struck both the stock and gold exchanges. Shares sold at demand prices, whatever they might be. The old commodore, due to pay $1.5 million on a bank's loan to the Lake Shore Railroad, failed to meet the obligation, a stunning lapse, and with Vanderbilt's demur, faith in railroads vanished.

The trustees of the new museum put aside the contract with Cesnola, on which they had an option to sign, that extended through December 1. "The financial crisis. . . . made it necessary for the Trustees," their 1874 report read, "to suspend all further action upon it."

Earlier, Johnston had written Hitchcock that "the time" blocked any action being taken to buy the original collection from Cesnola or pay for objects found later. "I shall have to write him to that effect, which I regret," Johnston told Hitchcock, "but it is useless to attempt anything for the present and perhaps all Winter."[14]

The crisis, which was world-wide, would last six years, deadening markets throughout the western world and sending Cesnola on another frantic search for museums which would buy his Cyprian antiquities.

Now free to dig for himself, he concocted the Treasure of Curium, working under the double spur of the need for a career and the hope of impressing the Metropolitan trustees with new interest in his finds. Then he began his book about his digs in Cyprus. Since the trustees were not going to underwrite his volume, he was going to dedicate it "to a certain H. H.," he told Hitchcock, "my best and most faithful friend, and you must help me to make it worth [*sic*] of him."

He told Hitchcock he would send him the draft "to be thoroughly *revised, corrected* and *changed* or *cut away* anything you do not like. . . . I greatly count on your helping me in making my book worthy of you, and of some interest to the public; you can *add to it, subtract from* it, in fact do with it, as you deem best for the book."[15] He might have been discussing fiction.

Proofs of the first part of the book, which dealt with the ancient history of Cyprus, went forward a month later. The second part which he would write only after more excavating—in a word, after Curium and something more to write about—would be written from "notes on hand."[16] A nervous author, Cesnola asked Hitchcock less than two weeks later to hire a professional writer to revise the first chapters after Hitchcock had done that himself. He wanted a best seller, something on the order of Layard's breezy and exotic *Nineveh & Babylon*, that was propped up in the lap of many a mauve-clad woman on a chaise longue throughout the British Empire.

But he also had the more than simple task of making a real name for himself in archaeology. "To *make money* with it," he told his friend in a virtuous burst of self-denial, "is the *last* consideration I have. I want to make a name first if I can, and then a little money afterward if possible."[17] It was a perfect outline for the adventure tale spiced with the verisimilitude of exact dimensions of imaginary vaults.

Twelve

Now that he had his treasure and his book was under way, Cesnola could again work on more familiar ground. He was engrossed in selling his new collection to several museums at once. In the first days of 1876, he had sent a small collection to the Metropolitan but had no firm word whether the trustees would buy it, whether they would support his digs or whether they would, indeed, accept other proposals he had made.[1]

The General was hardly dismayed at such a turn of fortune. By now he had become accustomed to riding with the tide of battle, military or economic, and he showed at this time a basic lack of concern for the New York museum. After all, he had not heard from such formerly friendly trustees as Prime, Hoe and Blodgett, though he had written to each of them. His move as the American centennial year opened was to sell his collection to some Philadelphians interested in establishing a museum or, if that failed, to have it acquired by the Centennial Exhibition itself.

"Now that the New York Museum does not accept my last proposal I am glad . . . because there is more than a probability that something will be done with the Philadelphia people." He was as ready as ever to bargain. "I ask $60,000 but you may close at $50,000, if you cannot get more from them," he told Hitchcock. Some time later, he was willing to accept $40,000.[2]

Cesnola still liked interest, high interest, and he was again willing that only a portion of the purchase price be paid in cash provided interest on the remainder was paid regularly. Able to learn from the past, particularly about money, he pointed out to Hitchcock that the need for regular interest payments should be stressed, since he had not received them from the Metropolitan. If Philadelphia bought the new collection, he wanted to go there himself to arrange it. But he cautioned, "this must not be *said* to *them* as if they do not pay me, I cannot go to Philadelphia."

As usual, he left Hitchcock with a good deal to decide: whether to sell the guide book to his finds at the Exhibition later that year, "out of which a handsome sum might be realized," and other details. He handed over the whole package with, "Everything is left in your hands with full power to act."[3]

His agent on the scene in Philadelphia was a Mr. Baraezi, at one time second dragoman for George H. Boker in Constantinople; in 1876 Baraezi had become secretary of one of the committees for the Centennial of the American Revolution, and Cesnola thought he might be influential in pushing the sale there. The collector, pressed by a "quiet" investigation by the Turks of his latest finds, was most anxious to "*hurry* this *affair.*" He had already gotten more than a third of his new finds out of the island, paying eight percent export duty on each shipment. Such was his skill in managing Turkish functionaries, however, that it was he who set the value that determined what he would pay.

In his rush to get his treasure clear of Cyprus, he now had boxes of antiquities in Liverpool, Geneva, Marseilles, London and America. Most were in Europe because, as private property, they were subject to import taxes in America. Only after they had been sold to a public museum or the Centennial Committee could they enter the country free of duty. If either of the Philadelphia groups bought the finds, the twenty-seven boxes of Cyprian antiquities he had sent to the Metropolitan would be relabeled to replace the *NYM* with *LPC* to signify his ownership. He didn't want more than were necessary to know the steps in his business.

In this letter of January 12, Cesnola wrote about Curium much as a salesman would write to the home office. He was writing not to a dear friend with whom he would be frank about the basic facts of his new collection but to a manager to whom he was supplying good merchandise and provocative, appealing sales talk. This alteration in mode marked a crucial turning point in his relations with Hitchcock.

He was relying more on his family. As his wife and daughters now joined him in Cyprus, he remarked that if they had not come out to him he would, perhaps "have left Cyprus forever."[4]

Moreover, the idea of quitting the island rested on a still more practical ground. He had been having increasing trouble with the Turks who, in a burst of patriotism against his massive operations, had been stoning his diggers.[5] This was probably one of the factors that turned him toward buying antiquities. More to the point was his reputation as a buyer. He had made it a practice since his first weeks on the island.

Determined to repeat the scope and grandeur of his first collection, Cesnola spent money freely and the previous year had been lectured by Johnston, himself retrenching because of the depression. "It seems to me a pity," Johnston had written, "that you should invest in your diggings all what you are worth in money etc. etc." Johnston, Cesnola felt, had put him in an "unpleasant position" by saying that if the General *insisted* on being paid the $5000 due him from the museum in 1875, "that some way or other the money has to be raised etc!"[6]

Cesnola was impatient with New York. In late 1875 he exploded to Hitchcock about the trustees: "What *donkeys* they are if they let the two sarcophagi and the last splendid findings [Curium] be purchased by another Museum!"[7] The quantity and quality of his new collection rivaled the best in the world.[8]

He would sell his great treasure elsewhere. In a letter to Baraezi on January 12, 1876, Cesnola made his determination evident. If he were to switch from the museum to the national exposition, Cesnola would not hesitate to use the esteem he had won in New York to further his dealings with Philadelphia.

"You must tell to these gentlemen, that they have to rely upon what I tell them herein. The Trustees of the Museum in New York (to whom they can refer if they wish,) did so." Then he added without shame, "and their full confidence in me, was not misplaced." When he was in New York in 1873, the trustees, he recalled, "vied with each other, to give me proofs of their esteem," and before he left elected him, to his surprise, a member of their corporation "by unanimous vote."

This new collection "is worth more than that at New York. Its character however is different from the other; for, while that in New York is poor in gold, precious stones, silver, bronze, and alabaster, and rich in heavy bulky stone sculptures, this collection is just the opposite; being very rich in what the other is poor; and not deficient in what the other is rich." The list of items in his new collection of 7161 pieces included 511 in gold, 272 in silver and 440 in bronze and other metals.

The display of the collection at the Centennial Exposition foundered as European loans of paintings, most of them, other than the English representation, meager samplings of national styles, were put on display in Philadelphia. Canvases by Reynolds, Lawrence and Landseer from Britain, a single Murillo from Spain and second-rate oils by Italians were hung in profusion. The radical French Impressionists were ignored.

In his most agile manner, the General then went back to concentrating on the New York museum, and was pleased when Johnston offered to get a navy ship to transport his entire collection to America in care of the museum. This would bring him, finally, the fruition of a fond desire in a way that would at the same time spare him import duty.[9]

At the same time, he mentioned himself in the position of "superintendent" of the "New York Museum," telling Hitchcock in January of 1876 that Prime was working to secure the post for him. That would fit in well with his wish to provide a good education for his daughters. "We intend to educate them," he wrote, "so as to be worthy of marrying in that kind of society to which they have a right to belong by birth."[10]

But he was well aware that the museum and its trustees, however wealthy, were plagued by the long depression. Suppose he should go to New York and wait a year until he could supervise the removal to the museum in the park? What "if after *waiting* the plan of Mr. Prime is not successful?" was the way he put his dilemma to Hitchcock. "You know the new President will be elected in November next; and if I do not apply for some foreign mission *in time*, and the *superintendency* of the Museum is not created, that I shall find myself without the proper means of maintaining my family!"[11] It was an old and harrowing prospect.

The General, now forty-three years old, felt he should follow the "American example" and *do* something rather than wait for something to happen. Though what to do puzzled him, it took his mind off the problem of the curious Cyprian script on some of his antiquities. His mind focused on whether or not the appointment of a superintendent at the museum would be made by the trustees or the "City Authorities . . ."

Will it be a *permanent one* like in Europe, or subject to the whim, and caprices of politicians? You may be sure, that a position like that, if not a *permanent* one has no attraction for me indeed! The Superintendent of the New York Museum no matter who will be selected for that place, if he is able and understand his duties, must be appointed *for life*, subject only to removal for *misconduct* or other *similar reasons.*[12]

Even before being offered the post officially, Cesnola was setting forth the conditions of his employment. Eventually, these very demands were met.

Getting out of Cyprus and over to New York was to prove a nip-and-tuck operation the whole way. The navy ship never arrived. Once more he was "very unlucky about obtaining a U. S. man of war coming here." Of the three he had expected, "none came to Cyprus!"[13] He had to send his antiquities and furniture off in a Greek bark in June 1876.

Then he took his family to Paris, dickered with the Louvre, the Berlin, the British museums and others who looked at the gold he had brought with him. Everyone admired, but there were few genuine offers. He began to complain that he had been hearing for too long from the "New York millionaires that 'hard times' prevail and that everybody is *poor*, and there is *no money* etc. etc. and all the sacrifices are expected from a *poor man* like *me* taking advantage of my foolish patriotic feelings towards my adopted country etc. etc."[14]

Once September and its cooling, busy days arrived, Cesnola took his family to London and settled down to finish his book on Cyprus. As he did so, he dealt simultaneously with the entire complement of museums. From Johnston in New York he had word that a purchase was out of the question. But Hoe, visiting the retired consul in London, was so taken with the gold he thought that the negative decision might be changed. The definite refusal from Johnston, however, so distressed Cesnola that for several weeks he referred to the gold as the "Rurium Treasure."[15]

He worried about everything that fall, from the prospects of selling in Europe to the condition of his piano and hair mattresses which he had shipped to New York.[16] And, as his hopes went down, his price went up. "Here in Europe, I ask and *shall receive* $100,-000," he wrote. His price to the Metropolitan was now $70,000.[17]

At the moment, this was beyond the trustees, and Prime, a leisured and ardent executive, suggested the museum "ought not to buy what it can't pay for" but should solicit funds for purchase by popular subscription.[18]

The building in the park was well along in construction, and Prime faced up to the fact that, once there, the museum would not be able to charge admission and would lose the grant it had been getting from the Park Commission while it remained in rented quarters. "The future presents the aspect of a Museum with valuable treasures," Prime noted, "without a dollar to pay expenses or debts." He thought it was time for New York State to "regard the museum as an educational institution as much as common schools" and to "tax the people to support and *enlarge* them." He estimated it would take two or three years to get the state accustomed to the idea. Meanwhile, he would put forward the notion of a general subscription to buy Cesnola's new collection. Prime knew his fellow trustees well enough to realize that, "if two or three men could be induced to take hold of it and go to see others, the thing could be accomplished. It must succeed or fail *at once.*"[19]

As it turned out, the sale was settled quickly; too quickly, in fact, for the British Museum's comfort. Discussing the proposed British purchase, Cesnola told Johnston that the trustees in London had offered him £10,000 or $50,000. In mid-November he notified Junius S. Morgan of this and the banker telegraphed New York that the museum there would have three days in which to act. Otherwise, it might lose the second Cesnola Collection to England.

Not having an answer from New York within the specified time, Cesnola accepted the British offer. He even stipulated that the spurious treasure be given his name. But the British proposal to buy had to be approved by the British Government. This ordinarily would not cause any trouble, as, Cesnola explained to Johnston, "the ex officio Trustees of the B.M. are the gentlemen at the head of the British Govert and their colleagues the highest men of England."[20]

At this crucial point, Cesnola received a letter from the New York trustees through Robert Hoe Jr., asking him to delay negotiations with London. Cesnola rushed back to the British Museum and picked up his antiquities, many of which he had put on display there to ease the men of culture and control into an admiring and purchasing mood. He gave the antiquities curator there, Charles T. Newton, forty-eight hours to complete the sale. (Or not.) Newton snapped back with the demand that Cesnola put that stipulation in writing for the British Government.

The next morning, the newspapers had the story. The London *Daily Mail* ran an article and editorial accusing Cesnola of double-dealing.[21] Cesnola was furious. He felt he had been placed in a "false light." Furious itself, the British Museum formally released him from any obligation to it that same day, and Cesnola was "free to treat with N.Y."[22]

Perhaps Cesnola found some relief, for he had long felt that the British were "haughty,"[23] and his wife longed to return to New York, both good reasons for a second sale there. However, the best and unmentioned reason was that he had a chance of a career in New York that he did not have in London.

Cesnola always insisted that he wanted to keep both his first and second collections together in America because of his devotion to his "adopted country"; but in view of the cloud which to this day hovers around the Curium find, that idea falls against shards of disbelief. Furthermore, he drove a sharp bargain with the New York institution.

In mid-November Cesnola was considering accepting $50,000 from the Metropolitan.[24] In a cable somewhat later, Metropolitan trustees Theodore Roosevelt, Johnston, Potter, and Hoe gave the collector the good news that the public subscription—one actually held among wealthy friends—was going well and that Miss Wolfe had given $10,-000. Morgan in London had pledged $2500; his son in New York pledged a like sum. Two days later, a second cable offered "$60,000 gold for all your collection. You to arrange collections in Park Museum without charge. Hitchcock approves. Details by mail."[25]

Cesnola did not bother even to answer the offer. He told Hitchcock privately later that he did not think his friend would bind him to work for nothing. The trustees tried again: "Public excited. Anxiously waiting reply. Museum liberally inclined for your services."

Cesnola ignored the hint of a job. He again brought up the British Museum, though it seems unlikely that that institution was, in fact, still considering buying his finds. "Am treating for Kurium only all of which is here. British Museum offers $10,000. Will you do as much?"

The Metropolitan replied it would pay shipment costs.

The General shot back: "If packing, insurance and compensation for arrangement is added to offer just received, will accept." It would give him an "in" to arrange the collection.

The museum wondered what the freight would be. "Fear raising more money impossible. State cost of packing freight, insurance."

Its future director told the museum trustees that shipment would cost $6000 and if it could not afford that, to buy only the Curium group—did he want to get it off his hands?—"or relinquish purchase altogether."

That did it. The trustees cabled. "We accept entire collection."

He applauded: "Allright. Three hearty cheers for our dear New York Museum."[26]

Since Cesnola had been moving easily in the ambience of upperclass Englishmen who invited him to their country estates and made a social figure of him in London that winter, he felt more and more pressed to add riches to his fame. He enjoyed going along with Sir John Lubback to his country seat and being a guest with three hundred robed scholars at a festival in Trinity College. He relished the almost lordly position he now held and began to feel he was entitled, as were these heirs of Britain who were his companions, to a sure and ample portion of the world's largess.

Since Hitchcock was in New Hampshire, it was his friend Prime who was keeping Cesnola posted on the state of affairs at the museum and was working behind the scenes to get him assigned as superintendent. A letter in January 1877 struck Cesnola as "not very encouraging. No doubt we must be very cautious as to what arrangement we ultimately conclude with the Trustees." It seemed that they were having so much trouble with finances that it was a question where they would get the money to pay him what they owed.

"If they do not intend to mortgage their collections," Cesnola asked, "what other security will they give us?"[27] He had adopted the British tone of assurance and it was his interests he considered paramount.

Counter-currents, however, troubled his relations with the trustees, particularly with Hoe, a volatile man like Cesnola himself. Now the trustee wrote a letter that Cesnola thought was entirely off-base. Cesnola, being on edge about trustees' feelings at the moment, snapped at Hitchcock that he did not intend to receive any other such letter "from him or from anyone else." The cavalier had lost none of the fire that had once made him pounce on the throat of a soldier he thought had insulted him.

The letter from Hoe cannot be found, but it must have dealt with the last sale. Cesnola could not see "what cause of complaint the New York Museum can reasonably have indeed but on the contrary I consider it has all the possible reasons to feel satisfied of having concluded an excellent bargain and proud of having secured the collection."

He was at a point where he was set to cancel the deal, and he wrote Hitchcock to "tell Hoe, Johnston or to any other Trustees of the New York Museum that rather than to know that any of them is discontented with the purchase" that he, Hitchcock, had the authorization to "annul the sale. . . ." Hitchcock was either to cancel the contract, and take possession of the finds, or "*close regularly, get the money* and invest it at once."[28]

The museum closed.

Hoe still had a knack, though, of raising Cesnola's triple exclamations. This time he telegraphed a reminder for the General to "*insure the Curium collection!!!*" If this was a sample of the way the trustees would act were he the superintendent, Cesnola griped, it might be "more pleasant & prudent for me *not to accept* that position if offered to me."

Ignoring completely that he had offered the spurious second collection to the museum only a month before the sale at $16,000 less than he finally received, Cesnola berated himself for not having demanded "$250,000 of my collection as *Castellani* did for his." The Castellani collection, a great quantity of very fine pottery, sold in Paris in 1878 for $406,000.[29] Had he first asked $250,000 and then accepted $66,000, Cesnola reasoned, "I would have been thought a *generous man.*" He had complained along these lines but to the worst possible confidantes. Junius S. Morgan and other American bankers in London had pointed out to him that he had gotten what he had asked and that was all he could expect. Cesnola saw the reasonableness of this view. "Having asked and sold to them my collection for *one third* of its real price," he admitted, "I have no reason to expect for any other acknowledgment."[30]

What bothered him also was the praise given donors to the subscription, particularly that given to the largest donor, tall, patrician Catharine Lorillard Wolfe.

"There has been more *generosity* and *patriotism* on my part than in Miss Wolfe or a dozen of them put together," he railed, "and I would not be surprised to hear by & by the remark that in endowing our Museum 'every Trustee had done his utmost while Genl Cesnola did nothing.' "[31]

Actually, his sale to New York sprang from practical considerations. Since it involved hope of a position in the city his wife longed to return to, it was sensible. But his own private yearnings were in his homeland, Italy. Were he to settle permanently in New York, he would see to it that he was treated with respect.

His anger during the exchange of telegrams—when he simply declined to answer at one point—stemmed from the museum's expectation that he would go to New York and spend a year arranging the collections "*at my own expense.*" This was absurd. Expressing the prevalent anti-Semitism, he saw it as "rather too Jewish."[32] Since he just did not believe that Hitchcock, knowing him so well, would commit him to such a course, he had felt free to ignore the proposition.

If he had not withdrawn the antiquities from the British Museum and they had eventually refused to purchase, he would have been in a bad position. Then the Americans would have been able to say, "You see, he could not sell the collection in Europe so now he is trying to sell all his rubbish to America."[33]

In more ways than one, the dealings with the two princely museums had been enervating. Cesnola's heart was not really in either sale; they involved but his bank account. His feelings actually were elsewhere. The truth was that Cesnola still longed for a position of rank of his European homeland. Ever alert politically, he was eyeing his chances of getting another, and better, consulate. Should Samuel J. Tilden, a friend of Prime's and a Democratic reformer who had destroyed the Tweed Ring be elected President, he thought he had a good chance of a suitable job. He was ready to accept any offer, "even in China!"

But, to him, "the Mission in Italy would be my *very highest aspirations & ambition. . . .* There I would be at home in every sense of the word." Behind the now richly adorned facade of fine clothes and heavy gold watch chain and jewelry, however, there still lurked the pain of uncertainty: he told Hitchcock, "I think that such a Mission will not be given to me being a *first class one.*" Despite these fears, he pleaded with Hitchcock to have Prime get word to Tilden on how the general felt about the consulate in Italy.[34] When the Electoral Commission that Congress set up to decide the disputed election of 1876 chose Rutherford B. Hayes, Tilden went into retirement. Again Cesnola's fortunes were tied to a personally disadvantageous political event. He took the disappointment in stride and concentrated on his book.

With his current status in London society, that was easy. The former Prime Minister, Gladstone, was a devotee of archaeology. Now he wanted to read Cesnola's manuscript. Soon Gladstone decided to recommend it to "the greatest of the London Publishers, Mr. Murray." Gladstone had already spoken to Murray, who had published the works of the pioneering archaeologists, from Layard on, and who, even now, was working with Schliemann on the German's first account of his work at Troy.

With such an entrée, Cesnola moved along with Murray as though the two were in tandem. Murray invited Cesnola to give him some manuscript. The General, taking with him C.W. King, a leading gem expert of Cambridge University, visited the Murray editorial office in Albermarle Street, four chapters in hand, each dealing with his digs in four different Cyprian sites. One was Curium.

Before he gave Cesnola his reaction, Murray invited him to a "splendid dinner at his princely country seat at Wimbledon." Only when Cesnola and some thirty guests were leaving for London at midnight did the publisher mention the book. Just before the carriage reached the door, Murray told the writer he had gotten in touch with friends, the Messrs. Harper of New York "asking them if they would join me in publishing your book."[35] They would. Cesnola was delighted. He expected to see his book sell in America as Layard's tale of living with wild tribes did in Europe. (Eventually, Cesnola's sold three editions.)

It would be unthinkable that his first work would not be read in Italy by his relatives and friends, and, to insure that, Cesnola arranged to translate the work himself and to publish a five hundred copy edition privately.[36] Before he left in the early spring of 1877 to return to New York, Cesnola had one small bit of business on hand, and that was to put him at an impasse on money with Junius S. Morgan.

The museum had asked him to go to the banker's London office and pick up the $5000 the Morgans, father and son, had pledged in the subscription. Straight off, the elder Morgan told Cesnola he had no intention of paying his son's pledge. He then asked the General to make out a receipt in duplicate. The banker took both receipts for $2500 and handed Cesnola a check for £500. Cesnola pointed out to him that "$2500 were more than £500; but he apparently got mad, and said that he did not intend to pay for *one penny more*, and kept nevertheless my two receipts for the full amount of $2500."[37]

If this seemed worth becoming disturbed about, Cesnola had further reasons for complaint regarding the manner in which the museum was paying him. He was soon to go to New York, having booked passage on the *Britannic* for April 26.[38] He depended on the interest of his payments, as well as installments, to enable him to buy a home and support his family.

Nevertheless, the Metropolitan paid $37,500 for him into the Union Trust Company at two percent, doing so on the advice of a trustee, Joseph H. Choate, one of New York's most prominent lawyers. Cesnola still had $26,000 coming and felt bitter at the low interest.[39]

Hitchcock was in Colorado and both the other trustees with whom he was closest, Hoe and Prime, had refused to "have anything to do" with Cesnola's money, so no one had been looking after Cesnola's affairs in New York. He had hoped to get good interest for three or four months on the entire MMA debt of $63,500 when he reached New York. Though that was now out of the question, he did not want to make an issue of it or "hurt the feelings of any of the trustees of the Museum."[40] The volatile cavalier also did not want to hurt his own chances. There was a reason for his control—he was, in fact, job seeking—but his strategy did not pay off. Almost as soon as he arrived in New York in May 1877, he was named secretary of the Metropolitan Museum of Art. His friends convinced him to work, as did the trustees, without a salary, and since he had advances from the New York and London publishers, he could afford to do so. Anyway, his duties in those early years while the new building for the museum was being constructed, were so light that he could keep on with his writing and handle museum business in two hours a day.

Cesnola established his family first in a boarding house, a practice then very common in the city. Most people felt the new apartment houses would surely fail. People sought privacy. Most wanted their own, one-family homes. It was only when they couldn't afford city prices that they rented their city homes and went to the country. Then, visiting New York, perhaps to see a round of plays and operas, they would go to favorite boarding houses.

The General decided he, too, should have a town house. He turned down one when the owner wanted $500 more than he was willing to pay and went with his family on vacation to Pennsylvania. When they came back, he bought a four-story home at 107 East 57th

Street. In those days such houses had a grand staircase, fireplaces in the main rooms, servants' quarters on the top floor and in the basement, place for a "well-bred and intelligent" housekeeper.

These personal problems settled, Cesnola turned to a more compatible task: competing with Schliemann. As Cesnola was dealing with the museum the previous fall for the sale of his Treasure of Curium, the German had been writing the King of Greece that he had unearthed in five simple, shaft graves at Mycenae, south of Athens, a dazzling offering of gold objects to the dead. Among them were gold cups, decorated daggers, clasps for clothing and fabulous death masks of gold sheet. One, the most splendid, was proclaimed the mask of Agamemnon himself, king of Mycenae, a flight of fancy on the part of the stolid Berliner. The gold in the treasure weighed eighty pounds. More important for scholars, it had, indeed, been found in one place, and Schliemann, by arrangement, had given the entire lot to the National Museum of Archaeology in Athens.

Though Schliemann, like Cesnola's workers at Golgos and elsewhere, had hacked through the hill of Hissarlik destroying for all time irreplaceable evidence of how men lived in the darkness before history, he worked at Mycenae with greater care. By evidence gathered at these excavations he placed the work of the Myceneans prior to that of the Greeks, and, by showing a similarity between the broken pieces of pots at Mycenae and in the Troad, where Hissarlik stood, demonstrated for the first time that the great Greek civilization arose from an earlier and distinct historical epoch. By doing this, he became not merely a collector of a vast and fabulously rich trove; he was beginning to realize what kinds of information would enable him or the others who followed him to reconstruct, in part, the life of the dawn people of mankind.

Cesnola hardly appreciated his work. He could see Schliemann as the "greatest discoverer of the age," soon after the celebrated discovery at Mycenae,[41] but he really relished the criticism that Schliemann, an irritating man with a single-track mind, was getting from the press. He recommended that Hitchcock read the July issue of *Frazer's Magazine*. In it was "a very severe article against Dr. Schliemann well worth reading." The piece made Cesnola glad that he had left out of his book his own theories and conclusions. He was going to avoid Schliemann's easily criticized pitfall. His book would be a *"clear plain & truthful* description" of what he did "avoiding anything which might appear to some of the readers *bombast* or *bragadocio."* He hoped his way of working would leave the critics of Europe and America with very little on which to vent "their *artistic spleen."*[42]

He had written a straight-faced and straightforward account which included the story of the fake Treasure of Curium. He was sending copies of the manuscript around, and the congratulations he received delighted him. One, from a French scholar, praised him for his "noble modesty."[43]

To sell his book, however, he needed the approval not just of the learned men, hidden away in their studies, but of the general public. What he needed, at this point, were articles in the general press. So he again encouraged Hitchcock to write about his work. This time, however, keeping in mind the wide circulation that *Harper's* had had and how many lectures Hitchcock had given, he suggested that his friend should not use his own name on the articles. He was too widely known as a Cesnola partisan. The New Englander took another writing chore on for his friend. He agreed to write—and wrote—a glowing summary of Cesnola's excavations in Cyprus. It was signed, or "fathered," as Cesnola put it, by John Taylor Johnson,"[44] the museum's president.

With his own home, an income from both publishers and the prospects of a reasonable return on his book in two continents, Cesnola and his wife moved in society with the pleasure of a couple long isolated. It was a period of accomplishment and promise, and Cesnola, garlanded with praise, put the museum in his debt by his work, with a few dedicated trustees, in preparing the exhibits to be moved to its permanent home, the great museum in the Central Park.

Thirteen

New York, as 1880 opened, stood hale but florid, flushed with the richness of ten-course dinners, alive with a yeasty stirring of plans that would change the face of the city. Though rich, it was not entirely sure of itself and found flattering the attention of Europeans. Charles Stuart Parnell arrived January 2 to get help for the Irish. Count Ferdinand de Lesseps, the hero-maker of the Suez Canal, came the next month looking for investors for the canal across Panama that he felt could well cap his career.

The rich looked the part. Their carriages bore liveried attendants. Their wives' clothes came from Paris. Their homes reflected richly diversified tastes. Fortunes inherited from two or three generations were spent with imagination and ingenuity. The twin palatial brownstones in Renaissance style rising for William H. Vanderbilt and his two sisters at a cost of $750,000 each, were decorated with fluted pilasters. Stone carvings of grapes and oak leaves softened their rectilinear Italianate lines.

Wealthy westerners, coming to New York, saw the sights of the town, drank and dreamed. "If a man wants to build a marble city, he can see a dozen patterns in one block," wrote H. Hudson Holly in 1878. "If he wants to build a brownstone city, there are five styles between. . . ." Broadway was a "most superb pattern-card,"[1] eye-catching and unattainable, for main streets that would give a metropolitan zest to prairie towns.

Here in the great metropolis, the Brooklyn Bridge, a decade in the making, was becoming a Gothic-arched span, the first from the great island city to one of its suburbs. Bedloe's Island, site of a fortress in the harbor, was being made ready for the Statue of Liberty. And, uptown, at Fifth Avenue and 82nd Street, the new art museum stood ready, only ten years after its founding, to receive exhibits in a permanent setting and take its place as the Metropolitan Museum of Art.

Throughout its first decade, the museum had been run by groups of trustees, wealthy, energetic men whose interests were not confined to their positions as bankers and railroad tycoons. Now they felt it was time to get one capable and knowing man to take on the job of director. It could be no one other than Cesnola. For two years now, he had been watching the new museum rise, visiting the site with Johnston, making suggestions for changes and alterations.[2] He had taken a critic whom he liked, Clarence Cook of *The Herald*, to see the building one summer day before the windows were installed.[3] Only Cesnola in all America could possibly catalogue his vast collection, as the European scholars insisted should be done, and, given the commanding presence of the general-count, an entertaining companion of those who controlled the museum, it was unthinkable that another would head the Metropolitan.

He was appointed director May 15, 1879.[4] By this time he had gotten across his main ideas about the position: that it was he who should sort out the duplicates, a job of classification that, he said, only someone with his knowledge of the antiquities could do, and, secondly, that the position must not be at the mercy of political whims and must be permanent.

Cesnola now supervised the move. With him worked several of the trustees, Johnston, the president, William W. Astor, and Rutherford Stuyvesant, Loring Andrews, Prime and others.[5] Beginning the task in March, 1879, they carefully packed and took the displays far uptown to the Fifth Avenue museum. There Cesnola ordered them about as the exhibits were arranged. When they finished in March 1880, it was the Cesnola collection that was the center of attention.

Press previews were numerous and lengthy. The *Times* concentrated first on Cesnola's Greco-Phoenician antiquities, then on Samuel P. Avery's Oriental porcelains, and, finally, the European paintings, which included Frans Hals' *Hille Bobbe*, Francesco Guardi's *Rialto* and Tiepolo's *Sacrifice of Abraham*. Today, the order of consequence would be reversed.

In the most conspicious and most carefully arranged space in the museum, Cesnola's statues and ceramics were entombed in glass cases, monuments to the Cyprian people; the mature male figures were larded with fat, their women stiffly erect. The artisans who had fashioned these statues and the culture they lived in, were plainly unappreciative of the male rib cage or the suppleness of the female body.

The building over which the Cyprian statues presided was no Louvre of the Americas. It was an old plan, conceived in 1868 by Calvert Vaux, one of the original designers of the park, and Jacob Wrey Mould, his English assistant. Mould had all the old world facility with detail which he had displayed in designing the Terrace in Central Park.

The lawyer-trustee, Joseph H. Choate, had drawn up an agreement between the museum and the Parks Department that to this day forms the framework for their relationship. It provides that the city owns the building, whose upkeep it maintains, and the museum, specifically its trustees, owns its contents.

As a result, the Parks Department had most of the say about the new building in the deer park. The first idea of holding a competition for its design—of the same sort that had won the development of the entire park for Olmstead and Vaux—fell under the weight of other projects. Vaux and Mould inherited the job of revising the museum plan of 1868, and, working for Parks Commissioner Andrew H. Green in the top room of the Bank of Commerce Building on Nassau Street, they did just that. Green had his office below and "used to come upstairs every half hour he could spare" to take a look at Mould's drawing boards.[6] The Parks Department coffers were not exactly a cornucopia of plenty. Vaux was limited to putting up the museum for a lesser sum—$560,000—than the cost of one of the Vanderbilt mansions.

When Vaux and Green were through, they reaped little satisfaction. To the *Tribune*, the interior looked like a railroad station, an accurate description of the huge hall, illuminated by a great skylight of iron and glass. Worse still, said the *Tribune*, the arching ribs of the building appeared "to be iron wrought into a pierced pattern, but they are in reality a cheap affair of iron rods covered with zinc—that last sweet thing out of architectural shams."

Despite all this, however, the hall presented, in the Cesnola collection, "a magnificent monument to its discoverer's energy and taste." Though much too big, the *Tribune* felt, the collection could not have been displayed more scientifically and more imposingly anywhere in the world.[7] Cesnola had obviously done quite right by himself.

Practically the entire main floor of the new two-story museum, then, was proof of Cesnola's collecting prowess. The trustees had committed the museum to spending its largest sum so far for the Cesnola antiquities and had now used the new building in the park to show them off to best advantage.

The very bulk of this huge horde, however, invited criticism. In a letter in the New-York *Times* of February 22, 1880, an unnamed correspondent compared the collection of the Metropolitan to that of the older Boston Museum. There had long been a rivalry between Boston and New York in the arts and literature, with Boston taking the field with ease. The writer continued this critical judgment; he thought the base of the Metropolitan's collection too narrow and he asked: "Take the Cyprian antiquities away from the collection and what would remain?" The answer, of course, was the picture gallery of European art, the King collection of antique gems, Avery's porcelains, the late Hiram Powers' sculpture, "California," a loan show of forty pictures by the late William Hunt and sixty pictures of contemporary American artists. Quite a bit, in fact.

But the writer was focusing on Cesnola's accumulation. He liked them no better than the *Tribune* man liked the building.

"There are too many of these Cyprian objects," he wrote flatly. "They may illustrate quite exhaustively a certain early period of art but, then, it's bad art and shocking bad art at that. Are they beautiful? Are the Cyprian statues, save with the rarest exceptions, either elegant or classic? Archaeologically, ethnologically, they may touch us a great deal but artistically hardly any."

The "endless quantity" of earthenware, he declared, was fit only for the British Museum. He thought it a sound idea for the Metropolitan to "sell nine-tenths of its Cyprian pottery and three-quarters of its Cyprian statues and replace them by objects of greater artistic value."

But Cesnola, who had a genius for arousing flat-out enmity in some and unquestioning devotion in others, had his champion.

Harper's, ever his advocate, took no such rigorous view. In an issue that appeared just as the museum opened in late March, the magazine declared that the Cesnola exhibit was of "great historical value." Side-stepping the art question completely, it stated that the Cesnola collection would provide "unprecedented information" about the Phoenicians. The magazine then anointed General Cesnola's discoveries as "the missing link in art so long sought."

As the day for the opening neared, even the *Tribune* softened its attitude toward the architecture. It decided the main hall gave a "delightful impression of space and light." For the very first time, it felt, Cesnola's Cyprus collection, finally classified, could really be seen. "Its arrangement," the paper conceded, "has been a true labor of love with General Di Cesnola, and he will have what reward he needs, in addition to his own enjoyment of the task, in the public appreciation and applause that are sure to greet the sight of his performance."

March 30, 1880, the day of the opening of the museum in its new red and black park building finally arrived, a scant ten years from the museum's founding. A Tuesday, it turned from cloudy to fair and the temperature at Hudnut's Pharmacy in lower Broadway, where official readings were taken, moved above freezing to forty-four degrees as the day progressed.

Even before noon, guests arrived.[8] A solid line of carriages—landaus, clarences, coupés and liveried hacks—stretched south down the graveled Fifth Avenue as far as one could see. They halted there, the horses stomping and whinnying in fret, until the doors opened at 3 P.M. In the snapping March wind, it was perfect weather for the ladies to make "a display of Easter toilets" that an inclement and early Easter had denied them. Now carriages brought them and their top-hatted husbands around the curving road to the new impressive building. The 3500 invited guests rustled through the "Long Branch cottage" entrance.

Within, Grafulla's band of the proud Seventh Regiment played operatic arias. It was the heyday of popularity for Verdi, prolific and melodious, and his and other familiar airs resounded under the zinc-coated iron arches as the brilliant gathering waited for the President of the United States. Rutherford B. Hayes, fifty-nine years old and a former Civil War major general, was to open the new building officially.

The crowd was so great that some hundreds of chairs provided for them could not be used. The guests stood as they chatted and listened to martial versions of lyrical songs. Meanwhile, the Presidential party were John T. Johnston's guests of honor at a splendid pre-dedication reception and lunch. Among the one hundred and fifty New Yorkers invited were J. Pierpont Morgan and his wife, the De Peysters, the Suydams, the John Jays, the August Belmonts, the H.G. Marquands, the Cesnolas, the Robert W. DeForests, Theodore Roosevelt, several Vanderbilts, the Joseph H. Choates and numerous trustees who enjoyed Johnston's hospitality before taking their carriages straight up Fifth Avenue to 82nd Street. They were properly late and conspicuously elegant.

The President and his wife were cheered as they arrived. Mrs. Hayes, Mrs. Evarts, wife of William Maxwell Evarts, Secretary of State, Mrs. Johnston and Madame Cesnola were escorted, once inside the building, to places reserved for them on balconies overlooking the platform. The men then disappeared into the "cozy and comfortable" trustees' lounge. Choate, the main speaker, was seen pacing about in the corridor outside the lounge, his head sunk on his chest, his hands clasped tightly behind his back.[9] He was to speak to an audience of the wealthiest men in the country.

Grafullo's men finally swung into "Hail Columbia" and the President, led by Johnston, entered the tapestry-draped hall. The men in the audience gave subdued cheers. Women waved lace-bordered handkerchiefs. The President, wearing a tight-fitting frock coat, shook hands with trustees and dignitaries already on the platform. Cesnola came next, with Secretary Evarts.

The program moved along briskly. It was to be followed by a party, not quite so exclusive as Johnston's, given by Mrs. John Jacob Astor. James F. Wenman, president of the Parks Department, delivered the building, "removed from the noise and shadow of the great city," to the trustees. In his view, the Cesnola collection was "a large archaeological museum of world-wide reputation complete in itself." President Hayes declared the building open to the public.

It was then that the eloquent lawyer, Joseph H. Choate, a partner in the Wall Street law firm of Secretary Evarts, spoke in a "ringing voice" that "mastered bad accoustics." He praised the museum for coming so far in only a single decade and quoted the Duke of Argyll as telling Cesnola on a recent visit that the British Museum had not accomplished as much in thirty full years. Choate looked at the long future and, privy to the aims of the museum board, declared that the Metropolitan "expects to make a more or less complete collection of objects illustrative of the history of art in all its branches from the earliest beginnings to the present time."

Choate met public grumbling from the poor over public support for the building by calling attention to the trustees' plan to set up a Museum of Industrial Art "for the direct and practical instruction of artisans." This would not only help the workers, he said, but Americans could expect the Industrial Art school to lead the way in training craftsmen so that consumers could buy well-crafted objects at home rather than having to import them from Europe.

Choate then moved to his main theme, the duty of rich men to endow the museum. His eyes watchful and intense, he had those qualities that make a first-rate lawyer, the special awareness and respect for his audience, be it judge, jury or dinner guests, and the carefully calibrated flow of persuasive language that could turn his listeners with their full assent, to his purpose.

Speaking to a throng studded with more millionaires per square foot than an Astor reception, Choate reminded his listeners:

Probably no age and no city has ever seen such gigantic fortunes accumulated out of nothing as have been piled up here within the last five years. They have been made in this city and out of this toiling people. Now all these lucky citizens owe something to the city and to the people out of whom they have made their millions. Their fortunes are not all their own; and where better than here can they pay their debt of gratitude? These trustees are too proud to beg a dollar, but they freely proffer their services in relieving these distended and apoplectic pockets. Think of it, ye millionaires of many markets, what glory may yet be yours, if you only listen to our advice to convert pork into porcelain, grain and produce into priceless pottery, the rude ores of commerce into sculptured marble, and railroad shares and mining stock—things which perish without the using and which in the next financial panic shall surely shrivel like parched scrolls—into the gloried canvases of the world's masters, that shall adorn these walls for centuries. The rage of Wall Street is to hunt the philosopher's stone, to convert all baser things into gold, which is but dross; but ours is the higher ambition, to convert your useless gold into things of living beauty that shall be a joy to a whole people for a thousand years.[10]

Then the blow came.

Soon after the opening a well-esteemed dealer in ancient coins and antiquities challenged the validity of some of the Cesnola collection.

Gaston L. Feuardent, a third-generation antiquarian, heir to the prime numismatic house of the old world, hit out publicly for the first time at "certain deceptive alterations and unintelligent restorations of some of the antiquities of the Cesnola collection."

His chief target was a tiny statuette.[11] He maintained it had been changed from the Elpis or Hope of the Greeks, a fairly common figure, to the rarer—and considerably more valuable—Aphrodite or Venus. Actually, Golgos was a principal site in Cyprus for the worship of Aphrodite.

Feuardent, who ran the New York branch of the Rollin & Feuardent numismatic firm of Paris and, of course, London, wrote his article for the August 1880 issue of the popular *Art Amateur, A Monthly Devoted to the Cultivation of Art in the Household*. He minced no words: "To endeavor to increase interest in a collection by deceptive alterations or restorations can only be called a miscalculation, a profanation or a fraud." The change had been accomplished, according to Feuardent, by the addition of a mirror, about the size of a nickel, in the left hand of the figure. This, and what he called other changes in other statues were attributed to craftsmen working "under the supervision of General di Cesnola himself." Feuardent gave three reasons for identifying the figure as that of Hope:

She was walking. She was holding up her garments with her left hand so as not to impede her progress. And, with the other hand, she was holding a flower. "These three actions combined were chosen by the ancients," Feuardent wrote, "to indicate Hope, sister of Sleep who suspends our griefs and of Death who terminates our suffering. From the earliest times Hope was represented as holding up her gown and 'passing by,' in order to show that she is an elusive being, and always escapes when one thinks of laying hands on her." The flower in her hand was a lotus, symbol of the Nile, itself the emblem of abundance in an unproductive land.

To change her to a little Venus, by placing a mirror in the hand that held up her gown, served only to make it "become a puzzle to future antiquarians," said Feuardent. Even more important for archaeologists, it robbed the figure of its basic function, that of revealing the customs and manners of the people who made it. "Antiquities," he observed, "must be absolutely trustworthy in the information they give."

The man who brought the charge was then thirty-seven years old. He had been in America since 1871 and had frequently made the journey between the New York and London offices. After establishing himself in a three-story building at 30 Lafayette Place, he had set about making a place for himself in the professional world of art dealers and the private community of leisured and wealthy men interested in antiquities. Trained by his father, Felix, in the Parisian headquarters that served the Louvre, Gaston had much to offer. Early in his stay in New York, he was elected a member of the American Numismatic and Archaeological Society in New York.[12]

He was a regular speaker at the group's meetings at Mott Memorial Hall in lower Madison Avenue, and respected for his knowledge and his careful presentations.

Contact between the Frenchman and Cesnola stretched back to 1867, when Cesnola first sent some antiquities to the firm's Paris office. The General had objected later to Feuardent's commissions, and felt that the dealer had been lax in failing to display his objects in London before he went there and arranged the exhibition himself.

For his own part, Feuardent had viewed Cesnola's character with some uneasiness which he showed in double-checking with the Hermitage. He had sought to compare pictures in the Russian museum's Cesnola catalogue with photos made by its curator and others made by Cesnola. Then, on July 8, 1871, Feuardent had sold to the British Museum five small Cesnola antiquities. The sale, which Cesnola never mentioned, amounted to £14 or $70.[13] It was the last time Rollin & Feuardent acted as agent for the collector.[14]

Thus, the August murmur nine years later was no new plaint. In fact, it suggests that the result of Feuardent's check in the summer of 1871 led him to ease his sales talk to the British Museum and was also the primary reason for his stated relief in *Art Amateur* of August 1880 concerning the British Museum's decision to pass up buying the General's exhibition hall full of Cyprian statues and artifacts. The institution, he wrote, followed the example of other European museums which were "quite unanimous in declining to purchase."

The Russian investigation was not Feuardent's only research. Two years earlier, in 1878 he had specifically questioned the "Little Venus" as well as another Cesnola statue, "The Sacrificer," a large limestone figure that holds an animal's head in its left hand.[15] Feuardent had spoken before the Numismatic Society when Cesnola's book on Cyprus appeared in New York that year, praising it as a "ray piercing through the dark history of Cyprus." But he was forthright in questioning Cesnola's designation of the statuette as "probably of Venus, Egyptian in character."

Now, just after the opening of the permanent museum, with Cesnola newly chosen as Director, the Frenchman put his charge against the statuette and six other Cesnola pieces before the general public for the first time.

His timing was miserable.

It seemed he realized this. He made it quite clear that he originally had no intention whatever of making the case public. He had gone to the museum, seen the statuette in a closed glass case, found that it was the "victim of a barbarous anachronism," and simply felt it was "no more than right that the authorities of the museum should be made aware of what was going on."[16]

So, when he met A.D. Savage, Cesnola's assistant, he told him the mirror had been added. Savage simply didn't believe him. "But as his opinion was quite indifferent to me," Feuardent wrote, "and I was satisfied with the accomplishment of a duty, I dismissed the whole affair from my mind."

It was Cesnola himself who pushed the quarrel toward public view. In a letter to Feuardent on May 19, 1880, Cesnola wrote that if the charge had been reported to him correctly, it was one "against the officers and employees of this Museum" and was "of such a serious character that I must have a most thorough investigation of it."[17] He adroitly made the accusation one against the entire museum and all its trustees and workers.

Feuardent retorted that he had seen the statuette in the 14th Street museum without the mirror and in the Central Park museum with it. Savage then admitted a change in the little figure, saying that it had needed cleaning and that the mirror showed up in the process. The figure had needed no cleaning, Feuardent held, pointing to the clear pictures in Doell's catalogue and in Cesnola's own book. He repeated his charge: "the antiquity of the mirror dates from the year A.D. 1879."[18]

In making his charge public, Feuardent tried in vain to keep it directed against Cesnola alone. That did not work.

Henry Gurdon Marquand, the side-whiskered acting president of the museum, got off a letter August 3 to the editor of the New-York *Times*, saying, "the General . . . was quite ill with acute rheumatism . . . and was trying the baths in Richfield Springs" Virginia but had telegraphed him to "deny *in toto* the slanderous assaults of the dealer." The gentlemen in charge of the affairs of the museum had decided that "the matter will not be allowed to rest in generalities but will be thoroughly treated in every detail by the Director of the Museum as soon as he returns to the city." It was not only Cesnola's plan but that of the board of trustees, then, to have Cesnola himself investigate the charges made against him.

Only two trustees were in town at the time the article appeared.

Both telegraphed Cesnola to "keep quiet." It was like asking a river not to flow.

Through a special correspondent, the New York *Post* obtained a long interview with Cesnola in Virginia. In it the General contended that all Feuardent knew about archaeology he had acquired while "cleaning old coins in the back room of an antiquity shop in Paris." The director denied all the accusations with the offer to have the little Venus soaked for a year to prove the mirror had not been recently added. As for the charge of concocting whole statues from unrelated parts, Cesnola said this was entirely false. He had an odd way of proving it. Everyone who had seen his collection in Larnaca, he said, had seen the mass of fragments that littered the two courtyards of his consulate and on his second tour of duty there, from 1873 to 1876, he had "selected from this mass the missing parts belonging to the statues already in New York." He had photographs of the incomplete statues in New York and "nothing was necessary but the selection of the pieces which evidently belonged to and which exactly fitted the original and mutilated objects."[19]

It was simply "ludicrous" for a "mere dealer" to attack him "when the best archaeologists of both hemisphere consider the discoverer himself the most competent restorer."[20] Feuardent was making the charges, Cesnola maintained, because he was a disappointed dealer whose offerings the Metropolitan had refused.

Feuardent, in a letter published in the New-York *Times*, countered by saying that, to him, Cesnola was the one who was really the "dealer." He had been an effective one at that, Feuardent noted ruefully, recalling that Cesnola had sold the collection of 35,573 objects to the museum and had received $121,866.95, with $17,000 still owed him. It was the largest group of Cyprian antiquities ever gathered by one collector. But of the vast horde, only about 200 are still on exhibition.

To a *Times* reporter, the French dealer dated the figurine as probably from 600 B.C. and the mirror as "a brand new thing."[21]

Suppose you had an antique Japanese statuette of the tenth century B.C., the antiquarian suggested, and under its arm what did you find but an English umbrella: "Would you not doubt the authenticity of the English umbrella?" The "little Venus" mirror was like no antique mirror he had ever seen. Its handle was just like a modern lady's brush. And it wasn't even very well done.

Feuardent quoted one of the museum's repairers, Charles Balliard, who had formerly been a repairer of musical boxes at Tiffany & Co., as saying Feuardent had complimented him on his work of carving the mirror. Not so, Feuardent snapped. It was a "most slovenly" job.[22]

By this time the dispute was avidly reported in the public press and was followed in great detail for the next three years. Rumblings of the storm have, in fact, echoed down the decades. In a rough sort of way, the papers took sides with the New York *Daily Tribune* and the Evening *Post,* pro-Cesnola, the *Times* and *Art Amateur,* pro-Feuardent.

When Cesnola returned to New York in late August, he wrote Johnston that he felt "rather worse" after his sulphur baths, probably because of the "dastardly attack by the French Jew dealer in an obscure monthly paper edited by a Jew."[23]

The director sent a letter to the *Tribune* calling the charges malicious and completely without foundation. A full investigation would be conducted. Wrapping his cause in the protective mantle of the museum, he said such an inquiry was due "not only to me but to the institution they (the trustees) represent and to the public." Cesnola expected the trustees themselves to make the study. He welcomed it. "Their standing in this community is such that when the result of their investigation is made public, it will, I hope, put an end to such attacks whether made from ignorance, malice or from interested motives."[24] He had the ear of the *Tribune* and was filling it with some charges of his own against the French dealer.

Cesnola then apparently set up rigid controls over the copying of objects in the Cesnola collection. One unlucky offender turned out to be the artist Wyatt Eaton, a teacher at Cooper Union and a founder of the American Society of Artists. Eaton said he was "ejected from the Metropolitan Museum of Art with unwarrantable rudeness" for making a sketch. The September *Art Amateur* reported the scuffle and the Metropolitan's subsequent apology. To the magazine it was apparent that the Metropolitan was enforcing its rules against copying "because of the Feuardent-Cesnola dispute."

No doubt about it: another artist, unfamed, unnamed but similarly ejected, reported to *Art Amateur* this conversation in the museum:

Artist: "Is there any objection to making sketches of things in the Cesnola collection?"

Savage: "Mr. Cesnola doesn't wish any sketches made in the interest of Feuardent. For any other purpose, we would be glad to have them made." Savage, obviously, was the arbiter of what was in the copier's mind. The artist found himself out on Fifth Avenue.

"Can it be," the editors asked, "that there are other Cyprian statuettes which the General might find it disagreeable for Mr. Feuardent to scrutinize too closely?"[25]

The same issue of *Art Amateur* carried a replay of Feuardent's charges, stated in a letter to the editor. In this letter, the Frenchman gave a detailed, chronological accounting of the case, including Cesnola's explanation, backed by the repairer Balliard, that the mirror had become apparent when the statuette was washed.

Feuardent even added a new accusation: false patina on some Cesnola bronzes. This patina had been applied after they were cleaned, "so although they may look pretty to the public with their modern green color, to the archaeologist they appear at first sight to be forgeries." To say the least, he ended, "it is curious for a museum to try to make antiques appear as if they were imitations."

The magazine pleaded for a truly disinterested inquiry by persons "outside the board" of the museum. It said the city, having spent $60,000 to prepare the exhibition hall for the Cesnola show, should be represented. To call Feuardent "a mere dealer" and Cesnola "the director," the magazine insisted, was beside the point.

"General di Cesnola either had tampered with the antiquities he has sold the Museum or he has not done so." The question of fact should be determined "by disinterested experts." Cesnola wanted to sue Feuardent, but Choate would have nothing to do with such a suit.[26]

The panel named to investigate the charges was such that Feuardent at first refused to appear before it. The Board of Trustees appointed three men and these chose two others.[27] Heading the committee was Frederick Augustus Porter Barnard, seventy-one years old, president of Columbia College for the previous sixteen years, and a leader in civic affairs. Although he had shared the platform with Cesnola at the museum's opening, he was willing to have Feuardent choose one panel member. But he was overruled.[28]

Two trustees sat on the inquiry board. Prime, the man who had worked to get Cesnola his directorship and a boon friend of the General, and John Quincy Adams Ward, a sculptor who had sculpted the figure of Horace Greeley of the *Tribune*, the paper that regularly backed Cesnola. A second lawyer on the panel was a famed judge, Charles Patrick Daly, Chief Justice of the Court of Common Pleas since 1871 and president of the American Geographical and Statistical Society. Sixty-four years old, he had run away to sea at thirteen and had kept a lifelong interest in geography from his seafaring days. To some he was an enigma. He was a quiet listener on the Common Pleas bench but on the Appellate Court he was garrulous to the point of blocking argument. He wore a full, soft beard and no mustache.

A minister, Roswell Dwight Hitchcock, D.D., president of the Union Theological Seminary, sixty-three years old, a man descended from the same family as Hiram Hitchcock, took fifth position.

It was a most distinguished panel. Feuardent, however, felt it was not objective enough. On December 19, 1880, the *Times* backed him in his plea for a member of his own choosing. The panel were superlative men, indeed, the paper observed, but not a single one was qualified to pass on the key question: the value of the collection. They were lawyers, a business man, a contemporary artist and an educator.

"This, at least, we are sure of, that no public or private collector in Europe would invest one dollar on the strength of their opinion in these respects, highly valued as it might be on some others."

"Nor have they any reputation in this country, public, or, we believe, even private, as experts on archaeological art. And these are men who are called upon to sit in judgment upon an archaeological art question, on charges made by an expert of long training, wide experience, and high reputation. It is safe to say that in no other country in the world would such a question have been submitted to such a committee by a body of the respectability of the Metropolitan Museum. . . . The Trustees of the Metropolitan Museum may rest assured that, whatever may be the actual state of their Cyprian collection, the verdict of their committee will add little to its reputation for authenticity. On such a subject, the opinion of one accomplished expert is worth a hundred times that of a hundred doctors of law who are not experts."[29]

Ten days later, the *Tribune* took the opposite tack. "If these gentlemen were less highly esteemed in this community than they are, this would still seem to be a justly constituted tribunal." It called Feuardent's appeal for a representative "absurd."[30]

The paper told Feuardent at the end of December that to question the board's impartiality in advance "is to acknowledge fear of it." This was in response to Feuardent's suggestion that Frederick Law Olmstead be given a chance to set up an impartial committee with no reference to either the museum or the French dealer.

Feuardent was ignoring both *Art Amateur* and the *Times*. These papers recommended archaeological experts for the case, but Feuardent only wanted men appointed by someone outside the museum.

The appointed panel moved briskly ahead. It reduced Feuardent's charges to a total of six lines for each object, sat around a table with two scrap books (which have since disappeared) and examined each piece minutely for the accuracy of the antiquarian's complaints.[31]. As reported in the *Times* December 12, 1880, a typical examination went something like this:

The charge was read: Statue No. 40, the figure of a man, found without a head or left forearm, had been fitted with the head of a child; the neck was modern.

The figure went up on the table. All took a good look. It was "mopped and scraped." Ward, the sculptor, and thus the man with the most experience in examining physiognomy, differed with the charge. To him the head was a mature one. In fact, he remarked, it had a slight double chin and a grown-up's teeth.

So it went.

As the study continued, the *Tribune* the next day had a more pleasant topic to report. The Consul of Italy in New York, Count Marefoselio, had delivered to General Cesnola a package sealed with the Royal Arms of Italy. In it was a parchment announcing that the King of Italy had conferred on "Count Louis Palma di Cesnola the

Royal Order and rank of Commander of the Crown of Italy." With
it came the Cross of Commander in the unit, one similar to France's
Legion of Honor.

During the first week of the New Year the committee, lacking
the observant Ward, met at Prime's home at 38 East 23rd Street.
Cesnola appeared to answer the charges. He showed himself as an
attacker who swooped on his opponent with the screaming, sweaty
thrust of a cavalry charge.

The complaints against him, he told the committee, showed a
"manifest display of ignorance in regard to ... ordinary archaeological facts and that the accuser was thoroughly dishonest, ignorant and
reckless." The committee, the General predicted, "would dismiss his
[Feuardent's] archaeology as charlatanism."

He had never made a "single restoration of any object or part of
any object in stone," but, "in the whole collection of thousands of
objects" there were only two instances, made by no less capable
hands than the British Museum, of restorations.[32] Obviously, he had
another definition for the joining parts of statues in his two courtyards in Larnaca with parts of other statues in New York.

Cesnola took a cavalier attitude toward Feuardent's charges of
the added mirror. "It would be a waste of time to review the extraordinary statements of the accuser."[33] He went on, however, to a fairly
full review. He repeated his contention that the mirror was revealed
after prolonged baths in 1879. This was, of course, after both sales,
and he had no reason to change the figure from Hope to Venus since
he already had "innumerable evidence of the worship of Venus at
Golgos."[34] As for the charge of a false patina, he simply denied it.

Repairs were another matter, Cesnola testified. He personally
superintended all of these and, in addition, he "kept pieces of each
statue separate from the moment of discovery and matched them
himself."[35]

He was so conscientious that he had "now in the Museum a ton
of fragments that have not been used because of his inability to
ascertain exactly where they belong. A lot more (had been) left behind in Cyprus."[36]

The heavy volume of broken arms and legs of his Cyprian statues
he blamed on native camels in Cyprus. They had a bad habit, he

explained, "of laying down without warning."

On the Sunday following this account, January 9, 1881, the
World carried a long story of Cesnola's report to the museum's executive committee the previous October. In it, Cesnola labeled Feuardent's bill "exorbitant," an adjective that touched the dealer on a
professionally sensitive node and later caused him to charge Cesnola
with libel. The resultant law suit was a sensation of the 1880s.

All this squabbling was getting thorough coverage by the many
New York newspapers. Hoe, the trustee who was as touchy as Cesnola himself, objected to the publicity. He threatened to move at an
executive committee meeting that the investigating panel be discharged.

Cesnola exploded. The mere idea revived his italics and mis-
spelling. Such a step would be "an *insult.*" His two years with the
Museum had cost him much in "labor, health & anxiety of mind." He
had gathered "only a harvest of *thorns* but no roses; and I am well
sick of it . . . In this dastardly attack upon me I have the simpathy and
goodwill of all the educated and fair minded persons of the country
—I ought to have *earned* that of the Trustees *by this time.*"[37]

Again, as he had when there was some question about his collection after the second sale, Cesnola gave the museum an ultimatum.
A true Canavesean, he required complete fealty. If he lacked the
Trustees' backing, he would resign immediately. The committee continued its hearings.

Feuardent finally appeared before it. Cooly, the dealer presented his case and observed that his charges raised questions of
veracity of himself, Cesnola and Balliard. The panel would have to
decide who was telling the truth.

It did so with dispatch. At the end of January 1881 the committee exonerated Cesnola completely. He had simply reunited "such
original fragments as existed and could be identified." Far from seeing that Cesnola had done any wrong, the five wished, in fact, that
he had done more of the same.

"We find in the store-rooms of the Museum a mass of fragments
which probably belong to objects exhibited in imperfect condition.
The fact appears before us that every fragment of a statue found at
Golgos was carefully preserved and that there now remains in Cy-

prus a large collection of such fragments which if brought to New York would possibly supply the original bodies of all the numerous heads now exhibited, coming from that spot."[38] In its premise about Golgos, the panel was incorrect since Cesnola kept heads more easily sold, and reburied bodies, heavy and expensive to ship.

The *Tribune* then said in an editorial what it had been hinting at all along.

Cesnola was known in New-York as an Italian nobleman who had abandoned his brilliant position at home to seek the distinction of an American citizen, who had worn the uniform of his adopted country and periled his life in her defense.

Feuardent was known as an enterprising son of a Hebrew dealer in antiquities, who had wished to sell certain objects to the Museum, and for whom a great pother had been raised because the Museum, though not without funds, had not hastened to buy his wares and pay him the price he asked. In short, Mr. Feuardent ... caused a suspicion that his real object was to advertize himself and his wares.

The *Tribune* called the charges "each and all without foundation ... vulgar in their origin and discreditable in the manner in which they were pushed."[39]

The museum's hearing, then, was over and done with and would never again be reopened. The little Venus remains on view at the Metropolitan as do about forty of the larger statues from Golgos.

Officially, the Board issued a resolution of its Trustees on February 21. They had always "known the falsehood of the published charges and have never ceased to entertain the highest confidence in his [Cesnola's] devotion and faithfulness to the interests, not alone of the museum, but of truth and scholarship and history."[40]

From *Art Amateur*, which had started the controversy, came a professional look at the Cesnola clearance. The magazine recalled it had suggested the previous summer that the Hope-Venus be sent to the British Museum or the Louvre when John Taylor Johnston was in Paris. Then, experts whose opinions would have been objective could have ruled on the charges. But, the magazine said, "the truth in the matter apparently isn't what the trustees have desired to arrive at."[41]

Fourteen

With a population of more than a million people, New York now was acquiring the look and accoutrements of a great modern metropolis. Telegraph wires draped Broadway. The first telephone exchange which had just opened had 252 subscribers who paid $60 a year for the service. As inducement, they had a one-month free-trial period. Thomas Edison had established his Edison Electric Light Co. in a small office at 65 Fifth Avenue and had won his first municipal client, Detroit.

Though expanded, the elevated railroads no longer frightened the horses. But the streets, considered the worst paved in the world, were as big a problem as ever. One small stretch, a single block in Fifth Avenue, was the scene of a three-year test of a new substance, asphalt, which was supposed to be a "noiseless pavement."

The first Catholic mayor had been elected and was serving without giving public money to Church schools. Jews were coming in even larger numbers to the Lower East Side, many of them from Russia where the reactionary Alexander III had persecuted them so severely that tens of thousands emigrated.

At Broadway and 30th Street, the famous stock company, Daly's

Theater, had begun its twenty years of Shakespearean presentations and the renowned Sarah Bernhardt made her American debut in New York on a cold November night in 1880. Simple pleasures persisted. Though many of the little ponds in the parks had been filled in, decreasing that enjoyment, others took its place. There was now a huge and popular toboggan slide at the northern end of Central Park. And, even more important to the general public, the bicycle had just been invented. Agreeably, it came just as the road overlooking the majestic Hudson River, Riverside Drive, was completed.

Women were wearing their hair in a "Marie Antoinette wave," admiring the low-priced India shawls at Arnold, Constable & Co., and, when spring came, buying North Carolina shad roe at twenty cents a pound. Bluepoint oysters sold for seventy-five cents a hundred.

Within their dark, massive homes the well-to-do amused themselves with games. One that was the rage of the town in 1881 was called "The Fifteen Puzzle." Players spent hours playing with a box of fifteen numbered blocks, trying to move them into consecutive order in an even number of moves.

Feuardent, having failed in his serious, straight-forward attack on Cesnola's countless finds, used another method to alert the placid leaders of Manhattan against fraudulent constructions. He had issued one card showing the statue of a priest with and without his right forearm and flat dish or patera. Cesnola was contemptuous. He told a reporter: "Now, sir, Mr. Feuardent may deluge this country with these cards but they won't do him any good."[1]

Yet people and papers began to take sides all over again.

Art Amateur held to its position. In April 1881, it ran a charge by Charles Osborne of Tiffany & Co. that the once hidden mirror of the little Venus had been rounded at its end so that it was then much more like an antique than before. The statue had been in Cesnola's possession throughout the panel's inquiry since "evidently the trustees supposed him incapable of doing anything to mislead them."

In May, Feuardent issued his second card. It suggested fifteen steps for the leisured to play at being archaeologists by making "A Composite Statue."

The first step was to cut off the head of the statue of a man, No. 213 in the Metropolitan's Cesnola catalogue, "place it in front of the trunk and compare the proportions of the two pieces." Feuardent listed fifteen such comparisons, then gave his "solution: the head belongs to a larger statue, the trunk belongs to another statue, that of an archer in a kneeling position; the lower part of the body belongs to still another statue, a standing figure."

At least one-third of the Cyprian statues in the museum, he asserted, had undergone such shifting changes.

Gradually, a group rallied to Feuardent's side. One of the first was the poet Clarence Chatham Cook, then fifty-three years old, a New Englander, a Harvard man and once editor of "The New Path," a pre-Raphaelite journal. In 1881 Cook, a critic who had made many enemies among contemporary American artists, printed a flyer on the Sacrificer, "Migrations and Transformations of a Statue in the Metropolitan Museum of Art of New York, numbered 39 in the Catalogue."

It showed the statue in five different versions: with a head on, with a head off, with one pair of feet, with a different pair, and with its base in various states.

The pamphlet attributed the head to Hitchcock's description in *Harper's*, the absence of the feet and base to the *Museum's Guide to the Cesnola Collection* of 1876, a base different from that pictured by Doell and, finally, a third, and new base. The charges against the Cesnola statues were appearing before the public in a very public way. Cook was convinced the statues were patched together in Cyprus and that the General had been duped by Cyprians, "adroit manufacturers of antiquities." Golgos, Cook felt, was an invention to promote sales. To most of the trustees, the best course seemed not to dignify the new attack by any reaction. Others were not so reticent. Barnard, at Columbia, wrote the sculptor Ward that Cook's charges were "much graver than those already dealt with."[2] They were, in fact, simply Cook's version of Feuardent's charges. Whomever they issued from, they enraged Prime. He wrote Johnston that he thought that the only "effectual answer . . . was a libel suit by Cesnola."[3]

Now in full pursuit of the director, Feuardent sent a letter to the editor of the *Times*, reprinted in *Art Amateur* with drawings, in which he gave a satirical lesson in "Phoenician-Italian Art Cookery." It was a "Receipt for Making an Antique Helmeted Bearded Female Figure," the Metropolitan Museum of Art's No. 23; Doell's No. 1 and No. 21 in the record of Sidney Colvin, an English commentator."

This was the male-female figure that Cesnola said in his book[4] "might represent" Venus herself. An English critic, W. Watkiss Lloyd, in his review of *Cyprus* which appeared in London's *Quarterly Magazine* in July 1878, recalled that "such a vagary" was not limited to Cyprus, that, on occasion, Aristophanes gave the Greek goddess of beauty's name the masculine ending of Aphroditos, and he quoted Rome's greatest lyric poet, Catullus, as calling the Cyprian goddess *duplex*.

Indeed, a close look at the well-padded Cyprian statues standing rather stiffly, man and woman a good deal alike, in the long corridor between the Ionic column and the Roman sculpture room in the Metropolitan presents a good case for the idea that the ancient Cyprians were the first society to arrive at the "unisex" concept.

Feuardent suggested that the "cook" pick out a body of stone of "semi-colossal size in order to fully impress the public." It should be unmistakably that of a female. "You are particular, therefore, that the development of the breast shall be prominent and that the garment falling in a double fold ... shall only cover one side of the chest, thus leaving one bosom bare."

Three long tresses fall on each side of the chest. "The next thing for you is to procure an unmistakable male head. In this you select one with a very full and curly beard and covered with a helmet." The hair that falls on the neck is to be "carved into tresses to meet the tresses on the female figure. Should you wish to connect your now bisexual statue with the worship of some divinity—Aphrodite, for instance—you add to your figure a right hand holding a cup and a left hand holding a dove. As the shape of the dove is not of great importance, you may change the bird at will. (See photographs of the Cesnola collection taken in London and the Statue No. 23 as it is now.)

"Break off a finger if it's too coarse, garnish with ornaments, then publish your unique work as follows:" and Feuardent quoted from Cesnola's book that such a statue "might represent the goddess herself." This is the statue that the museum now labels in a noncommittal manner as "A Votary."

Venus, Feuardent went on in his pamphlet, was depicted at Amathus in Cyprus as bearded and a statue in such exotic form "will be known over all the world and savants will write on it in all languages. You will have become famous and even the qualification of an 'archaeologist' will be accorded to you by a few and you can give yourself what titles you please. . . ."

After the trustees elected what a New York paper called "a Cesnola ticket" of officers on May 9, Cesnola reported to a newspaper man that Feuardent's charges were not even discussed.[5]

Things were not, however, moving along serenely. The next week Prime wrote Johnston that the articles in the *Times* were "worrying" Cesnola to the point where Prime felt the General "should go away from New York and newspapers for a month or two." The director was depressed, and these two leaders of the board moved to protect him.[6] They arranged for him to go to take a trip to Europe.

What was bothering Cesnola may well have been an editorial in the *Times* two days before Prime's suggestion to Johnston. The paper called for a careful investigation of Feuardent's charges. The trustees must begin to realize that their policy of silent contempt of Feuardent was inadequate. "If accepted as proved, or, what amounts to the same thing in this case, passed without challenge, it must place Di Cesnola in the category of imposters, and must discredit every enterprise with which he is prominently identified. If it be capable of disproof, it should subject its author to prosecution in the courts. One or other of these alternatives the Trustees and their Director must accept. The testimony against the honor of the methods pursued in the Museum is cumulative, convincing, apparently unanswerable. . . ."[7]

A few days later, Cesnola was home, ill. He wrote Johnston he would leave "the *Times* matter" in his hands.[8] Ten days later, on Sunday, May 29, 1881, the *Times* reprinted Feuardent's article on the bearded Venus, complete with pictures.

The effect, indeed, was becoming cumulative. In its June issue the *Art Amateur* wondered publicly "how long will the trustees of the Metropolitan Museum consent to pull the chestnuts out of the fire for their disingenuous director?" Choate, apparently, was still advising against a libel suit by Cesnola or the Museum. Neither took action. Feuardent did. Backed, finally, by the American Numismatic and Archaeological Society, he sued Cesnola for libel and defamation.

The action was forced upon him by the trustees failure to institute a "real investigation," Feuardent told the *Times*. No notice at all had been taken of a pamphlet in which he contrasted in adjoining columns Cesnola's statements to the board and his contradictory and earlier letters to the dealer. Feuardent had no wish "to press a legal investigation, if the Trustees would set an unbiased inquiry on foot and sift the matter thoroughly."[9] Now he was convinced there was no hope of that so he set the suit in motion.

Cesnola, due to sail for Europe that same day, met the issue with outward equanimity. He told a *Times* reporter the suit would not interfere in the least with his travel plans. His attorneys would handle the matter in his absence. Chief of these was Choate, the partner at law of the Secretary of State of the United States. He was soon himself to be American ambassador at the Court of St. James's.

Cesnola then went off on a four-month visit to Europe, visiting England, Germany and his cherished homeland, Italy. There King Humbert, who would give him a gold medal at the end of 1881 for his "services to science and art," told the Director he often passed the ruins of the Castle of Cesnola on his way to hunt in the Val d'Aosta. The king felt that the General "had made the little place quite famous."[10]

When his trip was over, Cesnola, his spirits healed, reveled in the scene at the museum in early November, a reception for the showing of the institution's latest acquisitions. The Jarves and Charvet glass shared attention with the antique gems of the Reverend C. W. King of England. Harvest of a lifelong search, these had been bought from the aging Trinity College minister by Feuardent. Johnston had not hesitated to purchase them from this source before donating them to the museum.[11]

The Feuardent-Cesnola lawsuit, under the guiding hand of Choate, was transferred from the New York Superior Court to the United States District Court on the ground that Feuardent was an alien. The

Times recognized that the switch would bring a lengthy delay. The federal court was crowded with cases; its new common law term would not take place until April 1882. Even after that, there would be delay. The newspaper felt the move one of "sharp practice and clever dodge."[12]

It would not be until the end of October 1883, actually, that the case, by then one of the great diversions of the decade, would open in the baroque federal building in City Hall Park. Its importance was lessened also by the generosity of wealthy New Yorkers to the museum. The gifts were rapidly overshadowing the Cesnola collection.

Then, in the Spring of 1882, the Cesnola finds became a spectacle.

Faced with constant, ever increasing criticism, the museum, which had declined to put the case before independent, archaeological experts, let the public judge each of two specifically accused statues. The museum completely reversed its former stand that Feuardent's charges were beneath attention. It called on sculptors, scholars, any member of the general public to make whatever tests they chose in determining, each for himself, the truth or falsity of the accusations.

It was an unrestricted, public scrutiny, unprecedented in the art world, one that showed how defensive some of the trustees had become.

Cook, with Feuardent as publisher, had now issued a second pamphlet combining the charge against the Sacrificer with another against a large statue called Aphrodite and Eros.[13] Cook quoted Feuardent as saying the Aphrodite (this one wholly feminine) was "a fraudulent patchwork of unrelated parts," and, furthermore, that it was not found at Golgos to which Cesnola had attributed it. Doell, the real authority who had seen Cesnola's first collection in Cyprus had never seen the temple at Golgos and referred to it in his *catalogue raisonné* as the "so-called Temple of Golgos." By the time Doell arrived the excavations had been filled in and the ground leveled. (Cesnola always held that his permit to dig in Cyprus called for him to leave the ground as he found it, level.)

Instead of being shown in London where some experts, sophisticated in archaeology, could have examined it, The Aphrodite had been sent direct from Cyprus to America. There, as Cesnola told Cook earlier, "nobody knows anything or cares anything about antiquities. They would never have bought my collection if they had not thought the British Museum was dying to get it."[14] It was Cesnola's belief in American ignorance and indifference, Cook declared, that led him to be less than meticulous in handling his finds.

Before a month was out, the museum's Executive Committee ordered the two statues, the Sacrificer and the Aphrodite, taken out of their glass cases and set up, unprotected, in the center of the Grand Hall.[15] They were placed where "ample light" would expose them and where they could be approached and examined on all sides."

The charges against them were blazoned on cards set up before them. The labels also stated categorically that the charges were false.[16]

Then the public and the experts were summoned. "Members of the Museum, the public and especially Editors of Public Journals, Sculptors, Workers in Stone, Scholars and all persons interested in the truthfulness of archaeological objects," were advised "to make the most careful examination of the Statues."[17]

They did just that.

It was a sensation.

In the same year that Oscar Wilde astonished New York society with his flowing hair and tight shining black doeskin trousers, the two mute statues under the metal arches at the Metropolitan attracted many thousands in a single fortnight.[18]

People came alone and in groups, sculptors, "gentlemen of intelligence," the knowing, the curious and the ignorant. Some brought chisels and hammered out small bits to be examined under microscopes. Some washed the stones with caustic potash and with other solutions to uncover suspected joining seams.

A group of architectural sculptors gave the two statues a complete going-over. Robert Ellin and three assistants had official approval beforehand to do as they "pleased so that the truth be ascertained."[19]

Aphrodite went under the knives and chisels first. The men

declared her to be of one piece with her original head replaced. Then one of the milling onlookers, who said he had talked to Feuardent, said that the seam across the curls at the nape of the head was a purposely misleading one and that, actually, the real joint was below, hidden under some newly carved hair. The sculptors chiseled a bit more. They found no such hidden seam. Aphrodite, they pronounced, was all Venus and a pillar of propriety. She had merely lost her head at one point, and Cesnola had replaced it.

They gave the same bill of health to the headless Sacrificer. It was true that at one time he had not had feet. But, they ruled, those attached to the statue now were the precise ones the original sculptor had provided. They were merely strengthened by a new base.

The general, professional approval of the statues stood, also, on reports from the prominent sculptors, John Rogers, Daniel French and Charles Calverley. Both Rogers and Launt Thompson, a sculptor of renown, cut, washed and filed the statues.[20]

Augustus St. Gaudens, whose *Farragut* now stood in Madison Square Park, made his own study. When he was through, he was uncertain whether each was a "patchwork" or not. To Prime, this attitude proved only that the sculptor did not want "to tangle with the *Times*."[21]

The fact was that St. Gaudens' heart went out to the pair of statues. He felt very definite about all those sculptors doing all that chiseling and filing, and he wrote Prime that he "disapproved" of those who were sawing off slices of drapery from the ancient Aphrodite.[22] He really thought a third investigation should be set up, one in which both sides, the Museum-Cesnola and Cook-Feuardent, should be represented. It was the old cry for an unbiased inquiry.

But, by this time papers as far apart as the Springfield, Massachusetts *Republican*, and the local *Il Progresso-Americano*, the latter calling the director "Il nostro illustre e benemerito compatriota generale di Cesnola," were agreeing that the clear implication of the sculptors' findings was that the charges were unfounded and had, indeed, been thoroughly squelched.[23]

But that was not so.

Art Amateur in May 1882 called for the museum to get the Feuardent suit heard quickly and thus test whether the $140,000

Cesnola received for the two collections was money well spent. The *Times* now took the leading trustees to task. These reputable citizens of "ample wealth and high social position," seemed to "deliberately sustain falsehood ... and to conceal the fact of their own deception by resisting all attempts to secure a fair investigation" of the charges "for which the Director of the Museum is responsible."[24]

Apparently alone of the metropolitan press, the *Times* had printed letters from A. D. Savage, an assistant to Cesnola who had resigned the previous November. Savage said he had quit when Cesnola had refused to reveal restorations that two elderly janitors, veterans of the 14th Street museum, had exposed during the General's absence in Europe. Instead, the General, accusing them of "unfaithfulness to the Museum" by not divulging their discovery only to him, had fired the pair. Savage had later given the *Times* a list of sixteen restorations, most of them plaster noses. They were all archaic Greek in form, which made it next to impossible to tell if the statues they adorned were of Greek or Phoenician (Semite) style.

In examining the case, the paper called the first investigation one-sided and the second "contemptible" by the use of invited testimony from friendly sculptors and the suppression of unfriendly verdicts.

In an editorial on May 18, 1882, the *Times* took note of a new mix-up. Two sculptors who had exonerated the two statues had declared other statues, admittedly restored (apparently those on the Savage list) showed no signs of having been tampered with. The editorial recommendation was that Feuardent and Cesnola face each other with professional archaeologists as judges.

No such sane course ensued.

Feuardent's backer, the American Numismatical and Archaeological Society, checked out the financial dealings he had had with Cesnola. It went to his banker in London, Frederick Burt & Co., to obtain his financial report of late 1872. This showed that Cesnola had been repaid $6,000 of the $13,000 the firm received for handling his antiquities. At its annual meeting in 1882, the Society declared the report "publicly vindicated Feuardent's reputation for honesty."[25]

Cesnola, as he had once precipitated the original public argument over the little Venus, again provoked disclosure of a judgment antagonistic to himself. At the end of May, 1882, Cesnola heard rumors around the Century Club, a brocade-draped haven of New Yorkers eminent in the arts, that Johnston had asked Lt. Commander Henry H. Gorringe to take a look at the statues and then had hidden the report. Cesnola begged to see it.

Gorringe, a naval officer with a sound archaeological background, was the current hero in New York society. He had just accomplished the seemingly impossible feat of removing the obelisk, "Cleopatra's Needle," from its ancient site in Egypt—where it stood in danger of being used for a hotel advertising billboard—and brought it safely to Central Park. William H. Vanderbilt had underwritten the move with a gift of $100,000.

Cesnola wrote Johnston that he felt he had a right to show the Gorringe report to his friends at the club, since Johnston's action, presumably in having the two statues examined publicly, "showed that he doubted the genuineness of the statues and disbelieved the assertions of the Director!!" The Director still wanted that direct and all-out Piedmont fealty. As for Gorringe's letter, even before he saw it, Cesnola did not care "one *iota* on its contents and what he says in it."[27]

Torn, Johnston said he felt it would be better to "let the whole thing fade out of public view as quickly as possible," since it was "not good for the museum."[28] Nevertheless, knowing the persistence of his director, he reluctantly sent him Gorringe's report.

The Commander had examined the two statues without touching them, had even talked to Feuardent personally, and had come away with a conviction if not a verdict.

On April 4 he had written Johnston that he was sure "there is sufficient ground to warrant a scrupulous and exhaustive examination of these statues by a fearless, disinterested committee of experts having full power to destroy them if necesary to determine the question at issue." The statues had little artistic value and since their archaeological value was zero while doubt remained of their genuineness, he believed "their destruction would be a small price to pay for the vindication of the collection and the destruction of its accusers."[29] Here was another call, equally unheeded, for an inquiry by experts.

Without commenting on what he told his friends at the Century, Cesnola returned the report to Johnston on June 1. It only reinforced his previous—unstated—opinion of Gorringe.

"I cannot understand," he wrote, "that men who have made a reputation for themselves and are clever in other things should be so utterly blind, prejudiced and ignorant in others! But such is human nature."[30] That is probably exactly what he told his fellow members at the Century Club.

Fifteen

The Metropolitan Museum of Art seemed to be in a "particularly unfortunate" state, said the *Art Interchange* of New York at the close of 1882. Cesnola had the confidence of "one or two trustees," and the rest were in the "pitiable plight of either asserting his innocence or of acknowledging that they have been thoroughly gulled and have comparatively no knowledge of art but are at the best moneyed amateurs."[1]

Almost a year later—on November 24, 1883—the *Police Gazette* topped a column on the Feuardent-Cesnola lawsuit with, "Cesnola's Bogus Antiques. Was a Worthless Collection Palmed Off on a Credulous Set of Old Fossils?"

Though glib and irreverent, the *Gazette* article had a number of the facts straight. For one thing, it referred to Cesnola as a colonel. The article added that the collector had tried to peddle his merchandise from one end of Europe to the other but had succeeded in selling only a few vases to the Berlin Museum. With the backing of the *Tribune's* Whitelaw Reid, the collection was "jockeyed into favor" and sold to the "amiable set of old fogies" for what the paper called "the unheard of sum of $130,000." He also got himself appointed director at the large salary of $5000.

The lawsuit, tried over a period of nine-and-a-half weeks at the end of 1883 and the beginning of 1884, brightened a dark and particularly hard winter. The Metropolitan Museum of Art felt the sting of ridicule as the Feuardent case, on the surface a personal dispute, changed over the months into a suit requiring the museum to defend its director and his collection. Not yet fifteen years old, the museum could not afford to allow the public impression that it had been duped.

The museum defended itself in the grand manner, hiring Joseph H. Choate as Cesnola's attorney. Choate, fifty-one years old, vice president of the museum, a leading lawyer, and an entertaining after-dinner speaker, enjoyed the small, courtroom audience. At the height of his experience and powers, he preferred cases that were not tiresome, used his humor to lighten the days and moved his adversary to follow this lead.

The Feuardent-Cesnola case, heard in the white and gold, balconied courtroom of Judge Nathaniel Shipman in the old Post Office Building at the foot of City Hall Park, was as popular as an opera. Trustees of the museum, Army generals who were friends of the director, ladies in plum velvet trimmed with white lace, all went downtown to relish the sallies of the brilliant lawyer and to see the statues, silent, pale figures, used as witnesses.

On the last day in October of 1883—after four postponements in the state court and a final shift to a federal court—Choate sat at the counsel table with Cesnola beside him. Cesnola wore his *pince nez*, his greying hair still parted rigidly down the middle of his head. His eyes often blazed with indignation. His dark, luxuriant mustache swept downward, hiding the set line of his mouth.

The pair faced Feuardent, balding, a black silk cravat tied into a bow under his wing collar.[2] With him was his lawyer, Francis Bangs, through whom Feuardent had sued Cesnola for $25,000 damages in a libel proceeding based on Cesnola's remark that Feuardent's charges were "maliciously made and absolutely without foundation in fact."

Two days later, with four trustees of the museum present, along with the members of the museum's investigating panel, including President Barnard of Columbia College, and the Reverend Dr. Hitchcock, the sculptor J. Q. A. Ward, the testimony centered around what Cesnola had ordered done to his statues before the show at 14th Street.

On the stand was an Arizona miner, Henry G. Hutchings. He had been an assistant superintendent at the museum when it moved to the Douglas Mansion on 14th Street in 1873. He first saw Cesnola's collection in packing cases in the basement and on the first floor there. Some of the statues were unpacked; some were still in their cases. "Many statues were without arms or legs; there were loose heads and great quantitites of fragments."

At that time, Theodore Gehlen was hired to repair the entire collection, Hutchings testified, and he had seen Gehlen "place hands, legs and arms on statues. I saw him repair separate heads. This was before the exhibition of these objects—while the collection was in the basement. Wherever joints were made they were so manipulated that the lines of juncture were not apparent when they were placed on view." Gehlen used his hands and also a saw and a brush to fashion statues that, when he was done with them, seemed to have been found in perfect condition. He had a certain "wash of his own composition," one ingredient being filings of Cyprian stone, that made the additions and the original look identical. Gehlen, Hutchings continued, also repaired statues by adding stone and plaster, filing the pieces smooth after glueing them together with another mixture of his own concoction. On exhibition, according to Hutchings, the statues, looked "perfect." The tail of the dove on the bearded Venus was a Gehlen creation of plaster-covered wood. The little Venus with the mirror had no such mirror when Hutchings saw it packed at 14th Street in April 1879 for the move uptown.

Choate made his move. The only defendant he argued, was General Cesnola. No one else was on trial, especially not Mr. Gehlen. The witness had not attributed the changes or the command to make those changes to Cesnola. The lawyer observed that Cesnola for many years was far away in Cyprus while his first collection remained in New York, quite obviously at the mercy of any repairer who came along.

Bangs met the point squarely. The plaintiff expected to make Cesnola responsible for all the repairs and changes made while the collection was in 14th Street.

The issue was joined.

Bangs then led Hutchings through an account of letters he received from Cesnola in Cyprus. In these letters the collector asked for a supply of Gehlen's special glue and praised the repairer's skill. Gehlen could have a certificate of satisfaction, Cesnola had written, any time he wanted it.

In cross examination, Hutchings said he saw nothing improper in Gehlen's filling the cracks of statues with plaster. Bangs was on his feet the next second, objecting to Hutchings' statement as personal opinion. The only points being contested, Bangs argued, were the restorations made by Cesnola and the libelous accusations of Feuardent by Cesnola after the public charges. It was then that Arthur Stickney of Choate's staff contended that the only reason the whole group was in court was Feuardent's charge of "fraudulent" repairs. The defense was going to hold the Frenchman to proof of that accusation. Since "fraudulent" was never clearly defined, that was going to be quite an order.[3]

Already twice examined, the case was all too familiar, and the papers—and Choate—began to concentrate on new details. One witness provided the information that the patched-up nature of the statues had been exposed only because the fledgling museum was too poor to have the Douglas roof mended and rainwater, dripping on the mended Cyprians, had dissolved some of Gehlen's cosmetic wash.[4]

When Choate asked one witness what Bangs considered an immaterial question, Bangs told the witness: "Don't mind anything Mr. Choate says. He envies you your position and wants to give testimony —don't let him. He's got a habit of saying funny things to make people laugh. Now, go on with your story—don't mind him."[5]

Puck pricked up its ears and printed a director's imaginary talk with a restorer who had added arms to the Venus de Milo. The trustees, however, put no impertinent questions to their imperious director. Instead, they treated him with deference.

It was a time of enormous growth for the museum. The financier

and philanthropist who would soon follow Johnston as museum president, Henry G. Marquand, had just spent $100,000 on a set of old
master portraits in Europe, and now he lent them to the Metropolitan. As the trial got under way, visitors to the museum saw for the first
time the "Portrait of Prince Baltazar Carlos" by Velasquez, Rembrandt's "Portrait of a Man," once owned by the Marquis of Lans-
downe, "Miss Carew" by Reynolds and the "Portrait of a Man" by
Frans Hals. The masterpieces outshone all else, dimming the newly
acquired two hundred copies of European paintings and pushing the
antiquities further aside. The multimillionaires of the day followed
Marquand's lead and the long and binding rule of European masters
at the museum was under way.

In court, the cabinet-maker Gehlen, a Pennsylvanian of German
extraction, speaking in a heavy accent, took the stand. He struggled
with Bangs' long questions until he finally pleaded he "no could
understand sooch high English."

Gehlen said Trustee Sturgis and Cesnola hired him and that
Cesnola told him to restore the statues "so as to be as like the originals
as possible." Cesnola in some cases had marked which parts should
be put together. In others, Cesnola brought him the pieces and told
him what to do. He had pursued the work energetically, using "saws,
chisels, gravers, a bit and brace, rasps and hammers." He put the
parts together with plaster of Paris and a secret cement mixture that
he meant to keep secret. He covered the whole with a wash that
included the dust of Cyprian stone. He had sawed off legs and parts
of statues and then replaced them in order to get them to stand
properly. He had made parts of heads and limbs with plaster. He had
specialized in noses.

"Who told you to make the noses?" Bangs asked.

"General di Cesnola."

"How did he tell you to make them?"

"As nearly right as possible."

"Yes. But how did you know what kind of a nose to put on—a
Grecian or a Roman, for instance?"

"I made the nose to correspond to the nation of the figure to be
restored."

"How many of these national noses did you put on?"

Gehlen failed to understand.

"Did you make the noses all of one nation or of a variety of nations?"

"I adapted them as well as I could to the fragments on which I was working; if the fragments were of a Greek figure I put on a Greek nose."[6] Later it was brought out that thirty to forty noses, some Greek, some Phoenician, had been supplied and had been removed after Feuardent's complaints.[7]

One newspaper, commenting it had once thought the trial would "never come off," observed, "Now that it is on, and certainly must 'come off,' it seems, from the evidence so far produced, that the 'noses, toeses, ears and new poses' of the archaeology in question have 'come off' too."[8]

Mrs. Lucy M. Mitchell of Staunton, Virginia, who was preparing a book on antique sculpture, testified sternly that she thought the public should accustom itself to statues without noses.

Gehlen was quick to admit that his work had been undone for the exhibit in the new museum. It seemed to him, in fact, that the Hercules, as shown uptown, had "grown."[9] He did not recognize a good many of the statues when he went to look at them uptown. They had been soaked, taken apart and, in some cases, put together again. Choate's questions showed he felt Gehlen had put the left leg of Hercules together improperly downtown and that the statue was only put into proper shape when his work was redone.

Charles Henkel, a watchman and janitor, told of seeing Charles Balliard, the repairer uptown, soak the Hercules, separate its parts and then assemble them again differently. One leg, Henkel said, was plaster. As the elderly man droned on, Choate demanded: "There is no dispute about that, is there? Why do you gentlemen not prove some fraudulent restorations?"[10]

Bangs later sought to have definitions introduced of "restoration" and "repair," saying that in doing so he was following Choate's example.

"Oh, leave me out of it altogether," Choate said.

"No, no," Bangs contended. "We could not leave Mr. Choate out of the case any more than we could leave out Venus."

"Oh, well," Choate came back, "if you leave both me and Venus out together I won't object."

Venus was going to be very much in the center of things. The testimony chugged along. Savage's account of his departure from the museum because Cesnola did not go through with his announced plan to admit changes in some statues; a discharged worker's report that Cesnola fired him when he refused to deny restorations he had seen being made; the worker's testimony that he saw and heard Cesnola giving Balliard instructions on what to do.[11] One witness, Charles Osborne, a designer and manufacturer of silverware, submitted sketches he had made of the little Venus in the summer of 1880 and in March 1881. They showed, the *Times* noted on November 14, that the mirror "had been changed materially."

Even Feuardent, suave and determined, had little new to offer. But when he came to the stand in late November he did show a difference in Cesnola's measurements of the temple of Golgos: the door in its east wall was eight feet wide in his report to the Royal Academy of Science at Turin and four feet wide in *Cyprus*. Again, he showed a photograph labeled in Cesnola's handwriting that gave Salamis as the site of the discovery of several statues and that, in *Cyprus*, were attributed to Golgos.[12]

Despite such new details, the trial seemed monotonous. The jury looked tired, the two counselors squabbled and yet another sculptor took the stand. It was on the twenty-first day of the testimony, when a single star of fireworks burst forth. The witness, Olin A. Warner, who had just completed a statue of Governor Buckingham for the State Capitol at Hartford, Connecticut, mentioned that the restoration of Venus was in his view the work of two persons.

"How do you arrive at that conclusion?" Bangs asked routinely. "Because I find six toes on one foot and five on the other."[13]

The six-toed Venus shot into brilliant notoriety, and the declaration, some weeks later, that the sixth toe was actually a sandal strap never quite caught up with the original accusation. It is easy to see why: the "strap" that holds the sandal to the foot does not curve around the toes at all.

By now, the case had elicited at least two cartoons. One, in *Puck*, showed Cesnola, grey hair parted in the middle, *pince nez*, drooping dark mustache and black frock coat, standing between a mutilated, armless "bearded Venus" and a "restored bearded Venus." The latter held an enormous round mirror in her left hand.

Cesnola, as the "Injured and Innocent Restorer," was commenting in wonderment: "I can't understand what all this fuss is about, gentlemen. *I* don't see any difference between these two statues."[14]

The other cartoon depicted "How Modern Museums Are Supplied with Genuine Antiquities." There were boxes of arms and legs in the workroom and a very busy workman was setting an arm on an antique statue.[15]

Some of the trustees were beginning to find this sort of treatment of the case abrasive.

President Barnard of Columbia College, once head of the museum's panel investigating Feuardent's charges, came to the stand to admit that all its conclusions had been based on uncorroborated assurances from Cesnola himself.[16]

Challenged by Bangs, Barnard's exchange with the lawyer went like this:

"When the committee found that there was no necessity for the addition of a mirror to the figure of Venus, because the collection already contained ample evidence of the worship of Aphrodite at Golgos, on what did you base your conclusion?"

"On General Di Cesnola's testimony."

"Now, what was there in the collection to warrant such a conclusion?"

"I cannot recall anything."

"Not a single figure?"

"No."

"You remember the Aphrodite and Eros?"

"Yes, Sir."

"Was there anything to back up the assertion of Di Cesnola?"

"Nothing that I recall."

"Can't you think of some other evidence of the worship of Venus at Golgos besides Di Cesnola's statement?"

"I know of no other; his statement was satisfactory evidence to me."

"What did he say that made the evidence satisfactory?"

"I can't remember. Three years have passed, and I can't recall anything he said."

"About what did he say then that warranted any such conclusion on your part as you have set forth to the world?"

The *Times* then reported that "very angrily" Barnard answered: "I have answered the question once as best I can, and I won't answer it any more."[17]

After four hours on the stand, the seventy-four-year-old educator stomped off to continue his drive for $4 million to make Columbia a university of national scope.

Augustus St. Gaudens followed him to the stand and held the little Venus for the first time, turning it slowly as he spoke. His verdict: the mirror was modern.[18]

At last, on December 11, 1883, the defense opened in a courtroom jammed with handsomely dressed women and notable men, trustees, Hiram Hitchcock (back now at the Fifth Avenue Hotel), Richard W. Gilder, editor of *The Century*, and others. They listened to assistant-counsel Stickney retrace the entire case in a two-hour speech. The lawyer attributed the suit to malice on Feuardent's part and said the defense would prove two key questions in Cesnola's favor. Not only would Feuardent's charges that the statues had been made a "fraudulent patchwork" be proved false but, further, the defense also promised to prove that the dealer knew that his charges were untrue. In addition, it was completely untrue, Stickney asserted, that Cesnola had asked the dealer for a false bill in order to get paid quickly by Johnston.[19]

Cesnola then took the stand. He spoke rapidly as Choate guided him through an account of his general excavations and the discovery of treasure at four different sites in Golgos. The *Times*, called the witness "Mr. Cesnola," thus emphasizing the fact that Choate failed to ask him "who or what he was."[20]

Two days later the drapes came off the statues, and the Sacrificer, the bearded Venus and Hercules shared with the little Venus the public's scrutiny.

Feuardent had his Sacrificers mixed up, Cesnola insisted. For the first time Cesnola stated that another statue existed. It was uncanny how like this first Sacrificer the second one was, but it was not identical. It was, in fact, two-and-a-half times larger. And it had gone to the bottom of the sea in the *Napried* fire.

The museum's Sacrificer had indeed been repaired. It was of one piece from the neck to the knees. Below that, the bits of leg found were not strong enough to support the statue. Therefore, a block of Cyprian stone was put into the base and cut into support and heels. These were attached to the body by rods used as dowels. But it was found that when this section was joined to the base, the feet on it did not match. A stonecutter sawed them off. One foot was then moved about two inches, the other about one-half inch, and the whole process, as Cesnola saw it, amounted to repair not restoration.[21] The work had been done on the advice of the sculptor Ward. That sculptor, of course, had been a member of the original panel and had reported favorably on the statue after its public inspection.

As for the bearded Venus: he-she was found West of the temple of Golgos, its legs and arms missing. But, apparently with the help of Layard's book, Cesnola had managed to get them back from the "peasants who had carried them off"[22] and then restored them to the statue. He had forgotten all about this restoration until Feuardent's charge reminded him of it. Thus, through oversight he had not called the attention of the first inquiry panel to this restoration. The bearded head on the statue was the original. (Actually, this head, as the lines of breakage today show, was once separated from the body.)

Cesnola moved tediously, step by step, through a description of what happened when the museum's executive committee—a most prestigious octet of Johnston, Prime, Daniel Huntington, Stuyvesant Rutherford, Robert Hoe Jr., Marquand, W.E. Dodge Jr. and Rhinelander—told him in 1879 "to repair the collection thoroughly."[23]

After the order, which tied the trustees to his fate, Cesnola had Balliard and another repairer undo all Gehlen's work. They first put the doctored statues in a bath which softened Gehlen's glue, separated the parts and then doweled them together, cementing the lines of juncture. Cesnola explained the 1879-1880 cosmetic wash by saying that "there was still dampness present that would assist disintegration" and to keep the damp New York atmosphere from harming the statues, a special wash—this time of glue, milk and filings of Cyprian stone—was brushed over the seams. It united the various parts perfectly, although Cesnola asserted, "I would have preferred not to conceal such seams, but I deemed the wash indispensible for the preservation of the stone." He had spent two months developing the wash and had called on his familiarity and experience with the repair rooms of both the Louvre and the British Museum.[24]

When Bangs had a go at Cesnola, the proceedings became quite lively. Feuardent's lawyer asked the General what he did after he found statues spread out in many places at Agios Photios.

"I put together such pieces as by the fracture and the grain of the stone plainly belonged together."

"Did you use glue?"

"Yes."

"Did you consider yourself an archaeological scholar then?"

"Yes."

"How did you determine the age of different pieces?"

"By the roughness of the surface."

"What was the age of the oldest piece found at Golgos?"

"About seven hundred years before Christ."

"And the newest?"

"About one hundred years before Christ."

"Lead forth the dog," Bangs ordered, and an attendant carried in a controversial small stone dog. It belonged to the museum.

"May I pick it up?" Bangs asked.

"Certainly, if you are strong enough," said Choate agreeably.

"I wasn't afraid of that," snapped Bangs. "I was afraid it might come to pieces."

Judge Shipman had to gavel for order.

Straight-faced, Bangs held the little animal toward Cesnola.

His query was direct: "How old is the dog, judging by its coat?"

General Cesnola looked at the little beast with plain distaste. He did not touch it. He changed his mind about dating on the merits of the surface of stone. Color and the style of art involved—Grecian, Phoenician and the like—had to be taken into account. The dog departed.

As for the little Venus, the director said the statuette and the mirror were both of the same stone.

Bangs, turning the statuette in his hand, then asked: "With what did you put the feet of the Venus on at Cyprus?"

"Glue."

"Do you call this a restoration or a repair?"

"An attachment."

"Oh, an attachment. Then we have three names for the same thing—attachment, repair, restoration. When a wash was added in the Central Park Museum, to conceal the joints, what did you call that?"

"A repair."

Without a change in tone, the director testified that one-fourth to one-third of the 1200 to 1300 stone pieces at the museum had been similarly "repaired."[25]

Bangs moved on to a report Cesnola had made to the inquiry panel at the museum about dirt incrustation on some statues. "Where are the photographs," he asked, "which show the original incrustation of dirt around this button?" He was pointing to the mirror of little Venus.

"Why do you call that a button?" Choate demanded.

"Because I know a button when I see one," Bangs replied evenly. "If you knew the best use to which buttons can be put, you would not talk so much."

Choate stared at him for several long seconds. Then he put on his coat and hat and left the courtroom.[26]

All told, Cesnola was on the witness stand for six full days. The jury, according to at least one newspaper, was beginning to look like a collection of martyrs. It was observed, however, that they perked up when the questioning centered on Cesnola's titles. In addition to being a General and Count, he had an honorary title of Doctor of Laws and therefore responded readily when addressed as "Doctor."

Bangs gave him trouble with his Army rank. He had noticed that Choate addressed him as "General," and he asked if that was an honorary title or one he had received by commission.

Cesnola responded, "I had not a commission, but I had the title."

"How did you get it. Whom did you get it from?"

"Mr. Lincoln."

"How."

"Before I was sent out as consul to Cyprus."

"How, by mail or otherwise?"

"I received it verbally."

"What is the next lowest grade in the Army to general?"

"Colonel."

"It is Lieutenant-General, isn't it?"

"Yes, sir."

"And then Major-General?"

"Yes, sir."

"And then Brigadier-General?"

"Yes, sir."

"And then Colonel?"

"Yes, sir."

"And you go by the name of General?"

"I don't know. I am called that."

"Here is the title-page of your book, which says, 'By General Louis Palma di Cesnola' "

"I know it is there."

"Do you know of any man in the United States who held the rank of General except Grant, Sherman and yourself?"

"No, sir. I never pretended to know."[27]

The court limited the examination, remarking that Cesnola now knew he had "no legal right to the title." In addition, it was established in court that his right to be called "Count" was one of courtesy, since the rank, one of male primogeniture, went to his older brother, Alerino. He was, in actual fact, a younger son, a cavalier. Bangs began referring to his own client as "General Feuardent."[28] The lawyer tried in other ways also to lighten the trial. When he had Prime on the stand and the little Venus was being sponged to show its rosy color, Bangs commented under his breath that it had a "Venus blush." Prime thought her a simple dancing girl, and future curators downgraded the little Venus even more. Today she is labeled "a girl walking."

The trustee and friend of the General—for Cesnola was called that to the day he died—took a great deal of the onus for change in the statues on himself. In fact, Prime said he was present when Cesnola told Balliard what to do to get the collection ready for the 1880 opening and had protested when Cesnola ruled that no restorations were to be made. Prime said he also approved of the covering wash. As for repairs, his attitude was a pragmatic one: "It is proper to do what is necessary to make a statue stand up."[29]

Before the jury retired for its deliberations, Hiram Hitchcock, Charles Balliard, sculptors John Q.A. Ward, Charles Calverley, and Launt Thompson, trustees Robert Hoe Jr. and William L. Andrews and other testified to the validity of the statues. The sculptors had some trouble doing so since the mirror on the little Venus had been rubbed experimentally so many times. They let it be known that they felt the statues had been tampered with more during the law suit than they had been before. The judge and jury under the gentle guidance of Ward, a trustee, visited the museum one mid-January afternoon.

But it was Cesnola himself who, sitting in thought in his library at home in the evening, came up with the trump play.

He simply resurrected and embellished Gorringe's idea. And it was a stunner. One morning in a quiet court a clerk read a memorandum from the defendant. Cesnola offered to let Feuardent saw any of the controversial statues into pieces to prove they were not "patchworks of unrelated parts." The Frenchman could have the figures washed in potash baths or could do anything he wanted with them.

It was Bangs' turn, now, to sit silent for an impressed moment. Then, recoiling in horror, he declined the offer.[30]

On January 29, 1884, the largest crowd of the long suit gathered to hear Choate's summation. The lawyer presented the jury with a practical view of things. He stressed that the 1880 work, which should have taken two months, had taken only two weeks. President Hayes had told the museum unexpectedly that he could not open the new building in either April or May so it had been moved up to the end of March.

The lawyer's main thrust spiced the practical with ridicule of the Frenchman's stand. What should they do with such a collection? Fail to restore feet? Hang it by its head? Pin it to the wall like butterflies? It was a miracle that, in the rush of the 1880 preparations, only half a dozen statues could justify challenge.

Choate pitted the formidable group of defense-witnesses, men the jury knew, "Messers. Hitchcock, Barnard, Ward and Judge Daly ... against the criticisms of Gaston L. Feuardent." He concluded by saying that the museum's trustees were standing by Cesnola "because they know he has been the object of malignant prosecution."[31]

When Bangs' chance for summation came, he flourished a picture of the Tweed Ring before the jury, a cartoon in which each accused official was pointing to another, shifting the blame to others for the repairs and restorations, for photographs in his book, even for his picture with the star of a Brigadier General.

The lawyer poured invective on the little Venus. He was fed up with her. "I despise her. She is not in my mind as good looking as many an American woman I know. She is not as well built as an ordinary ship of war." Reviewing the testimony, he recalled that the "mirror" had been also called at one time or another, a butter plate or a tambourine, and this general confusion should point clearly to the accuracy of Feuardent's charges.[32]

Arriving at a verdict was a grueling process. For twenty-eight full hours, without sleep but with a break for a good meal, the twelve men, two of them former soldiers, pondered the General's fate. Finally the jury members, unshaven and pale, gave their decision. They found for Cesnola on two counts, denying Feuardent redress for Cesnola's accusation that the charges were "maliciously made and totally without foundation," or for the director's castigation of his opponent as a "charlation, ignorant of archaeology." Apparently the jury felt such strong language came naturally to the fiery cavalier and should not be held against him. The panel failed to find for either man on another count, that Cesnola had wrongfully accused Feuardent's firm of not making a real effort to sell his collection and of overcharging him.[33]

Sixteen

The huge city, its elevated trains now riding spines of iron up its east and west sides, rumbled with the clamor of precipitous growth. Nearly two years of almost frantic building had put second generation immigrants along both rivers. Families, working to escape from feverish slums, moved as they could afford to each year. German refugees had brought with them vague Socialistic aspirations that grew in the long hours of the six-day work week into more specific aims. New York marked its first Labor Day in 1882. The garment cutters, the ship carpenters, plumbers and others began slowly and painfully to organize, to join together in what the Knights of Labor called "the great brotherhood of toil." Men who lived in a world of cold water and embittering conditions joined together in a binding camaraderie.

In the mid-1880s, the great worlds of finance and merchandise moved aboue these "toilers" in an insulated cocoon. Pullman cars were sheathed in plush, their ribs of dark, thickly varnished mahogany. The deep-piled, rich material draped high windows of the brownstones, covered theater seats and formed the curtains that parted for Richard Mansfield, Henry Irving, Ellen Terry and the ten-year-old prodigy, Josef Hofmann.

The era was one of new and overblown dimensions. Along Wall Street institutions which controlled the finances of the continent replaced the small, family size structures that had once lined the narrow street.

Even the diversions of the fashionable world had veered toward new fields. Tom Thumb had died in 1883 at the age of forty-six, and the public had a new hero, Richard Wagner. The men of the new age awaited his annual winter work with solemn anticipation. The leaders, men who knocked heads together or, if the heads belonged to railroad presidents, softened them on yachting excursions, had developed a prodigious certainty. This sureness, backed by vast wealth, was set in a world where the British Navy maintained half a century of peace. It filled the city with generally bright expectations, with hope for the future. The musical band of John Philip Sousa drew thousands to the park, the thrust of its brass ornamented with arabesques of woodwinds or piccolos much as the sturdy form of an iron gate in Piedmont gave substance to a baroque froth of metal. In the confident and joyous marches, the temper of the times breathed and found its spirit.

On Fifth Avenue close to the park, the managers of men and money built their mansions, some gaudy, some restrained, all expensive. Cesnola and his family lived a few blocks east on Fifty-Seventh Street. They had now also acquired a country estate in Westchester County, a seventy-six acre property in Byram Lake Road, Mount Kisco. This was the family's beloved "La Favorita," haven for Madame or the Countess Cesnola, as she was called, and, with its eight servants, the seat of the family's social life.[1] Often remaining in the country while her husband poured his energies into his work at the museum, Mme. Cesnola busied herself with benevolent activities. She founded the Italian Orphan Asylum in Manresa on the Hudson, not far from the Cesnola home, and, in the city, helped to establish the Cristoforo Columbo Hospital. For this and other work, she eventually received a personal blessing from Pope Leo XIII. The Cesnola daughters received every chance to mingle with the leading families of the day. They appeared at formal openings at the museum with the socialite youth of upper Manhattan.

In this they followed the tradition of their father who, adhering through the years to the ancient family Savoyard tradition, attached himself to the most powerful through bonds of loyalty and service. First it was to John Taylor Johnston, Cesnola's patron and friend. Then after Johnston's health failed and he relinquished the presidency of the museum in 1889, it was to his successor, Henry Gurdon Marquand. Seventy years old, his white side-whiskers a halo about his strong face, Marquand put a real estate, railroading and banking fortune to a sound Renaissance end: he had built for himself a princely mansion at 11 East 68th Street and filled its dark and cavernous rooms with ancient and exotic treasures. There was a Japanese morning room and others individually designed for his Persian, Arabic and Hispano-Moresque acquisitions. One of the most liberal benefactors of the Metropolitan, Marquand had already given the museum masterpieces of painting, the Della Robia altar-piece and reproductions of gold and silver objects in the Imperial Russian Museum. Like Prime, he favored Princeton, where his son Allan was professor of art and archaeology, and to that institution he gave not only a chapel but its first gymnasium.

Cesnola, son of the magnificent Savoys, could understand such a man, and he worked with the vigor and *brio* of his Cyprus days to run the museum to the president's liking. In this, he had Marquand's complete and unfaltering support. Metal-studded shoes sounding a rat-a-tat warning as he paced the marble-floored galleries, Cesnola, heavier now in his middle fifties, swept past guards who humored him by stiffening, as if to military attention, as he passed.[2] And if, in the humid heat of August, the heavy air coming through open windows into the museum should melt the mixture that bound the head of an ancient Cyprian statue to its body, the faithful guards would quickly remove the sculpture. They acted as though they were medical corpsmen taking a wounded soldier from the field of battle. The General very definitely ran a one-man museum. He was that man, the operating counterpart of the president of its powerful Board of Trustees. During the 1890s when other museums, notably the Boston Museum of Fine Arts, acquired superb collections of ancient classical art, Cesnola persisted in buying inferior specimens from his Italian friends. He declined Samuel Avery's important collection of prints and, in general, ran his own show.

For his work Cesnola received a relatively small salary. He had begun his career with the Metropolitan by working *gratis* for a year or so after the sale of his second collection. As a Trustee and Secretary of its Board, he was following the example of other trustees and could afford the generosity. He had received money from the sale of his second collection and expected income from his book. He had begun working for the museum in 1879 at $5000 a year[3] and had had several increases. Now, however, he faced a bill of $32,000 from Choate. The trustees, feeling the charges had been against the museum as well as its director, had contributed $21,000[4] but, Cesnola confided to Hitchcock in 1884, he had "no idea" how he would raise the balance.[5] The General managed to sell some casts of famous statues, apparently some he had obtained on his 1880 trip abroad, and it is likely that he kept up a trade with these over the years. Otherwise, there is no explanation how he paid his legal bill and maintained his New York home and his estate in Westchester in the approved style of the day. He enlarged and landscaped a small lake on his country property and managed to live up to his annual salary which eventually reached $12,000.

Money had brought him difficulty throughout his life, and that was not to change now. The director-board secretary, responsible for all the cash that came into the museum, was, in fact, the treasurer as well. He paid the bills and directed the keeping of the books. And the proceeds of sales of catalogues at the front desk—catalogues that sold for a dime a copy—went to the director. In the course of the first ten years at the uptown building, Cesnola piqued a bookkeeper and ultimately found himself facing a trustee investigation of charges that he was pilfering cash receipts. The report of the museum's treasurer, Salem H. Wales, in October 1890 countered this accusation by holding that, on the contrary, Cesnola had $4315.42 coming to him from the museum. He was due the advances he had made to freightmen and to others whose bills he had paid.[6] In exonerating him after a long and meticulous probe, the Executive Committee formally expressed its sympathy for Cesnola in facing charges made by a bookkeeper for whose methods he had no responsibility. The study only confirmed the Board's confidence in their Director. The bookkeeper was fired.

Cesnola, meanwhile, was caught up in the rushing stream of

activity that, obscuring his antiquities, focused more emphasis on great pictures. As he turned to running the ever more important museum, he spoke to the mighty with straightforward, Canavesean aplomb. In the spring of 1889, he wrote Cornelius Vanderbilt II, the forty-six-year-old board chairman of the New York Central Railroad, that Raphael's *"Madonna di Loretto"* was for sale in Bologna—Cesnola had it direct from the Italian Minister to New York that very day —"and our Museum ought to possess it by all means if possible." Cesnola mentioned that, having sat in at trustee meetings for a number of years, he knew it to be useless to try to get them to raise the money. As a result, he was writing Vanderbilt with a forthright appeal: "It would be a great gift if you would buy that picture for our Museum." Actually, he went on blandly, the trustees had been urging him to take a vacation but he had nowhere to go and nothing to do. If Vanderbilt would make this grand gesture, however, he would hurry off to Italy, buy the canvas, and, with his contacts there, secure an exit permit for the picture from the Italian Government.[7] It was a lovely April dream. But, a rare Raphael nothwithstanding, Vanderbilt demurred, and Cesnola spent the summer at La Favorita.

Hard-driving, determined and set against loosening his hold on museum affairs, the General settled in to controlling them. He had a small office built for himself on the balcony of the 1880 building[8] and from it could overlook most of what was going on. One new building —a structure to the south which more than doubled the original space—had been erected in 1888 and a second one, its mate to the north, was creating dust, noise and other problems as it rose.

Not content with governing the museum's inner operations, Cesnola had posted at the door the rules regarding admittance. He wanted no one admitted who was "ragged and dirty." To get into the museum, Cesnola held, a man "must be washed and his clothes must be neat and he must have on a coat."[9] He fought to make his standards prevail. In the spring of 1889, one of his guards had refused to let a workman in overalls into the museum and had, in fact, gotten one of the museum police to put him off the premises. Cesnola upheld the action of the guard and the policeman.

The story appeared in the circuit of newspapers across the country. In general, they sympathized with the aspiring workman and

raised the question of accommodations for those who could not get
to the museum on weekdays. Saturdays were workdays, but many
employees now made informal arrangements among themselves for
half the force to leave at noon on alternate weekends. Presently the
city electrified the building, and the doors were opened, to rich and
poor, on Tuesday and Saturday evenings.

Inevitably, this led to more pressure for Sunday openings. Cesnola turned a cold ear to personal attacks such as that carried in a
letter in the Brooklyn *World* in May 1885, headed, "It was Cesnola's
Day." During Edgar Allan Poe Memorial exercises, the writer reported, all seats were reserved for Cesnola's friends and he brusquely
refused to let anyone else in, even if they were members or life
members of the museum.

Faced, however, with a constant barrage from both the public
and from newspapers who wanted the museum open on Sundays, and
from conservative ministers who wanted it tightly closed, Cesnola
yelped in indignation. Excited during an interview for the once
friendly *Herald,* Cesnola lost patience with the idea of Sunday openings. To do justice to his feelings, he echoed the words of William H.
Vanderbilt before an investigating committee: "The public be
damned!"

The public should get a few things straight, he felt, and he set
about seeing that it did. The museum was not a public institution.
"Some of the officials of the city government seem to consider it so
and try to treat it as such," he lectured the writer who interviewed
him at home. The public had no claim on the museum whatever. The
only responsibility the museum had to the city, he insisted, was to use
the building to display art. The art itself belonged to the trustees.
Anytime they wanted to, they could pick up these valuable marbles
and, on three months' notice, go off without any explanation, put up
a building of their own and forget about the city and its increasingly
vocal population. Even earlier—in 1882—Cesnola had been maneuvering to get Vanderbilt to put up a museum building on two blocks
he owned and endow the institution with a million dollars. The museum was to keep its own name while the building took that of
Vanderbilt.[10] The plan failed. The museum stayed where it was and
terms of the original contract signed between city Tammany officials

and the museum remain in force. Cesnola was impelled to deal with the fact that letting the public into the building free on four days a week did not change the legal verities. Furthermore, he was capable of recognizing that all the aspects of the contract did not represent the rosy-fingered dawn of a new day for the growing museum. The document tied the city to pay but $30,000 to the two uptown museums, the Metropolitan and the American Museum of Natural History. The thought not only of letting hordes of low-class people into the building but also of not getting more money with which to pay attendants made Cesnola boil over.

The city would undoubtedly increase the museum allowance but it could give the museum, he noted bitterly, "just as little as they want to. They might allow us one dollar each. Then I would not heat the building and let the public go there and freeze." As he said this, it was the dead of winter. "When they become stiff I would set them up among the other groups of statuary."[11]

The General, whom the reporter described as "in full tilt at Boards, Park Commissioners and people," snorted and wafted a fusillage of cigar smoke at the newspaper man seated opposite him in the snug Cesnola library on 57th Street.

What bothered the General most was that half a dozen men, a handful of generous trustees, had contributed $30,000 a year for the previous several years to pay the cost of keeping the museum open. To ask them now to pay another $15,000 to let in some 100,000 people on Sundays—people who would peel bananas, eat lunches, even spit—would be simply unthinkable.[12]

The next day Cesnola wrote the paper denying the quotations but, though he admitted some truth in the account, he did not specify where it lay.[13] Actually, in calmer moments the Director was for Sunday openings providing the city paid the cost and the public behaved.

Such an exchange, of course, caused all the old war horses to canter out of their stables, and, caparisoned in well-worn anti-Cesnola charges, lope around airing such notions as the one expressed in *Life* Magazine that Cesnola's opposition should be a supremely powerful argument for throwing the doors open on the sabbath.

However, despite urgings from the Park Commissioners, the

Board of Estimate and the Central Labor Union, Cesnola and the museum board held their ground. In December 1888, Mayor Hewitt, opening the new building (in which Cesnola's Curium treasure gleamed in a second-floor gallery,) publicly expressed the hope that it would be open every day. Prime, giving the main address, countered with the standard museum argument: the trustees had had to give $27,000 the previous year in order to open the building as often as they did. The agreement between the city and the museum was simplicity itself: the city had offered to provide a building and a portion of the running expenses if the museum would go to the park and educate the public. The founders had expected to meet the rest of the running costs by charging admission until they could afford otherwise.[14] Prime gave no inkling of when that would be.

It was an argument in which the trustees put the full and powerful weight of their professional acumen. Accustomed to duress in business, they were unmoved by the threat of the Legislature to attach a Sunday rider to the then current construction appropriation —this time for a north wing.

It was only when laboring men—some 100,000 of them within the city—drew up a special petition, when the public offered $4000 to pay expenses,[15] when the Board of Estimate threatened to withhold money for the new building[16] and when cartoonists showed the friends of trustees enjoying privileged Sundays at the museum, that the heavy doors swung open in June 1891 for the general public— some six full years after this was first sought—and the Metropolitan Museum of Art became a regular Sunday attraction.

Cesnola stood at the door to appraise these new visitors that first Sunday. Men in derbies led in women in long dresses and youngsters in high-heeled high-buttoned shoes. Cesnola was ready for them. He had locked the room that held his Curium gold,[17] and he had plenty of guards, his own regiment of police, fragmentary though it was, primed to handle any difficulty. But there was none. Cesnola went home early, remarking to a reporter who followed him, that, judging from the well-dressed appearance of those who came, the "poorer classes," from whom he obviously expected trouble, had not been interested enough to make the effort to come.[18]

Soon, however, crowds were pouring into the galleries on Sunday afternoons, 170,000 in all by the end of the year. Then the program ran into an old snag—lack of money. Eventually, the museum's friends in Albany appropriated $70,000 for Sunday openings, and the regular Sunday crowd of 4600 in a few hours was more than the attendance on any full weekday.

There was now plenty to see. In a grand gesture, Cornelius Vanderbilt II had bought Rosa Bonheur's "The Horse Fair" for $53,-000 and immediately turned it over to the museum. He wrote "My dear General" that he was making the present "as an evidence of my high esteem towards its very able Director, much abused by the ignorants, but highly appreciated by those who, like myself, know him for so many years, and have seen almost daily his hard work at the Museum."[19] With such an introduction to the painting, Cesnola viewed it with proprietary concern. Not long afterward the elderly Marquand, visiting the galleries, came on his director and an assistant retouching the hooves of one of the huge horses in the canvas. He called a halt to the work.[20]

The flood of art pouring into the museum was now so great, as the contagion of giving spread from one to another millionaire, that Cesnola mused wryly about the problem of space. On her death in 1887, Miss Catharine Lorillard Wolfe gave the museum not only all her paintings but $200,000 to care for them and to buy more. Most donors gave only art and Cesnola, seldom one to hide his opinions, made it known that he felt what the museum needed most of all was someone who would simply donate a large amount of money. He wanted no strings attached. The Director also alerted his attendants to give constant visitors the warm reception of family friends. He was himself careful in answering the questions of even men whom he called "$10 men," those who paid that sum for annual memberships. One, a strangely quiet visitor who asked Cesnola pointed questions about the great businessmen who ran the museum—the younger Vanderbilt, Morgan, the art connoisseur Avery and the patrician, Marquand—was a Jacob S. Rogers of Paterson, New Jersey. Rogers kept silent about his own business, the manufacture of locomotives, at which he made millions. He was a bachelor, and Cesnola saw to it that he was made to feel at home in the museum. When he died in 1901 he left the Metropolitan more than five million dollars.

240

The growing institution was now so crowded that only a little more than half of Cesnola's own prized collection—some 17,000 of 35,000 pieces—were on display.[21] The Cyprian finds were still controversial. Taking up the quest for accuracy in the chalk-dry hills of Cyprus were German, French and British archaeologists. They brought to the task the commitment of youth in new careers. It was a German, as it had been fifteen years earlier, who now spoke the words that again clouded the massive first treasure of the Metropolitan. Max Ohnefalsch-Richter, working on his doctorate, began excavating in Cyprus for Sir Charles T. Newton, the British Museum's first keeper of Greek and Roman antiquities. Then he applied himself to what he called "the imperative task" of sifting the material in Cesnola's *Cyprus*. In doing this, he found most of it unreliable and came out flatly with the professional verdict—the first since Dr. Friederichs—that "no honest man can any longer believe in the temple treasure of Curium or in the temple of Aphrodite [Venus] of Golgos, both being inventions of L. P. Di Cesnola."[22]

A fully trained field worker, Professor Ferdinand Duemmler, also German, put it even more flatly: "There never did exist any treasure vaults or any treasure of the temple or any temple of Curium." *The New-York Times* ran close to a column on the views of the two men.[23] The scholar pointed out that Cesnola was so remiss that he published two different ground plans for the temple treasure vaults that never existed.

The renewed attack against Cesnola's finds was so strong, his faults laid bare with such thoroughness that Ohnefalsch-Richter himself in 1891 accused the British researchers of having "sinned in the excess of their distrust. Cesnola is left without a single good point."[24]

Two years later, the German was back trying to re-establish the archaeological worth of Cesnola's finds. In commenting on a new report, one by W. J. Stillman, an expert for the American Numismatic and Archaeological Society, confirming the stand that the original Curium vaults never existed, Ohnefalsch-Richter offered to tell the Metropolitan Museum of Art trustees what to do to make the Cyprian antiquities of "solid value to the student as something on which he can rely. At present he cannot."[25] The trustees kept mum. At that point, they were perfectly willing to forget both Cesnola collections.

Cesnola himself had reacted to the new controversy by stating flatly that all his objects in gold, silver, alabaster and bronze had been found in four rooms at Curium and that Golgos was a real town. Although making no claim to high archaeological standards, he maintained a pugnacious insistence that all his finds were absolutely genuine. By this, he simply meant that they were found in Cyprus and represented its art. Until future archaeologists came up with a more convincing hypothesis, he insisted, Cyprus as seen through his discoveries would have to be considered the cradle of the art of ancient Greece.

And, indeed, so it was. Until Sir Arthur Evans of England resurrected the palace of King Minos on Crete in 1900 and, with the thoroughness of a carefully trained expert, did the archaeological work establishing a link between the Minoan island culture and that of Mycenae on the Grecian mainland, Cyprus seemed that link. However, once Evans' conclusions were published, Cesnola's contention that Cyprus was the fountainhead of classical Greek art faded in the strong light of the Briton's greater knowledge. Cesnola never made that same claim again.

He concentrated on other things. Somewhat earlier, a bright prospect had illumined the Cesnolas' family life as the 1890s opened. Hiram Hitchcock, a widower in 1887, spoke to his friend of long standing about marrying Cesnola's second daughter, Louise. Then, as Madame and the General sat in the rear seat of his private railroad car enroute to New Hampshire, Hitchcock proposed. The proprietor of the hotel in New York was exactly her father's age. Louise looked at him amazed.[26] She spoke of something else. A few years later, Hitchcock married his second cousin, Emily H. Howe, who was twenty years his junior.

Cesnola, as he moved into his sixties under the lash of constant public criticism, became even more positive, more rigid. He had long had a low opinion of American artists of such standing as the sculptor St. Gaudens and the painter William Chase, calling their work "monstruosities [sic]."[27] Some of the current "painting manufacturers," he told General McClellan, had tried to bribe him to get the trustees to buy their work. He had refused.

Now, as 1895 opened and he had sixteen years' experience at

the museum, Cesnola expressed himself emphatically on how a museum should develop. He disagreed vehemently with the "asinine
art-critics of New York" who were objecting to his covering oil paintings with glass for cleanliness. The stocky director, troubled with
rheumatism and chronic bronchitis, indulged himself in the heavy
meals of the day and consoled himself privately. In his handwritten
book of reflections, he observed, "It is wrestling against opposition
that makes Giants of men."

Presently, he had gargantuan opposition, a movement within the
ranks of the trustees to oust him peremptorily from his positions. The
attack—it was, in fact, a concerted onslaught by a group of young
Board members—came on February 11, 1895. Led by Robert W.
DeForest, a younger group of trustees undertook to have Cesnola
removed both as Secretary and as Director. They sent Marquand a
petition which they presented as signed by seven trustees, including
the powerful and once friendly Choate, the sculptor J.Q.A. Ward,
Avery, the professional in the art world, and others, saying they felt
it "for the interest of the Museum that General di Cesnola should
cease to be connected with it officially...." This was no hasty conclusion nor the result of a single act on Cesnola's part, but one that
resulted from "long observation and reflection." If the other trustees
did not agree with them, then, they told Marquand, the others should
bear the responsibility for Cesnola's "present control of Museum
affairs." Their main objection was the General's attitude toward other
museums in America and Europe, the art community, the public, and,
still closer to home, to individual trustees.

Avery sent the elderly president, whose wife had just died, a
softer message, saying he had long been Cesnola's apologist, one
willing to "wink at irregularities rather than be troubled," but that he
felt the General's known antagonism to certain trustees was blighting
their enthusiasm for museum work. He pointed out that the move
could be made smoothly, that, perhaps, Cesnola could be given a paid
holiday in Europe and that Professor Allan Marquand of Princeton,
the president's son, could be persuaded to take on the Directorship
if only temporarily.[28]

Marquand sat quietly in his Madison Avenue mansion and
thought the whole question through. A few days later he decided to

vote to keep Cesnola in the two controlling jobs. He reported to dissident trustees what he planned to do, informed Cesnola of the coming raid on his position, and he rallied aid from others.

When he went to the Board meeting several days later, on February 18, 1895, Marquand carried with him a letter that was the *imprimatur* for his vote. The writer told Marquand he was too busy to attend, but he had confidence in the ticket the president approved and no other. "You know better than any other Trustee the exact conditions of the Museum affairs and what is for its best interests and continued success. Any change which does not meet with your approval will not meet with mine. Our Museum is progressing so well that to make any change in the present administration of its affairs, against your wishes, it would not benefit but do harm to the Museum." The letter, which Marquand received in time to show to other trustees, was signed by J. Pierpont Morgan.[29]

News of the split soon spread. The *New-York Times* headed a column-long story "Di Cesnola Cannot Stay." It reported the protective action of the two business chieftains but also quoted a European archaeologist who said the Cesnola collection had been "picked up all over the Levant."[30] The paper cited an unidentified critic as saying that while the former soldier was "undoubtedly the man to get the collection, he was not the man to take care of it." Cesnola at sixty-three faced the accusation of lacking "scholarly equipment, strict conscientiousness, accuracy and artistic taste necessary for Director of a great museum. He has treated his statues like a dragoon, or, rather, let us say, like a martinet; he has brushed, touched, and patched them up to make a good appearance on parade, probably without at first fully realizing the harm he was doing. But most melancholy of all, after doing it, he had denied it, and even after the fullest private and public exposure, he had been sustained in his denials by gentlemen whose indorsement should be their amplest guarantee for the scrupulous fidelity of the official whom they publicly sustain and honor."[31]

The youthful group sought to postpone action but Marquand, fully on Cesnola's side, said he would resign if that was done. At the mid-February meeting, Choate, angry, demanded to know, in a stentorian, courtroom style, if "this board is to be bulldozed." Marquand studiously ignored him. The postponement issue failed as the two opposing forces produced a tie vote. The officers were voted upon and all were chosen unanimously except Cesnola, who received ten of the seventeen votes and E.D. Adams, a dissenter, who polled seven. Cesnola had proved himself again an enduring director.

A protective patron, Marquand shied clear of reporters until their young opponents had "got through their fire." Then he called his friends on the press together and gave them a full statement.[32] Hitchcock sent his "dear old friend" the urgent advice not to let Choate's union with the rebels bother him, encouraging Cesnola with the thought: "Your triumph is *complete,* your ability & integrity are recognized by *all the world*—the trustees *as a body* are *your friends* & you must now *laugh* at anything that comes up to annoy you."[33]

The *Times* reported Cesnola's retention not as a vote of confidence in the director but as a pledge of loyalty to the museum and Marquand.[34] The preeminent art museum in the Western Hemisphere had moved, as she had in 1880, to envelop in the cloak of her identity this errant cavalier whose treasure she had made her own. What the founding fathers decided would be best for the museum was the ruling guide of action, as it had been fifteen years earlier when Choate went into court at the General's side.

In those days there had been a certain comic overtone to the charges aimed at wandering limbs of ancient figures. Now, with these old accusations barely mentioned, with the full blast of opposition directed at Cesnola's qualifications for his post, the attack, one that came from within the museum itself and enlisted such figures as Choate and Avery, moved toward the tragic. The blank, white silence that ensued engulfed the controversy like a full winter's snowfall closing the alpine mountain fasts above Cesnola.

The restless cavalier subsided into routine, long repeated tasks at the museum and sought desperately to recoup the reputation that had been mangled in the trial. His military rank was of primary importance to him. His attempts to legitimatize his claim to the title of Brevet Brigadier General moved through various channels of veterans' organizations and official Congressional offices. Soon after the trial, in 1884, Cesnola had pressed an officer of his GAR post to have Congress issue his General's commission. But it was not to be so easy.

Even if Lincoln had made the appointment in writing, M.J. McMahon of George Washington Post No. 103 in Nassau Street, New York, told Cesnola, it would have become "null and void" had the Senate adjourned without acting on it. The current Senate was powerless to "remedy the case" as they had no authority over the records of previous Senates. The matter had been discussed "at length," McMahon told his friend, but it had been found "impossible" to "discover any method of accomplishing your wishes." The veterans' group went so far as having a private and thorough search of the records of the 1865 Congress made in the hope of finding some "memorandum in writing of any kind of Mr. Lincoln's which might throw light on the subject and be useful to you." None had been found and despite their "kindest disposition," officials in Washington had to admit their "inability under the law to do anything."[35]

Cesnola then went after the title by a circuitous course. He had the president of the Eleventh Army Corps, Augustus C. Hamlin of Bangor, Maine, write a complete report of his gallantry at Aldie to General Russell A. Alger, Secretary of War. With it, Hamlin sent a thick brochure attesting to Cesnola's valor through affidavits from Brigadier General L.C. Estes, who had given Cesnola his own sword, and through Thomas Morley who described the cavalryman's wounds. On December 3, 1897, by direction of the President, Alger awarded to "Col. Louis P. di Cesnola a medal for most distinguished gallantry in action at Aldie, Va., June 17, 1863."[36] The medal in hand, Cesnola then had Representative George Brinton McClellan, General McClellan's thirty-three-year-old son, introduce a bill in Congress empowering the President to confer on Cesnola the rank of Brevet Brigadier General of Volunteers. The bill, H.R. 9640 of the 55th Congress, went to the House Committee on Military Affairs but was never reported out. It was found no legal provision existed through which a President could confer commissions by brevet on ex-officers of volunteers. No action at all was taken on it formally, so it literally died in committee.[37] Even after receiving a Congressional Medal, Cesnola never attained the rank he had held informally for decades. None of his close associates, however, knew of these moves or ceased to call him "General." Nor did Cesnola himself drop the accustomed title. He was quick to supply editors with the "facts" about his appointment by President Lincoln. Public appreciation grew more important to him; he kept the medal he received from the King of Italy in 1882, just before the trial, in a public display case in the museum.

In seeking a pension in the summer of 1899, Cesnola insisted his rheumatism would make it "next to impossible" for him to go to the pension office for an examination. In a flash of his old bravado, he asked that a medical examiner come to him rather than the other way around. He and his family now lived entirely in the country at Mt. Kisco, and he went to the museum for only a few hours on Tuesdays, Thursdays and Saturdays. He tried to set a time for the pension doctor to see him there and was ready to pay for a regular home visit.[38] But the pension office had its regulations, and they did not provide an accommodation such as this. The correspondence petered out. To the cavalry officer there would never come either the rank or the small financial reward for his war service. The rank had long ago been barred by the pistol episode; without it, he surely would have maintained his leadership in the brigade and have won, eventually, the title that went with it.

Now, as he began to stiffen with age, Cesnola turned his anger at the very trustees who had maintained him in his unique position as director of the museum. "The princely liberality of rich New Yorkers towards the Metropolitan Museum of Art (so often printed in the papers) is all bosh," he declared in 1895, "as is the statement that for many years Trustees paid the running expenses out of their own pockets."[39] Cesnola himself had been the one to publicize the trustees' financial generosity. His story now was different: conservative trustees had kept the museum out of debt by the strictest of economies and he had provided the necessary margin on which to keep the institution out of the hands of city or state politicians by raising the number of members from three hundred to an income-producing two thousand.[40] *"Silence* and *action* coupled with *activity"* had been his rule in excavating Cyprus[41] and they had been his by-words at the Metropolitan. For the most part, he went his own way, conferring only with Marquand about museum affairs. As they saw the museum's role, it was a private corporation which leased a building from the city. It could go elsewhere on three months' no-

tice.[42] The public was to be told nothing about plans the museum projected to avoid objections and advice from the public and the press.

Cesnola outlined the official museum position to an Italian professor: "The New York public knows nothing of the plans of the museum and shouldn't know them. Otherwise, they will shower the museum administration with suggestions and then the local press would try to force them to follow up the public will and this the Trustees do not want."[43] Joseph W. Drexel, a trustee, urged Cesnola, in fact, to keep the museum as a "proprietary" corporation. "Admit the public freely but only as a courtesy not as a right," he wrote. "When it has the right, then it will assume the direction and politics will rule the whole."[44]

The trustees did want their increasingly irascible director to take more vacations. Finally, in 1900 after his daughter, Eugenia Gabriella, made a marriage of which he disapproved, Cesnola took his wife and other daughter, Louise, on what amounted to a triumphal tour of Italy. "We had a really royal welcome in my little native city of Rivarolo," Cesnola wrote back to trustee W. Loring Andrews. "I believe the whole population was at the railroad station waiting for our arrival from Turin!"[45] Madame Cesnola was "very much affected" and Cesnola professed himself "not a little embarrassed" by the throng of veterans of 1848–1849, townsfolk and relatives cheering their arrival. His hand hurt from shaking a thousand hands. The Cesnolas went on by carriage in mid-July to Cesnola where, protected from the sun by several varicolored tents, they were the guests of honor at a banquet on a large meadow. Civic, military and religious dignitaries from ten provincial towns "and 40 ladies" enjoyed the feast. Small Italian flags decorated the tables. A huge American flag flew overhead. The press called the double display "historic."

Cesnola, who had been suffering bronchitis, reported his health had "improved wonderfully and I feel quite a new man if it lasts."[46] An Italian doctor had him on a strict diet, telling him firmly he must not eat potatoes, pastry, sweetmeats nor drink wine. The Queen of Italy wanted to meet the Cesnola ladies who were presented to her in her summer residence in the valley of Gressoney. In time, the trip

began to pall. "With all this hobnobbing with high born people," Cesnola wrote, "I begin to long again to be at home in New York once more and return to my daily *mill grinding* & *grinding!*"⁴⁷ He had had forewarning of the elaborate fete the Canaveseans were preparing for him and he brought with him to Italy four young Negroes. When they distributed superb cigars after the banquet the Italians laughed heartily. Deeply offended, Cesnola stormed off in a huff.⁴⁸ He was now quite accustomed to be received as a "great Italian—the founder and stern administrator of a grand institution."⁴⁹

Back in America, his hair now white with age at sixty-eight, he ran the expanding museum with disciplined austerity. He dismissed those who objected to his actions or his manner as malcontents, and even after the deaths of Hitchcock and Marquand at the turn of the century, the aging director, obese now but erect as ever, fought any move to oust him from his managerial position. Madame Cesnola died in 1902, removing a gentle influence from the Cesnola household in Mt. Kisco, and her husband erected over her grave a replica of a handsome Cyprian stele. A year later, in the summer of 1903, the seventy-one-year-old director successfully parried a new attempt to remove him as director by calling on two veteran trustees, William C. Prime and William E. Dodge, to review the terms of an agreement between Cesnola and a delegation of trustees in April 1879. The men —Johnston, Dodge, Hoe and Prime—had visited him at his home to offer the General the position of Director of the Museum. Cesnola told them he would think it over. A week later he told the men on their second visit that he would accept the post under certain conditions. He had them written out. The museum's president, Johnston, and the trustees read through a list of half a dozen conditions. They were glad to accept all unanimously. The list gave Cesnola "full control of the internal administration of the Museum" and insured that he could not be removed from office "except for a grave cause."⁵⁰

Cesnola kept his controlling position at a big oak desk in his museum office until the day he died. He had moved into the Hotel Seymour to avoid commuting to Westchester and handled museum business as usual through the week ending Friday, November 18, 1904. A veterans' group had invited him to their annual dinner, the night before and he had spent a long and pleasure-filled evening with

his friends. The heavy meal was too much for the elderly General. He became ill Friday night and remained in bed on Saturday, recovering slightly. On Sunday he suffered a relapse and that evening, with his daughters at his bedside, Cesnola died. The cause was given as acute indigestion,[51] but this was often a mistaken diagnosis for a heart attack.

The most prestigious trustees escorted his casket down the main aisle of St. Patrick's Cathedral, and the man who had been director of the Metropolitan Museum of Art for a quarter of a century received the public acknowledgment of his position from J. Pierpont Morgan, the Vanderbilts and the full Board of Trustees.

Somewhat later, that body issued a memorial resolution honoring his regime:

"His fidelity, his minute attention to his duties, and his capacity for work during his long career of service, merit great praise. Other distinctions and other interests in life, if not forgotten, were permanently laid aside, and the welfare and growth of the Museum became his single interest and absorbing occupation. His military training, when joined to his public experience, gave him distinguished powers of administration; and, while critics are never wanting, his capacity to administer the Museum and adequately to exhibit its contents has not been questioned.

"Whoever shall become his successor, and with whatever gifts he shall be endowed, the martial, independent figure of General di Cesnola—somewhat restive in opposition and somewhat impetuous in speech and action, but at all times devoted to his duty and winning the affection of his subordinates and associates—will long remain a kindly and grateful memory."[52]

The memorial made no mention of his Cyprian finds and after his death most of them were gradually withdrawn. Ten years later—in 1914—the Oxford University archaeologist chosen by the Museum to evaluate and catalogue Cesnola's statues and pottery, John L. Myers, Ph.D., published his handbook on the Cesnola antiquities. With the publication of this booklet, the "Treasure of Curium," was labeled a "mystery that cannot be cleared up" and was dispatched to the metal vault in the depths of the massive museum. It has not been seen publicly since.

Notes

ONE

1. A. Manno, *Patriziato Subalpino*, (Torino).
2. *Enciclopedia Storice Nobiliare Italiana* (Milano, 1932), vol. V, p. 674.
3. L. D., *Famiglia Palma di Cesnola di Ivrea* (Firenze, 1905), p. 41.
4. Violet Baker Cook, Cesnola's granddaughter, interview December 10, 1968.
5. Cesnola to Mary Reid Cesnola, December 4, 1863, *Dartmouth*.
6. L. D., *Famiglia*, p. 39.
7. L. D., *Famiglia*, frontispiece.
8. L. D., *Famiglia*, p. 6.
9. L. P. Cesnola, *Cyprus* (New York, 1878), p. 294.
10. Cook interview.
11. *Ibid.*
12. *Ibid.*
13. Turin State Archives, United Section, Sixth Infantry Regiment, Staff Roll of Officers of the 2d Regiment of the Aosta Brigade, p. 155.
14. *Ibid.*
15. *Ibid.*
16. L. D., *Famiglia*, p. 42.
17. Turin State Archives.
18. Turin State Archives.
19. *N.Y. Gen. & Biog. Rec.* (New York, 1942), XXXVI, p. 85.
20. Cook interview.

TWO

1. Cook interview, December 10, 1968.
2. Cesnola memo for lawyer in libel suit, 1880, MMA Archives.
3. George Templeton Strong, *Diary*, edited by Allan Nevins and

Milton Halsey Thomas, (New York, 1952), Vol. II, p. 392.
4. New York *Herald*, January 4, 1858, p. 6.
5. Strong, *Diary*, vol. III, p. 52.
6. Strong, *Diary*, vol. II, p. 409.
7. Cook interview.
8. Cesnola to Seward, F. W., National Archives.
9. Docteur N. Reiss, *Excursion á New York, en 1850* (Bruxelles, 1851), pp. 66–67.
10. *Ibid.*
11. New York *Times*, June 22 & 23, 1859.
12. Genealogy, Matthias Hitchcock, Dartmouth.
13. Cesnola to Mary Jennings Reid, April 1, 1861, Violet B. Cook.
14. Bridal couple's copy of church record, June 11, 1861, Violet B. Cook.
15. Classified ad in unidentified paper, Violet Baker Cook.

THREE

1. *The Blue and the Gray*, ed. by Henry Steele Commager, (New York, 1950), pp. 21–22.
2. Fitz-James O'Brien, *New-York Times, The Rebellion Record*, Frank Moore, ed. (New York, 1862), pp. 148–154.
3. Cook interview, December 28, 1968.
4. *Ibid.*
5. *Ibid.*
6. Edward Dicey, *Six Months in the Federal States*, (London,

1863), pp. 23–25, 219–220, 101, 96.
7. *Ibid.*
8. *Ibid.*
9. *Ibid.*
10. *Ibid.*
11. Frederick Pfisterer, *New York in the War of the Rebellion*, 3d ed. (Albany, 1912).
12. Thomas West Smith, *Story of a Cavalry Regiment* (New York, 1897), p. 10.
13. Henry Murray Calvert, *Reminiscences of a Boy in Blue* (New York, 1920), pp. 1–18.
14. *Ibid.*
15. *Ibid.*
16. *Ibid.*
17. *Ibid.*
18. Mil. Dist. Wash., July 8, 1862, National Archives.
19. Anonymous letter to P. H. Watson, Asst. Secy. War, July 16, 1862, AGO, National Archives.
20. Cesnola to McClellan, July 8, 1862, National Archives.
21. *Ibid.*
22. *Ibid.*
23. *Ibid.*
24. Edward P. Tobie, *Service of the Cavalry in the Army of the Potomac* (Providence, 1882), pp. 8, 13, 101, 103.
25. *Ibid.*
26. Cesnola, October 14, 1862, Hdqtrs Fourth Regt. N.Y.S.V. Cavalry, Albany, N.Y.
27. *The War of the Rebellion, A Compilation of the Official Records of the Union and Confederate Armies* (GPO, Washington, D.C., 1880-1901), vol. I, XXI, p. 19.
28. *War Reb.*, vol. I, LI–I, p. 965.

29. A. J. H. Duganne, *The Fighting Quakers* (New York, 1866), p. 67.
30. *War Reb.*, vol. I, XXV–I, p. 4.
31. *War Reb.*, vol. I, XXI, p. 702.
32. *War Reb.*, vol. I, XXI, p. 703.
33. *War Reb.*, vol. I, XXI, p. 757.
34. Judge Advocate General's Office, January 31, 1863, National Archives.
35. L. C. Baker to P. N. Watson, 1863, JAGO, National Archives.
36. Cesnola to Baker, January 10, 1863, JAGO, National Archives.
37. Officers' Casualty Sheet, February 2, 1863, National Archives.
38. Cesnola to Watson, February 12, 1863, JAGO, National Archives.
39. Cesnola to Stanton, undated, JAGO, National Archives.
40. *Ibid.*
41. Cesnola to Stanton, February 25, 1963, JAGO, National Archives.
42. G.O. 50, JAGO, National Archives.
43. Cesnola to Corning, March 10, 1863, George R. Loeb, Philadelphia.
44. Cesnola to Hitchcock, May 24, 1863, Dartmouth.
45. *Ibid.*
46. Leslie's, February 28, 1863.
47. Cesnola to Hitchcock, May 24, 1867, Dartmouth.
48. Rev. Frederic Denison, *Sabres & Spurs* (Central Falls, R. I., 1876), pp. 209–212.
49. New York *Times*, June 20, 1863.
50. Tobie, *op. cit.*
51. Augustus C. Hamlin, 11th Army Corps, Army of Potomac, to Secretary of War Russell A. Alger, October 19, 1897, National Archives.
52. Casualty Sheet, August 5, 1863, National Archives.
53. Thomas Morley, affidavit, July 29, 1897, National Archives.

FOUR

1. Louis Palma di Cesnola, *Ten Months in Libby Prison* (New York, 1865), pp. 1–6.
2. *Ibid.*
3. Thomas Morley, Affidavit, August 29, 1897, National Archives.
4. F. F. Cavada, *Libby Life* (Philadelphia, 1865), vol. 24–25, p. 1.
5. U.S. San. Com., *Narrative of the Privations and Sufferings of U.S. Prisoners . . . in the Hands of the Rebel Authorities* (Boston, 1864).
6. Rev. Louis N. Beaudry, *Historic Records of Fifth N.Y. Cavalry* (Albany, 1889).
7. *Libby Chronicle*, (Albany, 1889).
8. *Ibid.*
9. Cesnola, *Ten Months, op. cit.*
10. *Ibid.*
11. *Ibid.*
12. *Ibid.*
13. *Ibid.*
14. *Ibid.*
15. Madame Cesnola to Hitchcock, January 30, 1864, Dartmouth.

FIVE

1. Cesnola School brochure, December 8, 1864, National Archives.
2. Cesnola to Madame Cesnola,

December 4, 1863, Mrs. Cook.
3. *Ibid.*
4. Strong, *Diary*, vol. III, p. 427.
5. Cesnola to Hitchcock, May 23, 1864, Dartmouth.
6. *Ibid.*
7. *Ibid.*
8. Cesnola to Hitchcock, June 24, 1864, Dartmouth.
9. *Ibid.*
10. *Ibid.*
11. *Ibid.*
12. *Ibid.*
13. *Ibid.*
14. *Ibid.*
15. Cesnola to Hitchcock, July 11, 1864, Dartmouth.
16. Cesnola to Madame Cesnola, June 25, 1865, Mrs. Cook.
17. *Ibid.*
18. *Ibid.*
19. Cesnola to Hitchcock, August 1, 1864, Dartmouth.
20. *Ibid.*
21. *Ibid.*
22. Cesnola to Hitchcock, August 1, 1864, Dartmouth.
23. AGO, March 23, 1868, National Archives.
24. Cesnola to Hitchcock, Christmas, 1864, Dartmouth.
25. Lloyd's *Pocket Companion Guide Through New York* (New York, 1866), p. 56.
26. *Harper's Weekly*, December 16, 1865.
27. *Ibid.*
28. Executive Committee, New York Historical Society, August 14, 1860.
29. Building Committee, New York Historical Society, August 30, 1865.
30. Cesnola to Brig. Gen. E. D.

Townsend, December 1, 1864, National Archives.
31. *Ibid.*
32. *Ibid.*
33. Cesnola to AGO, March 25, 1865, National Archives.
34. *Ibid.*
35. New York *Herald*, March 5, 1865.
36. Strong, *Diary*, vol. III, p. 581.
37. Cesnola to AGO, March 25, 1865, National Archives.
38. AGO to Cesnola, March 29, 1865, National Archives.
39. Cesnola to Hitchcock, July 6, 1865, Dartmouth.
40. *Ibid.*
41. *Ibid.*
42. Harris to Brig. Gen. J. E. Mulford, Summer, 1865, National Archives.
43. Cesnola to Stanton, August 20, 1865, National Archives.
44. Grant to AGO, October 14, 1865, National Archives.
45. Nationalization record, August 16, 1865, U.S. Dept. Just., New York.
46. Cesnola to Hitchcock, November 30, 1865, Dartmouth.
47. *Ibid.*
48. *Ibid.*

SIX

1. Cesnola, *Cyprus*, (New York, 1878).
2. *Ibid.*
3. *The Dartmouth*, March, 1873.
4. Sir George Hill, *A History of Cyprus*, (Cambridge, 1952) vol. IV, p. 248.

5. Blackwood's *Edinburgh Magazine*, 1905, p. 622.
6. Cesnola to Seward, February 1, 1866, National Archives.
7. Cesnola to Hitchcock, February 22, 1866, Dartmouth.
8. Cesnola to Seward, January 7, 1866, National Archives.
9. Cesnola to Seward, February 4, 1868, National Archives.
10. Cesnola to Hitchcock, September 16, 1867, Dartmouth.
11. Cesnola to Hitchcock, May 7, 1866, Dartmouth.
12. Cesnola to Hitchcock, June 20, 1867, Dartmouth.
13. *Ibid.*
14. Cesnola to Hitchcock, February 4, 1868, Dartmouth.
15. Cesnola to Hitchcock, September 12, 1868, Dartmouth.
16. *Ibid.*
17. Cesnola to Hitchcock, September 16, 1867, Dartmouth.
18. Cesnola to Hitchcock, November 22, 1868, Dartmouth.
19. Cesnola to Hitchcock, February 7, 1869, Dartmouth.
20. *Ibid.*
21. *Ibid.*
22. Cesnola to Hitchcock, June 14, 1869, Dartmouth.
23. Cesnola to Fish, May, 17, 1868, Dartmouth.
24. Executive Committee, August 14, 1860, New York Historical Society.
25. Committee report.
26. Cesnola to Hitchcock, November 22, 1868, Dartmouth.
27. Cesnola to Hitchcock, March 30, 1869, Dartmouth.
28. Cesnola to Hitchcock, June 14, 1869, Dartmouth.

29. Cesnola to Harris, July 6, 1869, Dartmouth.
30. Cesnola to Hitchcock, October 29, 1869, Dartmouth.

SEVEN

1. Cesnola, *Cyprus.*
2. Cesnola to Gedeonov, January, 2, 1870, Hermitage.
3. Gedeonov to Hofmeister, January 17, 1870, Hermitage.
4. Cesnola to Gedeonov, March 17, 1870, Hermitage.
5. Gedeonov to Hofmeister, March 21, 1870, Hermitage.
6. Hofmeister to Adlerberg, April 4, 1870, Hermitage.
7. Cesnola to Fish, March 30, 1870, National Archives.
8. G. Colonna-Cecealdi to Cesnola, April 27, 1870, Hermitage.
9. Cesnola to Gedeonov, May 25, 1870, Hermitage.
10. Gedeonov to Consul Johnson, June 9, 1870, Hermitage.
11. Adlerberg to Gedeonov, May 31, 1870, Hermitage.
12. Cesnola to Gedeonov, July 4, 1870, Hermitage.
13. Cesnola to Gedeonov, August 2, 1870, Hermitage.
14. *Ibid.*
15. *Ibid.*
16. *Ibid.*

EIGHT

1. Cesnola to John T. Johnston, July

256

1871, MMA Archives.
2. Cesnola to Hitchcock, August 3, 1870, Dartmouth.
3. Cesnola to Hitchcock, March 13, 1871, Dartmouth.
4. *Ibid.*
5. Cesnola to Hitchcock, October 11, 1871, Dartmouth.
6. *Ibid.*
7. *Ibid.*
8. *Ibid.*
9. Cesnola to Hitchcock, January 17, 1872, Dartmouth.
10. *Ibid.*
11. *Ibid.*
12. *Ibid.*
13. *Harper's Magazine*, July, 1872.
14. *Ibid.*
15. *Ibid.*
16. *Ibid.*
17. *Ibid.*
18. *Ibid.*
19. *Ibid.*
20. *Ibid.*

NINE

1. Cesnola to John T. Johnston, February 3, 1872, MMA Archives.
2. Cesnola to Hitchcock, May 4, 1871, Dartmouth.
3. Catalogue of sale, 1-9 & 10, 1871, Dartmouth.
4. Cesnola to Hitchcock, March 13, 1871, Dartmouth.
5. Cesnola to Hitchcock, May 4, 1871, Dartmouth.
6. Cesnola to Hitchcock, March 13, 1871, Dartmouth.

7. Letters to author.
8. *Harper's Magazine*, July 1872.
9. Cesnola to Hitchcock, August 14, 1872, Dartmouth.
10. *Ibid.*
11. *Ibid.*
12. Hall to Hitchcock, September 20, 1872, Dartmouth.
13. Feuardent to M. le Directeur, August 8, 1871, Hermitage.
14. Cesnola to Doell, January 5, 1871, Hermitage.
15. Cesnola to Doell, August 14, 1871, Hermitage.
16. Cesnola to Doell, October 2, 1872, Hermitage.
17. Cesnola to Hitchcock, September 25, 1872, Dartmouth.
18. John T. Johnston, to Hitchcock, August 31, 1872, Dartmouth.
19. Hitchcock to John T. Johnston, October, 1872, Dartmouth.
20. Cesnola to Hitchcock, September 23, 1872, Dartmouth.
21. *Ibid.*
22. *Ibid.*
23. *Ibid.*
24. *Ibid.*
25. Cesnola to Hitchcock, September 25, 1872, Dartmouth.
26. *Ibid.*
27. N. Ignatiew to Cesnola, April 20, 1872, Dartmouth.
28. Cesnola to Hitchcock, October 18, 1872, Dartmouth.
29. *In Memoriam*, W. T. Blodgett, (New York, 1875).
30. Cesnola to Hitchcock, October, 18, 1872, Dartmouth.
31. *Ibid.*
32. Cesnola to Doell, October 19, 1872, Hermitage.
33. Cesnola to Doell, November 3, 1872, Hermitage.

34. J. S. Morgan to John T. Johnston, November 16, 1872, MMA Archives.
35. Agreement of Sale, November 11, 1872, MMA Archives.
36. Cesnola to John T. Johnston, November 16, 1872, MMA Archives.
37. Cesnola to Hitchcock, December 2, 1872, Dartmouth.
38. Cesnola to Hitchcock, December 16, 1872, Dartmouth.
39. *Ibid.*
40. John T. Johnston to Hitchcock, December 14, 1872, Dartmouth.
41. Cesnola to Doell, December 25, 1872, Hermitage.

TEN

1. New York *Herald,* January 29, 1873.
2. John Myers, *Handbook of Cesnola Collection* (New York, 1913).
3. New York *Herald,* January 29, 1873.
4. Cesnola to Hitchcock, early 1873, Dartmouth.
5. Cesnola to Hitchcock, January 18, 1873, Dartmouth.
6. Cesnola to Hitchcock, January 23, 1873, Dartmouth.
7. New York *Herald,* February 5, 1873.
8. *Ibid.*
9. Board of Trustees, February 17, 1873, MMA Archives.
10. Cesnola to Hitchcock, early 1873, Dartmouth.
11. *The College on the Hill,* ed. by

Ralph Nading, (Hanover, N.H., 1964).
12. *The Dartmouth,* March, 1873.
13. Cesnola to Hitchcock, 1873, Dartmouth.
14. *Ibid*
15. *Harper's Weekly,* March 4, 1873.
16. New York *Herald,* March 8, 1873.
17. Charles Balliard, June-July 1907, MMA Archives.
18. Testimony of Defendant, Feuardent v. Cesnola, 1884, p. 27.
19. Cesnola, *Cyprus,* p. 127.
20. New York *Herald,* May 23, 1873.
21. *New York Times,* January 6, 1873.
22. New York *Herald,* July 11, 1873.
23. *New York Times,* July 6, 1873.
24. Memo of Agreement, 1873, MMA Archives.
25. Heinrich Schliemann, *Ilios,* (New York, 1880) p. xvi.

ELEVEN

1. Cesnola to John T. Johnston, December 23, 1875, Dartmouth.
2. *Ibid.*
3. *Ibid.*
4. *Ibid.*
5. Cesnola, *Cyprus,* p. 349.
6. *Ibid.,* p. 294.
7. Cesnola to John T. Johnston, December 23, 1875, Dartmouth.
8. Cesnola, *Cyprus,* pp. 293-337.
9. *Ibid.*
10. Cesnola to Hitchcock, September 12, 1875, Dartmouth.
11. Charles D. Warren to Cesnola, December 5, 1875, Dartmouth.

12. John L. Myers, *Cesnola Handbook*, First Proof, Cyprus Museum, Nicosia, Cyprus.
13. Cesnola to Hitchcock, May 20, 1874, Dartmouth.
14. John T. Johnston to Hitchcock, November 7, 1873, Dartmouth.
15. Cesnola to Hitchcock, May 20, 1874, Dartmouth.
16. Cesnola to Hitchcock, June 17, 1874, Dartmouth.
17. Cesnola to Hitchcock, June 30, 1874, Dartmouth.

TWELVE

1. John T. Johnston to Cesnola (copy), December 7, 1875, Dartmouth.
2. Cesnola to Hitchcock, December 12, 1875, Dartmouth.
3. *Ibid.*
4. Cesnola to Hitchcock, February 7, 1875, Dartmouth.
5. Cesnola to Hitchcock, April 27, 1875, Dartmouth.
6. Cesnola to Hitchcock, August 6, 1875, Dartmouth.
7. Cesnola to Hitchcock, October, 1875, Dartmouth.
8. Cesnola to Hitchcock, October 7, 1875, Dartmouth.
9. Cesnola to Hitchcock, January 27, 1875, Dartmouth.
10. *Ibid.*
11. *Ibid.*
12. Cesnola to Hitchcock, February 7, 1876, Dartmouth.
13. Cesnola to Hitchcock, April 4, 1876, Dartmouth.
14. Cesnola to Hitchcock, July 14, 1876, Dartmouth.

15. Cesnola to Hitchcock, September 24, 1876, Dartmouth.
16. Cesnola to Hitchcock, October 1, 1876, Dartmouth.
17. Cesnola to Hitchcock, October 4, 1876, Dartmouth.
18. Prime to Hitchcock, November 13, 1876, Dartmouth.
19. *Ibid.*
20. Cesnola to John T. Johnston, December 13, 1876, Dartmouth.
21. Cesnola to Hitchcock, November 26, 1876, Dartmouth.
22. Cesnola to John T. Johnston, December 13, 1876, Dartmouth.
23. Cesnola to Hitchcock, November 14, 1876, Dartmouth.
24. Cesnola to Hitchcock, November 24, 1876, Dartmouth.
25. Cesnola to Hitchcock, November 26, 1876, Dartmouth.
26. *Ibid.*
27. Cesnola to Hitchcock, December 2, 1876, Dartmouth.
28. Cesnola to Hitchcock, December 19, 1876, Dartmouth.
29. MMA Loan Exhibition Catalogue, 1877,
30. Cesnola to Hitchcock, December 24, 1876, Dartmouth.
31. *Ibid.*
32. Cesnola to Hitchcock, November 26, 1876, Dartmouth.
33. Cesnola to Hitchcock, November 14, 1876, Dartmouth.
34. Cesnola to Hitchcock, December 17, 1876, Dartmouth.
35. Cesnola to Hitchcock, December 24, 1876, Dartmouth.
36. *Ibid.*
37. Cesnola to Hitchcock, March 14, 1877, Dartmouth.
38. Cesnola to Hitchcock, January 24, 1877, Dartmouth.

39. Cesnola to Hitchcock, March 14, 1877, Dartmouth.
40. *Ibid.*
41. Cesnola to Hitchcock, December 27, 1876, Dartmouth.
42. Cesnola to Hitchcock, August 27, 1877, Dartmouth.
43. Cesnola to Hitchcock, August 28, 1877, Dartmouth.
44. Cesnola to Hitchcock, September 28 & October 24, 1877, Dartmouth.

THIRTEEN

1. H. Hudson Holly, *Modern Dwellings in Town and Country,* (New York, 1878), p. 140.
2. Cesnola to Hitchcock, August 18, 1878, Dartmouth.
3. Cesnola to Hitchcock, August 30, 1877, Dartmouth.
4. MMA Archives.
5. *New York Times,* January 8, 1880.
6. *New York Times,* May 1, 1880.
7. New York *Tribune,* March 28, 1880.
8. *The World,* March 31, 1880.
9. *Ibid.*
10. *New York Times,* March 31, 1880.
11. Cesnola, *Cyprus,* p. 157.
12. Howard L. Adelson, *The American Numismatic Society* (New York, 1958), p. 84.
13. British Museum purchase record, July 8, 1871.
14. *Ibid.*
15. Pamphlet, American Numismatic Society, 1878.

16. *Art Amateur,* August, 1880.
17. *Ibid.*
18. *Ibid.*
19. New York *Post,* August 6, 1880.
20. *Ibid.*
21. *New York Times,* August 6, 1880.
22. *Ibid.*
23. Cesnola to John T. Johnston, August 21, 1880, MMA Archives.
24. New York *Tribune,* August 26, 1880.
25. *Art Amateur,* September, 1880.
26. Cesnola to John T. Johnston, January 18, 1881, MMA Archives.
27. Barnard to Feuardent, December 8, 1880, MMA Archives.
28. *Ibid.*
29. *New York Times,* December 19, 1880.
30. *Daily Tribune,* December 29, 1880.
31. Board of Trustees, MMA Archives.
32. *New York Times,* January 6, 1881.
33. *Ibid.*
34. *Ibid.*
35. *Ibid.*
36. *Ibid.*
37. Cesnola to John T. Johnston, January 18, 1881, MMA Archives.
38. *Daily Tribune,* January 28, 1881.
39. *Ibid.*
40. Board of Trustees, February 21, 1881, MMA Archives.
41. *Art Amateur,* March, 1881.

FOURTEEN

1. *New York Times,* March, 1881.

2. Barnard to Ward, March 21, 1881, MMA Archives.
3. Prime to John T. Johnston, May 18, 1881, MMA Archives.
4. Cesnola, *Cyprus,* p. 132.
5. Anonymous paper, May 10, 1881, MMA Library.
6. Prime to John T. Johnston, May 16, 1881, MMA Archives.
7. *New York Times,* May 14, 1881.
8. Cesnola to John T. Johnston, May 19, 1881.
9. *New York Times,* June 1, 1881.
10. Anonymous paper, October, 1881.
11. *New York Times,* November 2, 1881.
12. *New York Times,* November 8, 1882.
13. Clarence Cook, *Transformations and Migrations of Certain Statues in the Cesnola Collection* (New York, 1882).
14. *Ibid.*
15. Executive Committee, March 27, 1882, MMA Archives.
16. *Ibid.*
17. *Ibid.*
18. Executive Committee, MMA Archives.
19. *Evening Post,* March 24, 1882.
20. New York *Herald,* March 23, 1882.
21. Prime to Ward, March 19, 1882, MMA Archives.
22. St. Gaudens to Prime, March 18, 1882, MMA Archives.
23. *Springfield Republican,* March 26, 1882.
    Il Progresso Italo-Americano, March 25, 1882.
24. *New York Times,* March 17, 1882.

25. Adelson, *American Numismatic Society* (New York, 1958), p. 91.
26. Cesnola to John T. Johnston, May 31, 1882, MMA Archives.
27. *Ibid.*
28. John T. Johnston to Cesnola, May 31, 1882, MMA Archives.
29. Henry H. Gorringe to John T. Johnston, April 4, 1882, MMA Archives.
30. Cesnola to John T. Johnston, June 1, 1882, MMA Archives.

FIFTEEN

1. *Art Interchange,* November 21, 1882.
2. *Daily Graphic,* November 12, 1883.
3. New York *Tribune,* November 2, 1883.
4. *Evening Post,* November 2, 1883.
5. *Truth,* November 2, 1883.
6. New York *Herald,* November 8, 1883.
7. *New York Times,* January 10, 1884.
8. Anonymous paper, August 17, 1883, MMA Library.
9. *Daily Graphic,* undated, MMA Library.
10. New York *Tribune,* November 8, 1883.
11. *Evening Post,* November 12, 1883.
12. *New York Times,* December 5, 1883.
13. *The World,* December 8, 1883.
14. *Puck,* November 8, 1883.
15. Anonymous paper, November

24, 1883, MMA Library.
16. *New York Times,* December 7, 1883.
17. *Ibid.*
18. *Ibid.*
19. New York *Herald* and *New York Times,* December 11, 1883.
20. *New York Times,* December 12, 1883.
21. *New York Times,* December 13, 1883.
22. *Ibid.*
23. New York *Daily Tribune,* December 12, 1883. See also Cesnola, *Cyprus,* p. 130.
24. New York *Daily Tribune,* December 12, 1883.
25. Testimony of Defendant, p. 69.
26. *Commercial Advertiser,* December 26, 1883.
27. Testimony of Defendant, p. 41.
28. *New York Times,* December 22, 1883.
29. New York *Tribune,* January 30, 1884.
30. *Ibid.*
31. *The Sun,* January 31, 1884.
32. *Ibid.*
33. *The Sun,* February 3, 1884.

SIXTEEN

1. Cook interview.
2. MMA curator.
3. MMA Archives.
4. Cesnola to Hitchcock, March 21, 1884, Dartmouth.
5. *Ibid.*
6. James C. Young to Salem H. Wales, October 10, 1890, MMA Archives.
7. Cesnola to Vanderbilt, March 25, 1889, MMA Archives.
8. MMA officer.
9. New York *Advocate,* May 4, 1889.
10. Cesnola to Hitchcock, December 5, 1882, Dartmouth.
11. New York *Herald,* January 2, 1887.
12. *Ibid.*
13. New York *Herald,* January 5, 1887.
14. Anonymous paper, MMA Library, Vol. I, p. 79.
15. New York *Continent,* May 10, 1891.
16. New York *Sun,* December 19, 1888.
17. New York *Recorder,* June 1, 1891.
18. *Ibid.*
19. *Progresso Italo-Americano,* March 27, 1887.
20. Anonymous paper, MMA Library.
21. *Troy Budget,* May 22, 1887.
22. *New York Times,* October 24, 1885.
23. *Ibid.*
24. Max Ohnefalsch-Richter, *Ancient Places of Worship in Kypros* (Berlin, 1891), p. ii.
25. New York *Collector,* September 1, 1893.
26. Cook interview.
27. Cesnola to McClellan, April 17, 1884, MMA Archives.
28. Avery to Marquand, March 14, 1895, MMA Archives.
29. J. P. Morgan to Marquand, February 18, 1895, MMA Archives.
30. *New York Times,* March, 1895, MMA Library.

31. *Ibid.*
32. Marquand to Cesnola, March 3, 1895, MMA Archives.
33. Hitchcock to Cesnola, January 10, 1896, MMA Archives.
34. *New York Times,* March 3, 1895.
35. Mahon to Cesnola, March 18, 1882, MMA Archives.
36. Record & Pension 515, 852, National Archives.
37. *Ibid.*
38. Cesnola to Clay Evans, July 25, 1899, National Archives.
39. Cesnola to W. E. Dodge, August 18, 1895, MMA Archives.
40. *Ibid.*
41. Cesnola to Reverend Dr. William Hayes Ward, April 25, 1887, Dartmouth.
42. Cesnola to Senator Elsberg, March 5, 1901, MMA Archives.
43. Cesnola to Prof. Rodolfo Lanciani, March 11, 1887, MMA Archives.
44. Joseph W. Drexel to Cesnola, May 29, 1884, MMA Archives.
45. Cesnola to W. Loring Andrews, June 27, 1890, MMA Archives.
46. *Ibid.*
47. *Ibid.*
48. Interview, Celesto F. Scavini, Rivarolo, June 9, 1968.
49. Louis Fagan to Cesnola, July 14, 1901, MMA Archives.
50. MMA Archives.
51. New York *Herald,* November 22, 1904.
52. MMA Archives.

Bibliography

PRIMARY

Adelson, Howard L., *The American Numismatic Society*, New York, 1858.

Beaudry, Rev. Louis N., *Historic Records of the Fifth N.Y. Cavalry*, Albany, 1869.

———, *The Libby Chronicle*, Albany, 1889.

The Blue and the Gray, The Story of the Civil War as Told by Participants, ed. by Henry Steele Commager, Indianapolis, 1950.

Calvert, Henry Murray, *Reminiscences of a Boy in Blue*, New York, 1920.

Cavada, F. F., *Libby Life*, Philadelphia, 1865.

Cesnola, L. P. Di, *The Antiquities of Cyprus . . . Exhibited by Messrs. Rollin and Feuardent . . . from*

selection made by C. T. Newton . . . of *British Museum*, London, 1873.

———, *Cyprus: Its Ancient Cities, Tombs, and Temples*, New York, 1878.

———, *A Descriptive Atlas of Cypriote Antiquities in the Metropolitan Museum of Art*, 3 vols., Boston, 1885.

———, *Le ultime scoperte nell'isola di Ciprio*, Torino, 1876.

De-Agostini, Giovacchino, *Cesnola in Cyprus*, 1871.

Denison, Rev. Frederic, *Sabres & Spurs*, Central Falls, R. I., 1876.

Dicey, Edward, *Six Months in the Federal States*, London, 1863.

Dornbusch, C. E., *Checklist of the War Department's Bibliography of State Participation in the Civil War*, New York, 1961.

Duganne, A. J. H., *The Fighting Quakers*, New York, 1866.

Enciclopedia Storico Nobiliare Italiana, Milano, 1932.

Gallo, Francesco, *Biography of Luigi Palma Di Cesnola*, 1869.

Hill, Sir George, *A History of Cyprus*, Cambridge, 1852.

Howe, Winifred E., *A History of the Metropolitan Museum of Art*, New York, 1913.

Lang, R. H., *Cyprus, Its History, Its Present Resources and Future Prospects*, London, 1878.

Lloyd, Thomas, *Pocket Companion Guide Through New York*, New York, 1866.

Lloyd W. W., *General Cesnola's Cyprus*, London, 1878.

Manno, A., *Patriziato Subalpino*, Torino.

Martin, Edward Sandford, *The Life of Joseph Hodges Choate*, 2 vols., New York, 1920.

Massarini, Tullo, *Cypro antica e moderne e il Generale L. P. di Cesnola*, Roma, 1899.

Ohnefalsch-Richter, Max, *Ancient Places of Worship in Kypros*, Berlin, 1891.

Pfisterer, Frederick, *New York in the War of the Rebellion*, 3 ed., 1912, Albany, 1890.

Reiss, Docteur N., *Excursion á New York, en 1850*, Bruxelles, 1851.

Roversi, Luigi, *L. Palma di Cesnola e il Metropolitan Museum*, New York, 1898.

Schliemann, Heinrich, *Troy and Its Remains*, London, 1875.

Smith, Thomas West, *The Story of a Cavalry Regiment*, New York, 1897.

Strong, George Templeton, *Diary*, ed. by Allan Nevins and Milton Halsey Thomas, 4 vols., New York, 1952.

Strong, Theron G., *Joseph H. Choate*, New York, 1917.

Tobie, Edward P., *Service of the Cavalry in the Army of the Potomac*, Providence, 1882.

U.S. District Court, New York Southern District, *Gaston L. Feuardent vs. L. P. di Cesnola, Testimony of Defendant*, New York, 1884.

U.S. War Department, *The War of the Rebellion, A Compilation of the Official Records of the Union and Confederate Armies*, 70 vols., Washington, 1880-1901.

Zucchi, Mario, *Manno, Antonio, barone, 1834-1918, Patriziato Subalpino*, Torino, 1950.

SECONDARY

Abbott, A. O., *Prison Life in the South*, New York, 1866.

Bemis, Samuel F., *The American Secretaries of State and Their Diplomacy*, 10 vols., New York, 1927-1929.

Blegen, Carl W., *Troy and the Trojans*, New York, 1963.

In Memoriam, W. T. Blodgett, New York, 1875.

Boatner, Mark M., *The Civil War Dictionary*, New York, 1959.

Brown, H. C., *Last Fifty Years in New York*, New York, 1926.

———, *New York in the Elegant Eighties*, New York, 1926.

Brown, Junius H., *The Great Metropolis, a Mirror of New York*, Hartford, 1869.

Burton, T. E., *Financial Crises of the United States*, New York, 1902.

Casson, Stanley, *Ancient Cyprus, Its Art & Archaeology*, London, 1937.

Ceram, C. W., *The March of Archaeology*, New York, 1958.

Chestnut, Mary Boykin, *A Diary from Dixie*, ed. by I. D. Martin and M. L. Avary, New York, 1929.

The College on the Hill, ed. by Ralph Nading, Hanover, N. H., 1964.

Crockett, A. S., *Peacocks on Parade*, New York, 1931. Chaps. I-XI.

Daniel, Glyn E., *One Hundred Years of Archaeology*, London, 1950.

Dewey, D. R., *Financial History of the United States*, New York, 1903. 370-414.

Doubleday, Abner, *Reminiscences of Forts Sumter and Moultrie*, New York, 1876.

Dyer, Frederick H., *A Compendium of the War of the Rebellion*, New York, 1959.

Fifth Avenue, Walton Advertising and Printing Co., Boston, 1915.

Gallenga, Antonio, *History of Piedmont*, London, 1855.

Gordon, Cyrus H., *Forgotten Scripts*, New York, 1968.

Holly, H. Hudson, *Modern Dwellings in Town and Country*, New York, 1878.

Johnson, James R. and Bill, Alfred H., *Horsemen Blue & Gray*, New York, 1960.

Kerrigan, Evans E., *American War Medals*, New York, 1964.

King's Handbook of New York City, Boston, 1893.

Lamb, M. J., *History of the City of New York*, 2 vols. New York, 1877-1880.

Layard, Austen Henry, *Nineveh and Its Remains*, 2 vols., New York, 1849.

Lynch, D. T., *Tweed*, New York, 1927. Chaps. XXV-XXXI.

McCartney, E. R., *Crisis of 1873*, Minneapolis, 1935.

McDonald, William A., *Progress into the Past*, New York, 1967.

Michaelis, A., *A Century of Archaeological Discovery*, New York, 1908.

Orton, Charles William Previte, *The Early History of the House of Savoy*, Cambridge, 1912.

Perrot, Georges and Chipiez, Charles, *History of Art in Phoenicia and Its Dependencies*, 2 vols., London, 1885.

Robb, Edward, *The Epic of America*, New York, 1966.

Sabre, Lt. G. E., *Nineteen Months a Prisoner of War*, New York, 1865.

Schlesinger, Arthur, *Learning How To Behave*, New York, 1947, Chap. IV.

Schliemann, Heinrich, *Ilios*, New York, 1880.

Schuchhardt, Karl, *Schliemann's Excavations*, London, 1891.

Seward, F. W., *Reminiscences 1830-1915*, New York, 1916.

Silverberg, Robert, *Great Adventures in Archaeology*, New York, 1964.

Stokes, I. N. Phelps, *The Iconography of Manhattan Island*, New York, 1926.
The Stranger's Guide around New York and Its Vicinity. What to See and What Is to be Seen with Hints and Advice to those who Visit the Great Metropolis, New York, 1853.
Thayer, William Roscoe, *The Life and Times of Cavour*, 2 vols., Boston, 1911.
Treat's Illustrated New York and Brooklyn, New York, 1874.
Trevelyan, Janet Penrose, *A Short History of the Italian People*, New York, 1956.
Unger, Irwin, *The Greenback Era*, Princeton, 1969.
Van Rensselaer, M. K. and Van de Water, Frederic, *The Social Ladder*, New York, 1924, Chaps. IV-VIII.
Wecter, Dixon, *The Saga of American Society*, New York, 1937., Chaps. IV-XII.
Wiel, A., *The Romance of the House of Savoy*, London, 1898.
Williamson, James J., *Prison Life in the Old Capitol*, West Orange, 1911.
Wood's Illustrated Hand-Book to New York & Environs, London, 1873.

PAMPHLETS

Balliard, Charles, *Report to MMA, The Metropoliton Museum of Art*, New York, June-July, 1907.
Blackwood's *Edinburgh Magazine*, 1905, Vol. 177, pp. 622-639.

Catalogue for Cesnola sale at Sotheby, Wilkinson & Hodge, London, 1871.
Catalogue of Collection of General Cesnola *** For Sale to Suit Amateurs, Cyprus, 1869.
Cesnola L. P. Di, *Report to Royal Academy of Sciences in Turin, Italy, on Cyprian excavations, 1871.*
Cook, Clarence, *Transformations and Migrations of Certain Statues in the Cesnola Collection*, New York, 1882.
L. D., *Famiglia Palma di Cesnola de Ivrea*, Firenze, 1905.
The Dartmouth, March, 1873.
De-Agostini, Giovacchino, *Luigi Palma Di Cesnola*, Vercelli, 1871.
Doell, Johannes, *Memoirs de le Academie des Sciences de St. Petersbourg*, VIIe Tome XIX, No. 4, "Die Sammlung Cesnola."
Guide to the Cesnola Collection at the Cruger Mansion, New York, 1873.
Harper's Magazine, July, 1872.
Leslie's Illustrated Newspaper, 1863.
Metropolitan Museum of Art *Bulletin*, John L. Myers, "Preliminary Note On Cesnola Collection," Vol. IV, No. 6, June, 1909.
Metropolitan Museum of Art *Bulletin*, Myers, "Interim Report on Cesnola Collection," Vol. IV., No. 9, Sept., 1909.
Metropolitan Museum of Art *Bulletin*, Myers, "Third Report on Cesnola Collection," Vol. V, No. 10, Oct., 1910.

Metropolitan Museum of Art *Loan Exhibition Catalogue*, 1877.

Myers, John L., *Cesnola Handbook, First Proof*, Nicosia, Cyprus.

——, *Handbook of Cesnola Collection*, New York, 1913.

——and Ohnefalsch-Richter, M., *A Catalogue of the Cyprus Museum; with a Chronicle of the Excavations undertaken since the British Occupation and Introductory Notes on Cypriote Archeology*, Oxford, 1899.

Narrative of the Privations & Sufferings of U.S. Prisoners & Soldiers while Prisoners of War in the Hands of the Rebel Authorities . . . Boston, 1864.

New York *Herald*, 1858-1904.

New-York Times, 1861-1904.

Perrot, Georges et Chipiez, Charles, "L'Ile de Chypre et son rôle dans l'Histoire," *Revue de Deux Mondes*, Dec. 1, 1878, Feb. 1 and March 15, 1879.

Putnam's Magazine, July 1870.

Vogue, Charles Jean Melchior de, "Inscriptions Cypriotes Inédites," *Journal Asiatique*, 6 serie, Paris, 1868.

Index